ESSAYS OLD AND NEW

1

BROWNING'S MIND AND ART

BROWNING'S MIND AND ART

RICHARD D. ALTICK

K. W. GRANSDEN

PARK HONAN

F. E. L. PRIESTLEY

GEORGE M. RIDENOUR

WILLIAM CADBURY

ARCHIBALD A. HILL

BARBARA MELCHIORI

W. O. RAYMOND

G. ROBERT STANGE

GEOFFREY TILLOTSON

Essays edited by
CLARENCE TRACY

OLIVER AND BOYD
EDINBURGH AND LONDON
1968

OLIVER AND BOYD LTD

Tweeddale Court
Edinburgh 1

39a Welbeck Street
London W1

First published 1968

Printed in Great Britain by
Robert Cunningham and Sons Ltd, Longbank Works, Alva,
Scotland

PREFACE

The title of this volume may appear pretentious for a collection of essays making no claim to be either systematic or definitive. The eleven writers whose essays appear here were chosen not because they belonged to a school of criticism or could present a consensus of critical opinion on Browning that so far does not exist, but because each of them had already made a valuable contribution to the understanding of him and his poetry. Even the casual reader will quickly discover that they often disagree with each other and with me. Lovers of neat critical systems may deplore the apparent confusion that results, but it does seem appropriate to a poet whose world view, we are told, is pluralistic, and it ought to have delighted Browning himself. If the great white light of final truth does not shine out on every page, at least it breaks through repeatedly in shafts of illumination.

Five of the contributors, Messrs Altick, Gransden, Honan, Priestley, and Tillotson, have written essays specially commissioned by me for this book. The remaining six have kindly allowed me to reprint their essays from recent books and journals. For permission to reprint them here, acknowledgments are due to: William Cadbury, "Lyric and Anti-Lyric Forms: A Method for Judging Browning", reprinted from *University of Toronto Quarterly* (1964-5) by permission of the author and the University of Toronto Press; Archibald A. Hill, " 'Pippa's Song': Two Attempts at Structural Criticism", reprinted from *University of Texas Studies in English* (1956) by permission of the Director of the University of Texas Press; Barbara Melchiori, "Dark Gold, or Devil's Dung" from *Browning's Poetry of Reticence* (Oliver & Boyd 1968), reprinted by permission of the author and the publishers; W. O. Raymond, "Browning's 'The Statue and the Bust' " from *The Infinite Moment*, 2nd edn. (1965), reprinted by permission of the author and the University of Toronto Press; George M. Ridenour, "Browning's Music Poems: Fancy and Fact", reprinted from *PMLA* (1963) by permission of the author and the Modern

v

Language Association of America; G. Robert Stange, "Browning and Modern Poetry", reprinted, with permission of the author, from *The Pacific Spectator* (1954).

I am much indebted to two of my friends, Dean Malcolm Ross and Professor F. E. L. Priestley, for their kindly interest in this project and for much helpful advice. I am also grateful to the Canada Council for a research grant that greatly facilitated the production of this book.

Professor W. E. Fredeman very generously read the proofs and rescued me from a number of errors.

All quotations from Browning's poetry, except when some other source is indicated, are taken from The Centenary Edition, ed. F. G. Kenyon, 10 vols., London, 1912 (reissued in New York by Barnes and Noble, 1966).

CLARENCE TRACY

CONTENTS

Clarence Tracy

INTRODUCTION

BROWNING SPEAKS OUT

That bard's a Browning; he neglects the form:
But ah, the sense, ye gods, the weighty sense![1]

Victorian readers often fitted Browning into a neat critical
antithesis. He was a great teacher of important moral truths, they
said, but, alas!, a clumsy artist. The poet joked about the formula
in the lines quoted above, but it was evidently found satisfactory
by most of his readers until the early part of the present century,
when his popularity, along with that of other Victorian poets,
began to founder, taking the formula down with it. Today, however, as critical attention is once more being given him, especially
in Canada and the United States, the antithesis tends to turn about.
Readers in the age of Auden, Pound, and Thomas are not much
deterred by the obscurity that weighed heavily against him in his
own time and find his cacophony and burlesque humour in tune
with their tastes. They are also impressed by his imaginative
stamina and by his irony, his mastery of several styles, his often
extraordinarily deft use of words and his ability to create character.
His reputation as an artist is rising and will rise higher. But his
reputation as a philosopher and teacher, on the other hand, is
undergoing a transformation. Reacting against the heavily pious
approach that used to be made to him by members of the Browning societies, and by innumerable preachers in search of inspiring
quotations, modern readers tend to think of him rather as a poet
of sceptical and rebellious temperament who expressed relatively

[1] *The Inn Album*, 17-18.

I

few convictions on either religious or moral issues. Though no critical consensus has so far emerged, and some of the essays written about him seem to have been prompted by little more than a naughty impulse to turn the old certainties upside-down, modern critics are doing Browning's reputation a service in telling us to look to him not for moral instruction but imaginative insight; to treat him, in other words, as a poet.

The new view of Browning as a sceptic who had no particular message for his readers results partly from the biases of the twentieth century, and the habit all readers have of making over in their own image poets whom they like. It also results from an increasing awareness of the warning repeatedly given by the poet himself that his poems are dramatic, "being", as he explained in a note to *Dramatic Lyrics* (1842), "though often Lyric in expression, always Dramatic in principle, and so many utterances of so many imaginary persons, not mine". Though intended at first to have only a limited application, to explain the inclusion of a collection of lyric poems in the *Bells and Pomegranates* series, which thitherto had consisted only of plays, the meaning of the warning was gradually extended until it seems to apply to *all* his work, so that the view has grown up that he never expressed himself but only made other men talk. "You speak out, *you*," he wrote to Elizabeth Barrett, "I only make men and women speak." His poetry, he went on to say, "evidences . . . a dramatic sympathy with certain modifications of passion"[2] – indicates, that is, an ability to create character but no more expresses himself than Shakespeare expressed himself in his plays.[3] Critics have always known of this warning but have sometimes behaved towards it cavalierly; believing that it was only a smoke-screen, they relied on their

[2] *Letters of Robert Browning and Elizabeth Barrett Barrett*, (*1845-46*), New York and London (1899) I, pp. 16-17.

[3] The notion which has grown up out of these and other remarks made by Browning that he would have liked to blurt out everything in his heart but was inhibited in some mysterious way seems to me to rest on too literal an interpretation of his often hyperbolical remarks about the nature of his own art. As Professor Priestley has said to me, Browning was willing to reveal some things and not others, as his late poems "House" and "Shop" suggest. He never felt any compulsion to conceal his thoughts or feelings on the perennial problems of life and faith, but the deeply felt emotional crises of his own intimate life he would not expose to the prying eyes of the vulgar.

intuitions to tell them when he was using one of his personae to speak for him and when he was not. Today critics tend to go to the opposite extreme. They draw our attention to the multiplicity and diversity of his characters and point out that support may be found among them for almost any conceivable feeling or opinion. He has characters of every size and shape, they say, characters whom we may call villains, if we will, rubbing shoulders indiscriminately with others whom we may call saints: but he makes the villains as convincing and often more convincing than the saints. So they tell us that we must treat each of his poems as an autonomous unit with its own internal logic, not as a section of the poet's theodicy. Consequently one of his critics calls him a "relativist" poet, one whose words must be read only in the context of the dramatic situations he created for them.[4] His universe has been described by another as "pluralist", a universe of bewildering diversity from which the Absolute has been banished.[5] By another he has been called a "faceless man", one without convictions or even a personality.[6] Recently an angry young woman has even declared that he is a Samuel Beckett, and that in all his religious poems his speaking characters are existentially waiting for a God who never comes, who in fact does not exist except in their own imaginations. These characters are caught in the act of plotting routes through an enigmatic universe, she says, and building little shelters for themselves "to keep out the vast and unresponding night".[7] How dramatically the critical climate has altered in fifty years!

But the notion that he expressed nothing of himself because he was a dramatic poet rests on a misconception of the nature of dramatic poetry. No poet can produce a poem of any sort – either dramatic or lyric – that has depth, complexity, and lasting interest without putting a great deal of himself into it. In a simple lyric, like "Oh, to be in England/Now that April's there", the

---

[4] Robert Langbaum, *The Poetry of Experience*, New York (1957).

[5] E. D. H. Johnson, "Robert Browning's Pluralistic Universe", *University of Toronto Quarterly*, XXXI (1961) pp. 20-41.

[6] J. Hillis Miller, *The Disappearance of God*, Cambridge, Mass. (1963). This book has been widely read and so has been chiefly responsible for propagating a, to me, fallacious view of Browning's personality and achievement.

[7] Patricia M. Ball, "Browning's Godot", *Victorian Poetry*, III (1965) pp. 245-53.

prima-facie likelihood, in the absence of evidence to the contrary, is that the poet was expressing a feeling that he had genuinely felt, even though only momentarily or with only a part of his personality. When reading such a poem, the reader enters into a one-to-one relationship with the poet and is asked to identify himself with the latter by accepting the feeling or opinion expressed as his own. The identification is readily made when the feeling or opinion is a common or basic one; and even when it is more esoteric, like the nature mysticism of Wordsworth, the death-wish of Housman, or the religious ecstasy of Crashaw, the reader will at least suspend his disbelief and may well go farther, responding to the poem's impact with some normally submerged part of his personality. In a dramatic poem the same identification between poet and reader is asked for, but a new element has appeared, the *persona* or speaker. In this kind of poem a three-way relationship is established – reader, poet, and speaker – and the poet invites the reader to stand by his side, share his point of view, and observe at a convenient distance the antics of the speaker, as he manoeuvres, defends, and betrays himself. (The other persons normally present in a Browning monologue do not have places in this relationship; their function is to help define the personality of the speaker and to create the dramatic tensions out of which the monologue has arisen.) The reader does not ordinarily identify with the speaker at all, especially, as often is the case in Browning, when the latter has been introduced by a fanfare of the grotesque:

> Gr-r-r – there go, my heart's abhorrence!
> Water your damned flower-pots, do![8]

The reader is delighted by this humour, of course, but nothing is so effective for keeping him at a distance. Similarly he has no impulse to identify himself with the Bishop of St Praxed's when the latter wishes to go up to heaven clutching his jasper bath-tub under his arm, or with the Grammarian grinding at grammar, or with Caliban sprawling in the mud. Even when the speaker is not ridiculous or evil, he is kept at a distance from the reader by being pinned down by the poet to a particular time and place, rather than put into a universal situation, and by being involved in complex moral issues that cannot be immediately resolved, and

[8] "Soliloquy of the Spanish Cloister", 1-2.

given verse to speak that has a high conceptual content. Sometimes, of course, some degree of identification between reader and speaker does occur; but, when it does, and to the extent that it does, the poem ceases to be strictly a dramatic one. Normally, however, the reader is invited to sit beside the poet on the bench for the purpose of making a moral judgment on the speaker. The very rhetoric of Browning's monologues suggests quasi-judicial situations: many of his speakers are engaged in defending or apologising for themselves, to the police, at the bar of public opinion, or in an actual court; others are fond of putting cases even when they are only thinking aloud. He habitually puts life on trial in his poetical court and compels it to defend itself.

Emphasis is laid on the distance separating poet and speaker (or subject) in Browning's writings on the poetical character. In "How it Strikes a Contemporary", for instance, a poem that Professor DeVane rightly held to be a parable of the function of a poet, the poet is presented as a spy, one of God's spies, who goes about enquiring into the ways in which the people of the town behave themselves and reports on them at night in letters (*i.e.*, poems) addressed to "our Lord the King" (*i.e.*, God). He is self-effacing and, like Carlyle's Herr Teufelsdröckh, isolated, austere, and unseen, his activities not fully known to the town that is the subject of his writing. One receives the same impression of aloofness from the first book of *The Ring and the Book*, which is Browning's most elaborate statement of his aesthetic. The poet's isolation from the rest of mankind is made abundantly clear as, absorbed in his reading of the "Old Yellow Book", the tumultuous life of the city flows past him unregarded on either side. He is elevated above the crowd and has a special mission, which he confides to us alone. After developing his unfortunate ring-analogy with its neo-classical implications, he launches himself much more convincingly into a romantic theory of poetry, likening himself as a poet to a necromancer (Faust) and to an inspired prophet (Elisha).[9] Then, seated on his terrace like Teufelsdröckh in his attic, he abandons himself to a flight of pure fancy. His romantic aesthetic, of course, implies a great deal more than the proposition

[9] His romanticism was a qualified one: the poet, he said, cannot create (for only God can do that), but he can "resuscitate". I do not think he was speaking only of the special case of *The Ring and the Book*.

with which this paragraph began: but, whatever else it proves, it shows that in his view the poet stands above and beyond the subject of his poem, holding only so much communication with it as a judge holds with a prisoner at the bar. In fact, as he says in "How it Strikes a Contemporary", the poet is "not so much a spy, / As a recording chief-inquisitor". He is, under God, a judge. As a judge, the poet must act according to some body of law, some expressed or implied moral principles. At this point critics today find difficulty, because, they say, being a dramatic poet, Browning never spoke out his own convictions, he merely made other men speak. There are two answers to this difficulty. In the first place, only a few of his poems are fully dramatic. In some of the others the poet speaks out in his own voice (there are not only the obvious ones like "One Word More" and "Prospice", but also several of the lyrics in *Dramatic Lyrics*, for example, the ones *not* covered by the prefatory warning). In a great many more the dramatic mask is sufficiently flawed to allow the poet's face to show through. For example, it is impossible to accept "Fra Lippo Lippi" as a fully dramatic poem. The situation, to begin with, is unconvincing: in the Renaissance no policeman would care two straws about a monk's possible moral lapses in the red-light district of Florence, especially after that monk has given his address as the Medici Palazzo, and so no real dramatic tension develops between the speaker and his interlocutors. Instead of presenting an objective or dramatic situation, Browning was getting something off his chest, using Fra Lippo as his spokesman for defending his own views on art at the bar of Victorian public opinion, with a few incidental observations thrown in on the ethics of monasticism. The poem, in fact, behind its façade of dramatic poem, is a verse essay. Though Fra Lippo's views on art are not exactly the same as those expressed in *The Ring and the Book* and in "How it Strikes a Contemporary", they are not incongruous and may be taken for special applications of the same basic convictions. In many of Browning's other poems the sensitive reader will similarly detect the overtones of his voice in the utterances of his speakers, especially when the dramatic situation is not very remarkable, or when he has put substantially the same line of thought or the same imagery into the mouths of two or more speakers of different characters. Guido, for example, expresses his religious beliefs in terms strikingly similar to those used by Caliban, and versions of the philosophy of the imperfect turn up in many poems. Recurrent imagery is also most important. Browning reveals himself often through his references to the moon, a star, gold, dung, as well as through several familiar archetypal patterns, such as a journey, or the Perseus-Andromeda myth, about which Professor DeVane wrote so well.[10] While this is treacherous ground on which to erect a system of Browning's thought, it is safe to use these things as means towards understanding his basic moral values so long as one remembers that he was a poet, not a philosopher, who operated with imaginative insights rather than with articles of faith.

In the second place, in order to maintain a distance between himself and his speakers, the poet occupies a known position in moral space. In other words, his moral values must be felt before those of the speaker may be ascertained. To some extent this positioning is achieved through reliance on common sense, through an unspoken sharing of values between poet and reader, both of whom are assumed to be men of good will, right thinking, and healthy feeling. This, of course, is nebulous, though no more nebulous than the relationship habitually established between authors and their "dear readers". Browning, like other authors, however, may do much and actually does much to crystallize this nebulous relationship by subtly influencing the reader's sympathies and suggesting to him grounds for judgment. The pointed reference in the closing lines of "My Last Duchess" to "Neptune taming a sea horse" has often been noticed as a particularly good example of the means used by Browning for indicating how we ought to sum up one of his characters. Other examples might be found in other poems; *The Ring and the Book* is full of them. Most of all, of course, he does so through the way he works out his poems, through the way he rounds off his "plots".

But it must be confessed that Browning sometimes takes too much for granted. Believing strongly in the power of poetical fancy, as he calls it in *The Ring and the Book*, and in its superiority to reason, he often relies too heavily on the ability of his reader to follow him in his flights. Readers of "Count Gismond", for

[10] DeVane, William Clyde, "The Virgin and the Dragon", *Yale Review*, XXXVII (1947) pp. 33-46.

example, formerly have assumed that the speaker was an innocent
woman saved from disgrace in the nick of time by a chivalric
rescuer, and in support of this assumption they were able to point
to the analogy of the Perseus-Andromeda myth, which is one of
the most significant pieces of recurrent imagery in Browning.
But inside the poem itself there is very little to support this
assumption. Browning has indicated that the speaker was an
orphan, that she had been brought up with her cousins as a kind
of Cinderella, and that since her marriage she has lived with her
husband "in the south". But he has not given us any certain clue
to her character. Moreover who the Adela is to whom she is
speaking and why she says what she does at that particular
moment are left obscure. Consequently four recent writers,
determined to overset the critical applecart, now tell us that she
is not a virtuous woman at all but either a scheming adventuress
who has procured the death of the man who knew the truth about
her, or that she is herself the hapless victim of her Bluebeard
husband.[11] Ambiguities are much in fashion now with readers of
poetry, even sevenfold ones, but the ambiguities in "Count
Gismond" do not enrich the poem for us; they merely confuse
and bore us. Another example of this failure of communication
is "Porphyria's Lover". The speaker in this poem is a strangler
who murdered his sweetheart when she paid him a visit in his
cheerless cottage, apparently on her wedding night while her
guests were making merry in the great house close by. He had
long been in love with her and had felt sure that his love was
secretly returned, an assurance that was redoubled when she came
to him then, though she was too weak to conquer her pride and
dissever the vainer ties that were about to bind her to a man she
did not love. Like many of Browning's heroes he saw what he
should do in a flash of inspiration: he wound her long yellow hair
three times around her throat and strangled her. Now her weakness has been conquered forever, and forever she will be his.
The man, of course, is mad. Nevertheless Shakespeare often

---

[11] John V. Hagopian, "The Mask of Browning's Countess Gismond",
Philological Quarterly, XL (1961) pp. 153-5. John W. Tilton and R. Dale
Tuttle, "A New Reading of 'Count Gismond' ", *Studies in Philology*, LIX
(1962) pp. 83-95. Sister Marcella M. Holloway, "A Further Reading of
'Count Gismond' ", *Studies in Philology*, LX (1963) pp. 549-53.

made fools speak deeper truths than his sane men, and it is by no means clear that in "Porphyria's Lover" Browning was not similarly using his protagonist to convey some of his own beliefs on life and love. Porphyria's lover has grasped one positive moral principle: that it is better for a woman to be dead than to marry a man she does not love, a principle no more insane than that of, say, "The Statue and the Bust". Yet Browning has fumbled the poem in its closing lines:

> And thus we sit together now,
> And all night long we have not stirred,
> And yet God has not said a word![12]

Was the speaker expecting and subconsciously wishing for punishment? Was he either waiting for God to express his approval or implying that God's silence was tantamount to his approval? Does the point lie in the irony of his astonishment that the universe has not been disturbed by his sordid crime? Or is there a God at all? In writing this conclusion Browning may have been thinking of the words that Othello uttered when he was at a similar stage in his life:

> Methinks it should be now a huge eclipse
> Of sun and moon, and that the affrighted globe
> Should yawn at alteration.[13]

The difference is that Shakespeare's frame of reference is perfectly clear and that the more we study his lines and their implications the richer his meaning becomes. But the more we study Browning's lines the more confused we become; his focus is blurred and his implications contradictory. Ambiguities like these indicate Browning's failure in these poems to provide enough room for his reader to sit beside him on the judicial bench.[14]

[12] "Porphyria's Lover", 58-60.
[13] *Othello*, v, ii, 98-100.
[14] Many critics feel that Browning's early monologues are merely objective studies of states of mind ("modifications of passion", as Browning himself said), and that the final lines of "Porphyria's Lover" reveal nothing beyond the a-morality of the psychotic mind. There is no doubt that before *Christmas-Eve and Easter-Day* Browning was more objective than he was afterwards, but I am not prepared to admit the absolute objectivity of such poems as "Porphyria's Lover", "Johannes Agricola in Meditation", and "Soliloquy

Whether or not he was aware of these failures I do not know, but in the greater monologues similar failures in communication do not occur, and in *The Ring and the Book* his method of avoiding them was specific. It is a dramatic poem in the sense that it consists of a series of monologues, each of them very like the monologues in *Men and Women* and the other volumes of shorter poems; but, taken as a whole, it shows the dramatic poem entering a new stage of sophistication. At points, indeed, Browning seems to have gone out of his way to prevent his poem becoming dramatic in the ordinary sense of the word. Since there is a whole cast of characters rather than a single significant one, we naturally expect these characters to confront each other and to act out their passions and sorrows before our eyes. Instead he presents each one separately and makes him account for himself in isolation. The pertinent analogy is again that of the courtroom rather than that of the stage, for instead of producing a drama Browning puts each of the characters involved – the innocent as well as the guilty and even the material witnesses, lawyers and bystanders – into the dock one by one where they stand trial for their words and deeds. Even the Pope, though he delivers a verdict in Book x, is also on trial for the way he discharges his awful responsibility before the bar of the reader's opinion, the ultimate tribunal recognised in the poem (I, 1220-1). Browning, however, has not left the reader this time without guidance in arriving at his own verdict.

He guides readers of *The Ring and the Book* in two ways. In the first place he has provided a framework story, of which there is no reasonable doubt that he is himself the speaker. The latter is not only not differentiated in any specific way from Browning, as would be necessary in order to authenticate a truly dramatic persona, but he is identified with Browning positively by the facts that he lives in Florence, in Casa Guidi, is a Protestant, is not beloved by the British Public, and is a widower whose dead "lyric love" was a poetess. Moreover Browning makes it clear that his version of the story is not just one among many, to be accepted or rejected in whole or in part by the reader at his own discretion, but one specially inspired and as close to the truth as it is possible for a mortal to come. At the start, the speaker tells

of the Spanish Cloister". There is no room to discuss the question adequately here.

us, he was led by Providence to discover the Old Yellow Book among the litter in a Florentine book-stall (1, 40 ff.), and the sense of his special mission dominates the whole monologue. After reading through the documents contained in the book and mastering them, and after failing in his attempts to verify their statements empirically in Italian archives, he allows his "fancy" free rein as he goes over the narrative in his mind step by step, interpreting the motives of the characters, sorting out conflicts in the evidence and deciding each participant's degree of guilt or innocence. He writes as an omniscient author, his omniscience being of transcendental origin; not the result of creative and imaginative energy originating within himself, but a shaft of brilliant light sent down to him from heaven. His opening monologue similarly is a pillar of fire to the reader as he travels through the rest of the poem.

In the second place Browning has given his poem a significant structure. It has been said that this shows him to have had a pluralistic world view. Professor E. D. H. Johnson, who is the ablest proponent of that view, has this to say:

> The total impression created by [Browning's poetry] is of a pluralistic universe made up of people of all sorts and conditions, living in all ages and climes, each uniquely inclined to a course of action by character and circumstance. These actions portend no final resolutions; at best they are approximations more or less satisfactory according to the number of truths which they embody. . . . It is *The Ring and the Book*, however, which both in conception and form most comprehensively exhibits Browning's pluralism. . . . And however partial the truth emerging from most of the monologues, however much of it comes to us perverted by malice or the errors of self-delusion, we yet find that the limited awareness of each successive speaker has contributed to the total awareness which Browning is building up in our minds. The cumulative effect of so many conflicting versions is to evoke that kind of complex response to existence for which William James was to become the philosophic advocate. . . .[15]

[15] Quoted by kind permission of the University of Toronto Press from the *University of Toronto Quarterly*, xxxi (1961) pp. 22, 23.

Most of what Professor Johnson has written here is so true, especially that about Browning's building up a "total awareness" out of the limited awareness shown by each of his speakers, that it is rash to find any fault with him. But when the structure of this poem is examined more closely, it seems to me to suggest not William James's pluralism but a much older variety of that philosophy, the sort implied in the second term of Shelley's familiar contrast between the One and the Many. I have already referred to the powerful impression made in the first monologue by the poet's singleness of purpose contrasted with the manifold pluralism of the daily life of the streets of Florence going on about him, a key symbolism firmly planted here to illuminate the remainder of the poem. The whole structure, indeed, depends on this contrast between the One and the Many, or, to put the idea into other terms, on the irony subsisting between the truth as it is revealed to the poet and to us and the many partial truths enunciated by the characters. The principle behind it is not unlike one of the basic philosophic ideas in *Paradise Lost*: those characters in the poem who are obedient to the will of God are in possession of the truth in so far as human beings are able to apprehend it, and so their testimony has not only internal consistency but also substantial agreement with the testimony of other characters similarly situated; whereas those characters who have fallen away from God are like Milton's devils, "in wandring mazes lost". The difference between Milton and Browning in this principle is that whereas Milton's characters are mostly either angels or devils, Browning's characters are distributed throughout the moral spectrum. The chief function of Books II, III, and IV, as well as of Books VIII and IX, consequently, is to illustrate the extraordinary capacity human beings have in their varying degrees for partial truths, even those who incline to what the reader knows to be the right side sometimes failing as badly as the others. These five books might have been tedious in spite of Browning's extraordinary narrative skill, if they had not been necessary for establishing the ironic background of the poem. Against this, three separate lines of development are contrasted: the Caponsacchi-Pompilia monologues (Books VI and VII), the Pope's monologue (Book X), and the two Guido monologues (Books V and XI). These three sets contain most of the real matter of the poem. All of these characters have come close to the heart of the subject, and, though their versions by no means all agree with each other, nothing that any one of them says may be lightly dismissed.

The Caponsacchi monologue and the Pompilia monologue make up a single version of the story, for they fit together like the two parts of an indenture. Some facts may be mentioned in only one of the two, and others may be given different emphases, as is natural, but there is no significant disagreement between them. The truth of this assertion may be tested at many points: convenient examples are the incident at the theatre, which Pompilia and Caponsacchi report in almost identical terms (VI, 393-433 and VII, 950-90), and their first meeting (VI, 701 ff. and VII, 1359 ff.). Pompilia and Caponsacchi agree with each other not because they are conspirators but because they are telling the truth – the truth which is always one. Hence it is significant that Caponsacchi speaks only once, whereas Guido speaks twice: he needs to speak only once because what he says is the truth, of which there is only one possible version. He points this out himself to his judges in what a modern court might well rule a contemptuous tone; but his arrogance is that of the truth-teller and saint, the arrogance of a man who knows that he is in the right. Moreover, like all of Browning's saints and heroes, both Caponsacchi and Pompilia are able to see through the lies told by other people. She, for example, knew at once when the comfits lit in her lap at the theatre that he, whom she had never seen before, could not have thrown them (VII, 982-3), and similarly knew that the love-letters brought to her allegedly from him could not have been written by him (VII, 1125-7). In the same way he has no difficulty in seeing through the complicated web of lies told him by the infamous Margherita (VI, 676-82 and *passim*) and recognises Pompilia for the saint she is when he first meets her alone (VI, 701 ff.). He arrives at all the decisions he makes not by processes of careful logic but by inspiration (VI, 937 ff.), and his moral code is as unconventional as that of Porphyria's lover. The only sin he confesses to is failure to commit the crime of murdering Guido on sight (VI, 189 ff.). Proof that Caponsacchi and Pompilia represent the truth as Browning saw it and as, within the context of the poem, we are meant to see it is that the Pope corroborates it. Browning avoids the narrative error of having him repeat the story already told by Caponsacchi and Pompilia, but there is no doubt of his concurrence in it. Moreover, his monologue occurs in the climactic position in the structure of the poem, where all the lines of interest intersect, and it stands alone. The truth for Browning is always one and his truth-tellers do not need to repeat themselves. The Pope, of course, is not to be identified with the Absolute, with the One, because Browning presents him throughout as a human voice, not the inspired pontiff or the incarnate voice of God. But he comes as close to the truth as a mortal man can.

More will have to be said about the Pope presently, but before I do so it will be well to contrast Guido with Pompilia-Caponsacchi. Guido is the most interesting character in the poem and, as Professor DeVane has said, makes a very clever defence of himself. But Browning's success with him boomeranged, like Milton's success with Satan, who as a result has attracted a good deal more sympathetic interest than he could have been meant to. Guido, however, in spite of the depth of his characterisation and the incidental sympathy he is entitled to, is not a truth-teller. By this I do not necessarily mean that he tells lies, because throughout both his monologues he is remarkably frank and even at times clear-sighted. But he does not tell *the* truth because it is not in him. Significantly, he speaks twice, doing so because truth does not come naturally to his lips and he has to beat his way with difficulty toward the apprehension of it. The process is interrupted half way through by the Pope's verdict and sentence of death, but his two monologues make up one protracted, painful, and confused effort at self-analysis, undertaken without the aid of the transcendental insights given to Pompilia, Caponsacchi, and the Pope, and sweated out under the spur of suffering and the immanence of death. Professor Cook in his *Commentary on "The Ring and the Book"* has noted that Guido is not always consistent in his defence of himself. This is an understatement. Guido flounders through both his monologues, grasping at straws, making excuses, feeling sorry for himself, and hurling *tu-quoques* at the corrupt churchmen who confront him. At the end, though he has achieved some self-knowledge, he has not achieved enough moral strength to enable him to face death, and he collapses in utter defeat and humiliation.

The most interesting feature of the arguments that he brings forward in his self-defence is that few of them are calculated to win the assent of either the Victorian or modern reader. He makes a good deal of rhetorical capital out of his claim that a husband has the moral and legal right to kill, with his own hands, his adulterous wife, a point that had been canvassed at length in the Old Yellow Book with many precedents cited from Leviticus, and that puts him on the same level with the Duke of "My Last Duchess"; he asserts his privilege as an aristocrat to do whatever he wishes; and he declares that the Bible nowhere forbids revenge. Indeed Guido was for Browning not just a bad man but a man representing an early stage in human moral evolution, and consequently hopelessly out of date in seventeenth-century society, let alone that of the nineteenth century. Guido himself becomes aware that "the law of the game is changed" (XI, 116) and complains again against the law of moral evolution: "Why do things change"? (XI, 265). The most important evidence of the obsolesence of his moral position occurs towards the end of his second monologue (XI, 1910-2003), where he outlines his religious beliefs. He has never been a Christian, he says; he is instead "a primitive religionist" (XI, 1919), an Etruscan, like one of the aborigines described by Virgil in *Aeneid* VIII, 314-5, who were sprung from the soil and who worshipped Jove Aegiochus, the sender of storms and disasters. Men try to appease this Jove, who is "all-good, all-wise, and all-potent" (XI, 1972), but he is remote and communication with him difficult. So normally men confine their dealings to the lesser gods, the polytheistic gods of the Greeks, who fortunately are irrational bunglers and easily hoodwinked to men's sins. Guido's system of religion is similar in many respects to Caliban's, at least in respect to the concepts of higher and lower levels of divinity, the former having some resemblance to the abstract god of metaphysics, and the latter to the anthropomorphic gods. Guido, unlike Caliban, has some inkling of the idea of a god of love, but ludicrously misunderstands the concept, supposing it to mean only an easy-going, good-natured god who will wink at men's sins. At bottom, however, Guido's religion, like Caliban's, is the religion of a being who has only begun his moral evolution and whose gross clay is stirred only by the faintest impulses of real insight. There can be no question of the reader's siding with him rather than with Pompilia and Caponsacchi. The movement of the poem, then, is away from his partial, superficial, pluralistic truths and towards the centre where there is only one truth, even though it may be known only partially and in flashes.

The Pope has often been felt by readers to be Browning's spokesman and to have delivered his verdict on the moral and legal issues of the poem. Certainly there is every reason to question the dramatic nature of his characterisation, because he bears little or no resemblance to either the historical Innocent XII or any other pope living or dead, being, like most of Browning's clerics, a good Protestant at heart. Although I have said earlier that he too is on trial, he is given a speedy acquittal and remains on in the poem in the capacity of judge. As a judge, however, he spends little of his time addressing himself to the particular points of the case; for him, as for us who have read the poet's opening monologue, these are a foregone conclusion and a rehash of them would have been unnecessary and tedious. Instead he comments at large on the human situation as the events of the poem have revealed it, on man's ignorance and moral darkness, and on the power of religious insight and poetical imagination to penetrate that darkness and disclose the One behind the Many. His point of view is ambivalent: at times he speaks from the seventeenth century but at others, and on the whole more often, he is a contemporary commentator, aware of the problems and values of the modern world and possessed of enough imagination to see something of the history of man's whole moral evolution. He quickly wins our confidence and approval. To call him Browning's spokesman is to be too literal, but a great deal of what he says undoubtedly reflects what Browning was thinking about and the way in which he responded to life. He is not so much a spokesman for Browning as an ideal personality epitomising the basic values and feelings that the poet expects us to share with him and to put to use in judging the characters and events of his poem. He makes explicit in this poem what had been implicit in the other dramatic poems and had sometimes failed to become meaningful. He represents Browning's most considered attempt to express himself unmistakeably in a work retaining the outward appearance of a dramatic poem.

To study the Pope's character is not only to learn the clue to the interpretation of *The Ring and the Book* but also to let in light on many other poems as well. He is a man who combines a stern sense of duty with a warm humanity and a broad understanding of people and their problems. His outlook is ecumenical: he is sympathetic to the Molinists, he derives comfort and inspiration from the ancient Greeks, and he is prepared to include within the kingdom of God the hypothetical inhabitants of another planet. His richest scorn is poured out on the heads of clerics who consider the formularies of their church more important than the spirit of the loving Jesus. He is no dogmatist and no system can be put together from his words. He is deeply concerned over the presence of evil in the world, but he has no explanation of it entirely satisfactory to himself. To him the universe is ultimately mysterious and the ways of God past finding out. He also has an historical consciousness, intimating that the laws, dogmas, and myths that men put their faith in are all temporary and must give way as higher stages are reached in human development. Many of his opinions are individualistic and unconventional: he acknowledges the usefulness of religious doubt, is sceptical about most of the established institutions of church and state, and declares himself on the side of the soldier saints who do what their intuitions tell them is right in defiance of law and custom. These attitudes are essentially those of Browning himself, not perhaps of the Browning presented to us by his biographers, but of the Browning who projects his image to us in his poems when he invites us to look through his eyes at the vices and virtues, the follies and heroisms, the squalor and grandeur of his poetical world.

Richard D. Altick

"ANDREA DEL SARTO": THE KINGDOM OF HELL IS WITHIN

Andrea del Sarto was called "The Faultless Painter". If it were not that in Browning's poem the epithet falls short of being an unqualified term of praise, one might apply it to "Andrea del Sarto", probably the poet's greatest short dramatic monologue. Certainly few of his poems approach it in sheer intensity, fidelity, and mounting horror of psychological portraiture. The received interpretation, that Andrea is simply the victim of timidity or weakness, seems to me to fall far short of the whole truth. Has anyone yet sought to express in print the full measure of Browning's achievement in this picture of a man whose capacity for self-deception is tragically insufficient for even his momentary comfort?

Andrea's condition, as this essay proposes to demonstrate, is terrible beyond the reach of irony. Ordinarily in Browning's dramatic monologues we are superior to the speaker: we are able to see him as he does not, or at least we see more than he is aware of. But Andrea has an insight into himself that approaches our own, for he recognises as soon as we do, perhaps earlier, the illusoriness of what he calls Lucrezia's love for him, and more than that, his moral inadequacy which is manifested both in his weakness as a man and in his failure as an artist. Our response in this poem therefore is not governed by irony—irony such as we feel, for example, over the ignorance of Pictor Ignotus, who rationalises to his own satisfaction his refusal (actually his inability) to compete with the bright new stars of Renaissance painting, not knowing that the secret of great art lies in the artist's unfettered realisation of a passionate personal vision, and that he

18

is the slave of outmoded conventions. Although incidental ironies abound in "Andrea del Sarto", our response is chiefly one of pity, dictated not by the painter's ignorance but by his very lack of ignorance. He knows himself too well to find solace; no soothing balm of deception can alleviate his stark awareness of his nature and present situation. Browning elsewhere (as in "A Death in the Desert") celebrates God's mercy in providing clouds or eyelids by which man, a finite creature who cannot tolerate the absolute, is spared the blinding sun-rays of God's pure truth. In a similar manner, self-deception is a psychological device by which a human being is enabled to avert the whole intolerable truth about himself; it makes life, however less honest, a little more endurable. Andrea's tragedy is that he has no such refuge.

If this is the poem's implicit statement, it is worth repeating a few critical commonplaces to enlarge our realisation of the extraordinarily close relationship in this poem between technique and content. In "Andrea del Sarto" Browning's artistry intensifies the ultimate psychological revealment: to a degree seldom matched in dramatic poetry, the two are inseparable. Only when we comprehend the full emotional depth of his portrait of Andrea can we appreciate the degree to which poetic means here is the vehicle of poetic meaning.

As one of the finest examples of Browning's stream-of-consciousness technique, the poem has no logical progression. The speaker's thoughts wander, double back upon themselves. The setting as evening descends on Florence, his own weariness, Lucrezia, the fatality of God, his paradoxical triumph as a draftsman and failure as an artist, the cuckolding cousin, the superior gifts and fortunes of Rafael, Leonardo, and Michelangelo, the golden year at the French court and its sordid consequence when Andrea fraudulently converted to Lucrezia's pleasure the money the King entrusted to him to buy more art for Fontainebleau, a flicker of sexual passion not wholly spent – all these are interwoven in the natural involution of reverie. But this seeming aimlessness is actually reducible to one recurrent emotional movement. Andrea, brooding over the sterility of his life and the nullity of his prospects, clutches at a straw; he assumes confidence, attributes blame, or otherwise seeks peace in finding a reason, however untenable, or hope, however frail, only to have each comforting thought crumble as he grasps it. Only the disconsolate resignation born of weariness remains.

A second constant is the poem's pervasive tone, which has always been taken to suggest the technical perfection of Andrea's painting – even, lifeless, and dull – as well as his mood as he reflects on the failure of his life and seeks to divert responsibility from where he knows it really resides. The diction is no less colloquial than that of, say, Browning's other poems spoken by artists: but here is heard no lively (and slightly tipsy) "I am poor brother Lippo, by your leave! / You need not clap your torches to my face. / Zooks, what's to blame?" The music hath a dying fall. Andrea's cadences have a sad dignity which reduces our awareness of their colloquial nature; they are spoken, for the most part, in a monotone; and the fact that they belong to a soliloquy rather than a monologue – for Lucrezia can scarcely be called an auditor in the literal sense – further drains them of animation. The very exclamations seem muted. Yet beneath the lethargy and the surface placidity, beneath the gray ashes of Andrea's resignation the fires of restlessness still smolder, and once in a while they burst into momentary flame. There is not much suggestion of physical movement to relieve the prevalent mood of enervation. Once Andrea makes a gesture of still unmastered physical desire as he reaches out his hands to "frame your face in your hair's gold, / You beautiful Lucrezia that are mine!" And at another juncture he suddenly rises to correct a false detail of anatomy in a sketch by Rafael. But the impulse soon spends itself, is quenched indeed by his ready awareness of its futility: "Ay, but the soul! he's Rafael! rub it out!"

As in Andrea's painting, so in his present mood – "I often am much wearier than you think, / This evening more than usual" – and so in the poem: "A common greyness silvers everything". There is a Tennysonian perfection of sober, melancholy ambience in the lines

> There's the bell clinking from the chapel-top;
> That length of convent-wall across the way
> Holds the trees safer, huddled more inside;
> The last monk leaves the garden; days decrease,
> And autumn grows, autumn in everything.[1]

[1] "Andrea del Sarto", 41-5.

(One may believe that Tennyson would particularly have admired the choice of verb in the first line: a toneless, choked-off
clink rather than a full-voiced, resonant, freely echoing *ring*.)
The dominant colour throughout is the silver grayness of twilight.
But it too, like the prevailing silver tone of Tennyson's "Tithonus", a poem of perpetual dawn rather than of twilight, is
momentarily broken on several occasions. As in "Tithonus",
gold and fire intrude, symbolic here of two influences which led
Andrea to prostitute his gift – the celebrity and fortune he won
as a painter at Francis I's court and the irresistible attraction of
the golden-haired Lucrezia – and in addition ironically symbolic
of the fire of pure internal inspiration, the divine gift which belongs
to the true artist but was denied him, or perhaps, as he suspects,
which he threw away. The surface calm, a "perfection" of mood
corollary to the technical perfection and the neutral wash of gray
and silver tones that characterises Andrea's art, thus proves to be,
like his rationalisations, illusory. Underneath, in the succession
of quickly extinguished bursts of passion as he recalls what was
and what might have been, there is poignant disturbance. The
whole poem, so quiet in superficial impression, is in fact made
dramatic by the sustained tension between Andrea's wish to live
out what life remains to him in a sort of drugged repose and the
uncontrollable devil-pricks of his self-knowledge.

One thinks of Shakespeare's seventy-third sonnet:

In me thou see'st the twilight of such day
As after sunset fadeth in the west,
Which by and by black night doth take away,
Death's second self, that seals up all in rest.
In me thou see'st the glowing of such fire
That on the ashes of his youth doth lie,
As the deathbed whereon it must expire,
Consumed with that which it was nourish'd by.
This thou perceivest, which makes thy love more strong,
To love that well which thou must leave ere long.

But Andrea has no such comfort as is expressed in the last couplet.
Accompanying his awareness of his artistic and spiritual failure, as
his soliloquy continues its inexorable course, is the equally bitter
knowledge that, if he ever possessed Lucrezia's love, he does not

have it now. The very first lines begin with a sigh, and the true
nature of their relationship as husband and wife is at once plain:

> But do not let us quarrel any more,
> No, my Lucrezia; bear with me for once:
> Sit down and all shall happen as you wish.
> You turn your face, but does it bring your heart?[2]

The possessive "my" of the second line, here so unremarkable a
monosyllable, will acquire its own burden of irony as the situation is revealed, beginning in the very next line after these: "I'll
work then for your friend's friend, never fear."

   Unlike most of the attending figures in Browning's dramatic
monologues, Lucrezia is not a mere casual witness, a fortuitous
occasion for the speaker's revealment: she is the central figure in
his tragedy. None of Browning's unspeaking auditors is more
silent than she, and in none is silence more eloquent. Her
Gioconda smile tells more about her, about Andrea, and about
their history and present situation than could pages of dialogue.
It is the smile of a woman confident of her power over men, and
at the same time contemptuous of the man to whom she belongs,
not in fact but in name and in the transparent illusion to which he
so desperately clings. She has no interest in his art; she carelessly
smears with her robes a still-damp product of his brush. Nor
does she listen as he pours out his soul. She merely smiles, and
awaits the "cousin's" whistle.

   Lucrezia's relation to her husband, as the first ten lines of the
poem make clear, is limited to the interest defined by her very
name, which is etymologically suggestive of profit and riches.
She tolerates him, in his tired age, solely for the money he can
earn her through the dogged exercise of an admired but empty
art. Because of her, he suffers the ultimate degradation as both
man and artist. Not only is he reduced to painting frescoes,
portraits, and assorted artistic make-weights to order for a
wealthy patron ("Treat his own subject after his own way, / Fix
his own time, accept too his own price"): the commissions came
through the "cousin", her lover, and the money he is paid will be
devoted to liquidating – through the euphemism of "loans" –
that same lover's gambling debts.

----

[2] "Andrea del Sarto", 1-4.

Except for the moments when he frames her hair and essays to correct Rafael's line, Andrea's hand presumably encloses Lucrezia's throughout most of the monologue. If so, it sustains an irony initiated in the early stages of the poem. In lines 8-9, 14, 21-2, and 49, there occurs a hand-within-hand image normally suggestive of security and comfort. But the symbolic meaning is determined by whose hand holds whose or what, and in this case God's hand encloses Andrea (49), whose hand encloses Lucrezia's (14, 21-2), which will enclose the money Andrea expects from the patron (8-9) and which she in turn will hold for the cousin. Here we have no such firm belief in God's wise beneficence as is conveyed by the use of the same figure in "Popularity" – the image of "God's glow-worm", the unrecognised poet-genius, being held tightly in "His clenched hand" until the time comes for God to "let out all the beauty". Nor does "Your soft hand is a woman of itself, / And mine the man's bared breast she curls inside" have its ordinary implication of quiet, trusting intimacy. It is belied not only by the serpent-suggestion of "curls", but by the whole emotional context.

Nor, we are invited to believe, do the lover and the patron represent the limits of Lucrezia's sphere of influence. In lines echoing Dryden's "Your Cleopatra; / Dolabella's Cleopatra; Everyman's Cleopatra" (*All for Love*, IV, 1.297-9), Andrea celebrates

> My face, my moon, my everybody's moon,
> Which everybody looks on and calls his,
> And I suppose, is looked on by in turn,
> While she looks – no one's. . . .[3]

In a declension characteristic of Browning and far more devastating than Dryden's single line, the "my" gives way to the ambiguous "my everybody's", and thence to the brutal truth of the succeeding lines. Lucrezia is public property, at least so far as her superlative beauty is concerned; but she maintains the strategic distance, the cool lack of sole commitment, which is part of the desirable woman's armory of fascination. She has attributes of the *femme fatale*: her hand, inside his, represents her whole woman-self, curling snake-like against his breast; her hair is

[3] *Op. cit.*, 29-32.

"serpentining beauty, rounds on rounds"; and her low voice is like a "fowler's pipe" which the bird "follows to the snare". Physically she is the walking objective correlative of his art: she too is technical perfection, and as a work of art she too lacks the redeeming, crowning element of soul. She has "perfect brow, / And perfect eyes, and more than perfect mouth", and perfect ears into which she places pearls – jewels of the same grayness which "silvers everything" in the present setting as it does in her husband's art. "There's what we painters call our harmony!" Andrea exclaims; but it is a harmony limited to the eye, one that has no counterpart in their spirits.

Andrea seeks another kind of harmony, an acceptable simple interpretation of his life which will explain as it consoles:

> . . . the whole seems to fall into a shape
> As if I saw alike my work and self
> And all that I was born to be and do,
> A twilight-piece.[4]

And so begins the tortuous course of reflexions on his failure. Initially he is confident of his scope as artist. He

> can do with my pencil what I know,
> What I see, what at bottom of my heart
> I wish for, if I ever wish so deep – [5]

the last clause reminding us of the similar bold and unsupported claim of Pictor Ignotus: "I could have painted pictures like that youth's / Ye praise so." But boasts are cheap, and, unlike the forgotten painter whose success lies in his ability to construct tenable rationalisations for his failure, Andrea cannot delude himself for long. What begins as an assertion of superiority ends as an admission of inferiority. He is, beyond question, a facile artist, one with dazzling skills. He can do things "easily", "perfectly", "no sketches first, no studies" – "do what many dream of, all their lives". They strive, agonise, and in the end fail; he succeeds. The truth, however, as he realises, is that his is a lower order of accomplishment, the product of a "low-pulsed forthright crafts-man's hand". The striving he attributes to the rivals who envy

---

[4] *Op. cit.*, 46-9.   [5] *Op. cit.*, 60-2.

him his effortless command of technique is not, in the end, toward outward perfection but toward a quasi-religious vision that transcends colour and line.

> Their works drop groundward, but themselves, I know,
> Reach many a time a heaven that's shut to me,
> Enter and take their place there sure enough,
> Though they come back and cannot tell the world.
> My works are nearer heaven, but I sit here.[6]

True fulfilment in art occurs not in the creation but in the creator. The act of striving, stirred by the "truer light of God ... / In their vexed beating stuffed and stopped-up brain, / Heart, or whate'er else", results in no tangible evidence of success, but in an experience as supernal and ineffable as that of Lazarus or the mystics.

We have, then, the paradox that the closer a work of art comes to physical perfection, the wider the gap that separates it from true, or spiritual, perfection; and so with the artist himself. Perfection, as Browning asserts so often in his poetry, may be beyond the possibility of human achievement, but ceaselessly to struggle toward it is the impulse and deed that distinguishes man from beast, and artist from mere craftsman. "Even if the longed-for goal be never reached, even though the violence of the striving consume the soul utterly, yet it is enough that it should burn so nobly." So remarked Giordano Bruno, a philosopher of the generation just after Andrea's. In Browning's view, such struggle will strengthen, not consume, the soul. A man reaches in order "that heaven might so replenish him, / Above and through his art." But, overweighted with his special earth-bound powers, Andrea never reaches, never dares; he prefers the safety of a limited art, the perfectness, as Ruskin put it in *The Stones of Venice*, of the lower order. Unlike true artists with their fierce pride in their work, he is indifferent to praise or blame; he has no "sudden blood". His temperament is emblematised by the "length of convent-wall across the way" which "Holds the trees safer, huddled more inside"; he is, he says later, "the weak-eyed bat [a painter with weak eyes!] no sun should tempt / Out of the grange whose four walls make his world."

[6] *Op. cit.*, 83-7.

> In this world, who can do a thing, will not;
> And who would do it, cannot, I perceive:
> Yet the will's somewhat – somewhat, too, the power –
> And thus we half-men struggle. At the end,
> God, I conclude, compensates, punishes.
> 'Tis safer for me, if the award be strict,
> That I am something underrated here. . . .[7]

But can the man who values safety ever be said to struggle? The answer implicitly nullifies Andrea's momentary assurance. He is not entitled to number himself even among the "half-men" (those with the will but not the power, and those with the power but not the will). For he has not striven heroically, even in the face of certain futility, to round himself off into a whole man; therefore he will not earn God's grace. "In heaven, perhaps, new chances, one more chance", he says later – but the "perhaps" is a true measure of his confidence. The only struggle of which we have positive evidence that he is capable is the present one – the pursuit of extenuation – and it is not likely to be rewarded. Far from being attuned to divine inspiration his soul is "toned down" to the low seductive call of a callously selfish woman. On the one occasion in the poem when he looks upward, it is a physical gesture prompted by tired eyes, not a symbolic manifestation of inner desire; and the resulting vision is not of the New Jerusalem but of the walls of his "melancholy little house" cemented with the misapplied "fierce bright gold" of Francis I. He is a mercenary in a profession whose true *dévots* have a priestly vocation. At the same time – and this is the final turn of the screw – he knows that those same dedicated painters with whom he must constantly compare himself have in fact won a far greater measure of worldly fame than he has. At the end of a wasted life he has nothing to show for his ambitions but a certain ephemeral reputation for facility, while Rafael, Leonardo, and Michelangelo have enjoyed both fulfilment of spirit and ample earthly reward.

Faced with this bitter maldistribution of fortune, Andrea seeks to lay it to divine decree:

> Love, we are in God's hand.
> How strange now, looks the life he makes us lead;

[7] *Op. cit.*, 137-43.

How free we seem, so fettered fast we are!
I feel he laid the fetter: let it lie![8]

But the admission that men strive, and through struggle achieve a
glimpse of heaven, disposes of a foreordaining God as a scape-
goat. We are not "fettered fast": man's will is free. God not
serving his need, Andrea seeks some other reason for his failure –
and Lucrezia is at hand. In passages laden with past conditionals
(the subjunctive is the grammatical mode of regret), he considers
what he might have been and done:

I know both what I want and what might gain,
And yet how profitless to know, to sigh
"Had I been two, another and myself,
Our head would have o'erlooked the world!" No doubt.[9]

Had you . . . given me soul,
We might have risen to Rafael, I and you!
Nay, Love, you did give all I asked, I think –
More than I merit, yes, by many times.
But had you – oh, with the same perfect brow,
And perfect eyes, and more than perfect mouth,
And the low voice my soul hears, as a bird
The fowler's pipe, and follows to the snare –
Had you, with these the same, but brought a mind!
Some women do so. Had the mouth there urged
"God and the glory! never care for gain.
The present by the future, what is that?
Live for fame, side by side with Agnolo!
Rafael is waiting: up to God, all three!"
I might have done it for you.[10]

But this supposition is another product of a half-man. He has the
power to make it, but not the power to believe it. Its frailty is
summarised by "might have", and it is totally demolished by
what follows: "So it seems: / Perhaps not". This bleak con-
cession is neutralised for an instant by a return to the former
theme: "All is as God over-rules." But, having been destroyed
earlier, this assumption will no longer serve, and Andrea must
face the truth: "incentives come from the soul's self; / The rest

[8] *Op. cit.*, 49-52.   [9] *Op. cit.*, 100-3.   [10] *Op. cit.*, 118-32.

avail not". And the great painters he envies did not have wives, not even incomplete women like Lucrezia.

Nevertheless, this truth is not to be borne, and in his search for another incentive which would have availed him, he recalls one which indeed did once serve: "that long festal year at Fontainebleau!" This was, in retrospect, the Browningian "great moment" in Andrea's life. "I surely then could sometimes leave the ground, / Put on the glory, Rafael's daily wear." (*Could*: but did he? Rationalisation is often assisted by the merciful filters of memory.) "A good time, was it not, my kingly days?" As he describes it, however, his success even then was not of the order of a Rafael's or a Michelangelo's. He basked in the "humane great monarch's golden look"; but certain details of his description of the King suggests that Francis' favour is as irrelevant to the true source of Andrea's tragedy as is Lucrezia's lack of soul and the premise that "All is as God over-rules." The King's "curl" and "smile" link him with Lucrezia, and "his gold chain" recalls God's fetters. To be sure, there was a "fire of souls / Profuse" in those halcyon days at the court; but as far as we can tell it was in other souls, those of his admiring onlookers, not his. He was not a Rafael, "flaming out his thoughts / Upon a palace-wall for Rome to see". No: he was Lucrezia's husband, and in the end the gold of her hair worked more potently upon him than the gold of the King's patronage. "You called me, and I came home to your heart."

But was her heart – if she has one – really ever his? Certainly he does not possess it now. For as Andrea talks on, Lucrezia continues to smile, and as she smiles, the utter hollowness of his confidence becomes more pronounced. It is increasingly apparent that she dominates him absolutely, and that all he wins from her presence is the grim pretence they are bound by mutual love. His only concern in life is to satisfy her, so that she will continue to play what he well knows to be merely the meaningless simulacrum of a role. Whether or not Michelangelo was right when he told Rafael that Andrea would one day "bring the sweat into that brow of yours", all he now cares for

> Is, whether you're – not grateful – but more pleased.
> Well, let me think so. And you smile indeed!

This hour has been an hour! Another smile?
If you would sit thus by me every night
I should work better, do you comprehend?
I mean that I should earn more, give you more.[11]

Candid about his art as about his place in Lucrezia's life, he recog
nises that he is deliberately prostituting the unique talents he does
possess. But he persists in trying to persuade himself that the
purchase is worth the sacrifice. "Come from the window, love",
he pleads in phrases oddly prophetic of "Dover Beach": "Let us
but love each other". It is an empty wish, and he knows it, for
he undercuts it at once with "Must you go? / That Cousin here
again?"

His meditations in this latter part of the poem are a comming-
ling of rationalisation, realisation, and inadvertent self-reveal-
ment, all of which belie his assertion that "I am grown peaceful
as old age to-night". Not all passion is spent, for beneath the
surface, his feelings remain turbulent and conflicting. "Clearer
grows / My better fortune, I resolve to think" – but whatever
confidence is implied by the first five words is cancelled by the
succeeding revelation that it is generated by an act of will rather
than a sincere conviction. The subjunctive "would" and "should"
of lines 205-6, "If really there was such a chance" (201), and the
"Well, let me think so" (203) reinforce the contrary-to-fact tone
seen earlier in the use of frequent conditionals. "Well, let smiles
buy me!" (223), however, ruthlessly dispels the general ambivalence. Against such a blunt admission of his helplessness before
her, the succeeding platitudes – "Let each one bear his lot" (252)
and "No doubt, there's something strikes a balance" (257) –
are impotent.

The image of the walls of the New Jerusalem at the poem's end
is the culmination of a process that began in the early lines. The
"length of convent-wall" enclosing its safe huddled trees (42-3)
became "the grange whose four walls" make Andrea's – the
"weak-eyed bat's" – world (170), the idea of safety thus acquiring
the additional suggestion of cowardice and retreat. Later, the
walls turned into those of the house built with Francis' money;
their drabness gone, they were "illumined" with "fierce bright

[11] *Op. cit.*, 202-7.

gold" (216-7) and thus, by implication, tainted. Finally, the walls are transformed into those of "the New Jerusalem" upon which Leonardo, Rafael, Michelangelo, and Andrea (as he momentarily allows himself to believe) will fulfil their ultimate aspiration as artists (261-3). The concurrent expansion and alteration of the image from beginning to end of the poem is both illusory and ironic. Andrea's present confinement, symbolised by the convent wall, gives way to a vision of freedom and fulfilment. But we quickly realise, with him, that this seeming prophecy is but another futile dream.

These last ten lines of the poem contain a terrible sequence of truths, most of them ironic. There is heavy significance in the past tense of line 258: "You loved me quite enough, it seems to-night." The tense of "loved" is a slip of the tongue which adds substance to our conviction that he has a deeper subconscious awareness of the truth than his words normally express, and it renders additionally false the ensuing statement that, while Andrea's hypothesised co-workers on the celestial frescoes are without wives, "I have mine!" Neither the present tense of the verb nor the possessiveness of both verb and pronoun, we are certain by now, has any justification in fact. But the pretence persists. "There's still Lucrezia" (she is indeed still present – in the flesh) "as I choose." In this ultimate denial of the predestination he had earlier sought to embrace, he confesses that he has freely devoted himself to her, the embodiment of soulless physical perfection, rather than to the high, sacramental art to which the other three artists are dedicated. The choice may have been indefensible, as it surely was disastrous, but he alone made it.

"Again the Cousin's whistle! Go, my Love." Toward these last three monosyllables the whole poem has pointed. They are charged with the meaning of all that has gone before, as Hamlet's "Good night, Mother" is heavy with memory of the conflicting passions he has experienced in the closet scene. The verb, the possessive pronoun, and the noun: each has its bitter burden. His only comfort, and a cold one she is – the woman for whom he sacrificed his integrity as man and artist, in contemplating whom he saw mirrored at twilight the full failure of his life and character – no longer affords him even her physical presence. She leaves to keep a rendezvous with livelier company, and he resignedly watches her go ("my Love"!). He is left alone with himself, an awful fate. Like all men cursed with too much self-knowledge and lacking the saving grace of rationalisations that will stick, he carries the kingdom of hell within him.

William Cadbury

LYRIC AND ANTI-LYRIC FORMS: A METHOD FOR JUDGING BROWNING[1]

The bare face, the naked eye of the lyric poet which we watch roll in various frenzies in *In Memoriam*, *The House of Life*, and "Fern Hill", carries conviction so far as the diction of the poem, its imagery, its structure, make of it a pattern of feelings which bespeak a single vision.[2] We believe in the feelings which we see move before us, and so we believe in the poet who creates them. If the feelings are honest, coherent, and unified, we believe in the poem, in what it says. Feeling thus leads us to philosophy, not as observers but as participants, accepting what the poet says because we believe in him. Judging the worth of the attitude presented is thus the same as judging the worth of the poet who presents it, since, for the purposes of the poem before us, the poet *is* no other than the attitude.

The kind of poetry we are here describing is the lyric, which Northrop Frye tells us is characterised by the sense of the poet singing to himself and overheard by us, and which Paul Goodman

---

[1] Reprinted, after revision, from *University of Toronto Quarterly*, XXXIV (1964-65) pp. 49-67.

[2] As will become apparent, this paper is in part an attempt to bypass the perpetual argument about the nature of the dramatic monologue, by creating a terminology which will subsume the dramatic monologue and allow us to go on to other matters than its definition. For the history of the argument, see the second chapter of Robert Langbaum, *The Poetry of Experience: The Dramatic Monologue in Modern Literary Tradition*, New York (1957) and the fourth chapter of Park Honan, *Browning's Characters*, New Haven (1961) in part a refutation of Langbaum.

defines as the imitation of an attitude.[3] But there remains the poet's other face, the masked one. Here the rolling eye is not the poet's but his creature's, and the single vision is implied, not in what the creature says or feels, but in the ways in which the poet makes him say his say and demonstrate his feeling. This form we may call the anti-lyric, remembering that it differs from drama and from epic in that it is neither acted on stage nor sung directly to an audience, but that it differs from lyric too in that we do not see the poet plain – in fact, we can only make sense of anti-lyrics by remembering always to be aware of the difference between the poet and the words of the poem. If the poet does his job we believe in the *persona* as man, but we are not concerned to test the truth of what he says. Here again we come to philosophic thought, but now through seeing a worth in speech beyond what the speaker knows. The anti-lyric contains an attitude again, but this time we do not judge it or feel it directly; we must first feel the character who displays it, not the attitude itself, and so we may call the anti-lyric an imitation of a character. His feelings need not, in fact should not, be honest, coherent, and unified, for the fact that they are not informs us that we are not reading lyric.

We can only perceive a character as a character if we feel his distance from ourselves, and if we do this we must judge him, for better or for worse. When Caliban stones his twenty-first, for instance, we are prevented from sympathy with his otherwise seductive theology, and so we know how to take him, despite the brilliance of his arguments. We learn to know our man, and all his pleading only makes us know him better. And so the poet, to keep himself separate from his character, must invest him with special and distinctive attributes which will, like Caliban's brutality, enforce the reader's distance as well. Always we judge the statements of anti-lyric at one remove, not seeking to feel an on-going attitude directly, but seeking to feel it in its relationship to a created character.

But Wayne Booth and Simon Lesser point out from their widely differing points of view that we are ready and eager to

[3] Northrop Frye, *Anatomy of Criticism*, Princeton (1957) pp. 250, 272; Paul Goodman, *The Structure of Literature*, Chicago (1954); reprinted in Phoenix edition (1962) used here: pp. 184, 216, 272.

identify with almost *any* character.[4] If the character's perverse attitude is too compelling, we may lose our bearings, forget the poet who controls the creature, and so read as final what must be only intermediate, a step on the way to philosophic thought. The sprawl of critical opinions on "My Last Duchess" indicates the danger. The poem can be and has been read as depiction of a tough-minded realist putting off the sentimental woman who cannot distinguish between cherry-boughs and men.[5] Read this way, the rhetoric of the poem must be taken to make us feel that we are being stretched beyond the normal limits of our humdrum morality, that the duke's putting off his duchess is the lamentable but necessary consequence of his strong personality, and vital for its fulfilment. And yet we know perfectly well that such a reading is absurd; it is not the lover of cherry-boughs who is inhuman in her sentimentalism, but the possessor of the nine-hundred-year-old name in his. We must test the poem against our outside knowledge of what kinds of character Browning will create and how he will judge them, if we are even to begin to resolve the possible ironies. We must supply, from outside knowledge, awareness of the poet displaying his narrator, and to make the effort is to disrupt our reading of the poem.

But the problem is most severe of all in poems in which the touchstones of value must be accepted entirely on faith. In these we have insufficient evidence of the narrator's personality to feel him as real, and thus to know him or evaluate his feelings. Such a poem is "Count Gismond". Here again we are in no real doubt about values. Gauthier is bad and Gismond good; the woman, a calumniated innocent, has *not* committed adultery with Gauthier; Gismond and his rescuee escape from their vicious and sordid society to a tranquillity which that society cannot allow. Mulling over Browning's characteristic poetic patterns, we can see that "Gismond" is imitated in "The Glove", and that both are forecast

---

[4] Wayne C. Booth, *The Rhetoric of Fiction*, Chicago (1961) pp. 155-8; Simon O. Lesser, *Ficton and the Unconscious*, Boston (1957); reprinted in Vintage edition, New York (1962) pp. 201-3.

[5] Thomas J. Assad, "Browning's 'My Last Duchess' ", *Tulane Studies in English*, x (1960) pp. 117-28. B. R. Jerman, "Browning's Witless Duke", *PMLA*, LXXII (1957) pp. 488-93, takes what I think is an equally mistaken view, and is corrected by Laurence Perrine, "Browning's Shrewd Duke", *PMLA*, LXXIV (1959) pp. 157-9.

by the Jules and Phene episode of *Pippa Passes*. In all three poems, positive and direct social action cuts through sham. Aware of poetic structures, we see that all three poems are ironic comedies of Frye's second phase.[6] But this awareness is unfortunately not enough. Recognition of similarities in structure cannot create understanding of any given poem, although it can help us to recognise a poet or to place a given, already understood work in the whole context of literature. So we must always look to the rhetoric of the particular piece before we place it in its apparent structural niche. In the Jules-Phene episode and in "The Glove", the rhetoric clearly reinforces the structural pattern in a very simple and direct way. We can have no doubts about the unpleasantness of Lutwyche's morality, nor about the attractiveness of Jules'. In the monologue form of "The Glove" there is more possibility for confusion, but the narrator, the cynical and punning Ronsard, is fully realised; we know that he has no interest in lying to us, and so we can question what he says only by asking his relationship to it. Why, we ask, does he remain in a court, the depravity of which he sees so clearly? He remains precisely because of the operation of the humorous irony which is the tone of the poem. His defence against depravity, his ironic wit, makes particularly vivid the necessity for less ironic souls to get out.

"Gismond" is altogether weaker than these. Like "The Glove", it is narrated, yet we can see none of the excuse for narration which is present in "The Glove". We believe the woman's story because, as she reports it, Gauthier at his death admits his lie.[7] But without his admission, we would have no way to determine the truth; the woman might well have gulled Gismond into defending her depravity. If we test her tone as we tested Ronsard's, we find much to disturb us – the lady's image of the bloody sword which swings against her from Gismond's hip, and her final statement to Gismond (which we know to be a lie, though we may not know its purpose) that she has been describing her tercel's

⁶ This phase of comedy is described in *Anatomy*, p. 180.

⁷ Among the few recent discussions of "Gismond", we may single out Ina Beth Sessions, "The Dramatic Monologue", *PMLA*, LXII (1947) pp. 503-16, especially pp. 510-1. E. D. H. Johnson, *The Alien Vision of Victorian Poetry*, Princeton (1952) pp. 92-3; sees no possible ambiguities in Gismond's lady.

slaughterous prowess, might well be taken as imagistic proof of her mingled love of sex and violence. We cannot see in her tone, as we could in Ronsard's, a proof of personality clear enough to let us judge her or her story with conviction. We are, then, convinced of her innocence, not through knowledge of her character, but through Gauthier's admission of guilt, which is a result of the narrative of the poem, not of its drama. The anti-lyric form is not only unnecessary, but disrupting to accurate response, and so we feel it finally as a sentimental pose, an arbitrary device for achieving pathos.

The imitation of character which is the sign of anti-lyric is, then, only fully justified when it creates a response beyond what the imitation of attitude, the sign of lyric, could attain to. And it is particularly important that the choice of imitation be justified when, as so often, Browning intends to invert our normal responses, to demonstrate that an attitude we take for granted is insufficient explanation of life's complexities. He can, after all, always choose the lyric presentation. "Apparent Failure", for instance, quite simply tells us what Browning thinks and builds his case for thinking it; if we disagree that the poor suicides may be blessed, we do so in opposition to the attitude which it is the poem's point to create.

But when Browning chooses the other option, anti-lyric, the choice must be justified by a vision of character so complex that only the tension between the character and our perception of him as different from ourselves can sustain the vision. The Bishop ordering his tomb, for instance, is both a decadent churchman whose spirituality is riddled by materialism, and a typically Renaissance lover of art whose over-whelming aesthetic drive vindicates his trickery. No one simplification of his character could do him justice, and so we are made to hover, distant from him, between our possible judgments. Our scorn is undercut by sympathy with his desire that lapis delight the world, yet our sympathy is undercut by our certain knowledge that the lapis will not, that his sons are selfish and corrupt through the logical extension of his values.[8] Sympathy and scorn remain blended in a percep-

[8] Roma A. King, *The Bow and the Lyre*, Ann Arbor (1957) p. 56, sees the Bishop as largely contemptible, and so disagrees with Honan (p. 134), with F. L. Lucas, *Eight Victorian Poets*, Cambridge (1930) p. 29, and with me.

tion of integrity of character which could only come about through his own presentation of his case. This is the kind of complexity for which the anti-lyric is made.

"A Grammarian's Funeral" arrives at as fine a complexity, but, since the monologue is not the grammarian's but a disciple's, it justifies its technique in a different way. The dramatic situation here is not of central interest, since we are more concerned with the grammarian, the subject of the poem, than with the disciple, its narrator. Here, as in "The Glove", the conviction carried by the narrator's personality conditions our reaction. No matter how we might be tempted to doubt the worth of the grammarian, we see at least that he could inspire the disciple's wholly noble fervour. Through the disciple we see that the grammarian is both pedant and pioneer, and that he deserves his noble grave just because the disciple thinks he does.

We would see no need for the distancing narrator if the grammarian's goals were obviously high, if the subject of the poem were a theologian, say, or a scientist. But he is not; he is a grammarian who indulges in the most absurdly minute studies of the silliest possible things, and we would normally view him as a sell-out, someone who backs away from larger questions. If the attitude were Browning's, not the disciple's – if, in short, the poem were lyric rather than anti-lyric – we would have the choice of viewing him this way, of rejecting the imitated attitude. But because the object of imitation is the disciple's character, the choice is not open to us. What looks at first like a withdrawal from life is in fact a commitment to it on a deeper level than we might at first allow. And it is only through the creation of the disciple, living proof of the efficacy of the grammarian's personality, that such a daring inversion of our normal response can be surely established.

But the dangers of the subject of apparent failure are as real as the rewards, since it is so easy for apparent failure to become failure indeed. Like the poems which we have been describing, "Childe Roland to the Dark Tower Came" and "Love Among the Ruins" deal in anti-lyric form with the theme of apparent failure; since one succeeds and the other fails *through* their anti-lyric forms, they may stand as demonstrations of the criteria for anti-lyric.

"Childe Roland", like "A Grammarian's Funeral", "In a

Balcony", and many others, demonstrates the consequences of voluntary submission to bondage; and Roland's, like the grammarian's, is a bondage to a quest which is in itself a wasteland journey. But here the final success of the quest is not so clear, precisely because we see Roland as he sees himself, not as another sees him. If he were (like Norbert of "In a Balcony") to praise his own achievement, we would feel, as we do in that poem, that Roland had put himself beyond our sympathy with his arrogance; we could not share his attitude, and that attitude is all we have, since we lack a separate narrator. But all we and Roland know is that he somehow matches himself with his world in such a way that an illumination is possible for him which was not possible for his companions on the quest. His success lies in coming to the brink of action, not in the action itself. We never know if he wins or loses in his struggle with the tower, and it does not matter.[9] His ability to see the tower and to blow the horn is proof enough of his virtue. Our consciousness of Roland's character as different from our own enables us to judge the process of his action as we judged the Bishop's last moments, and as we judged the grammarian through his disciple. As participant, Roland must judge on grounds of what he can foresee of the end of his action; but as observers, we may judge of its process, what the narrator's attitude displays of his character.

We are conscious of our difference from Roland, and this consciousness allows us to judge his worth rather than the accuracy of his interpretation of life. But at the same time we are drawn to Roland's character through empathetic sharing of his universal quest. As in "The Glove", the poem's tone creates our response, and here, as there, the tone is created from two plaited strands. Stanza pattern and metre in "Childe Roland" support our distance, while the run-on lines which undercut the stanza pattern, and the rhythm which works against the metre, create our involvement. Stanza pattern is carefully interlocked, coming always to a full and predictable close and emphasising by its recurrence the integrity of each stanza; but rhythmical stress is varied freely in each line and run-on lines predominate. The threatened breakdown but constant control of a rigid pattern

---

[9] For a reading opposed to mine, see E. D. H. Johnson, p. 95, and for a reading with which I largely agree, see Langbaum, pp. 192-200.

make us feel that the pressure of experience will overrun the boundaries of metre and stanza, while we are always conscious that recurrence is there. We have, then, as the poem's prevailing tone, a sense of strong feeling leading in the direction of impassioned but informal prose rhythm and so enforcing identification with the knight, but at the same time we have clearly bounded rhyme, metre, and stanza, enforcing distance from the obviously *created* narrator. The feelings are patterned, but by their tendency to break their pattern they convince us of their pressure – despite its formality, the verse is on-rushing, involved.

Our involvement with the knight in the process of his search allows us to avoid assigning values to knight, wasteland, or tower, but our formal distance permits us to ask why this knight could see the tower when the others failed. As always in the best of these poems, the answer lies in the knight's shifting attitudes which we perceive as his character. Up to the point of his despair (section xxvii) he faces the landscape with courage, but he consistently errs in trying to give it meaning and pattern; each attempt to impose meaning is at once proved false. He expects to be able to orient himself to the road, and so the road disappears; he expects to discover that memory will give him courage, only to learn that memory is more appalling than perception of present horror; he expects that the river will divide the world he knows into recognisable moral opposites, and so he finds that the far side is as terrible as the near. But on the far side of the river we see that the landscape does present consistent reductions of the possibility of meaning. We see examples of meaningless disorder in various areas of human activity – signs of combat show no ending, neither corpses nor footsteps leading away; torture implements, evidences of human villainy, rust away[10]; agricultural leavings rot by villainous chance. The pattern of emptiness forces him in the end to accept lack of meaning and admit defeat in his search for pattern. It is then that he despairs; he realises that there is no moral value in the world for him to find. He

[10] David Erdman, "Browning's Industrial Nightmare", *Philological Quarterly*, xxxvi (1957) pp. 417-35, takes "the engine . . . fit to reel / Men's bodies out like silk" to be "rusted industrial equipment" (p. 423), in keeping with his thesis. The image contains medieval and modern brutalities, but I think it is a device for torture, not a part of a factory, that Roland sees.

escapes, as do the heroes in Auden poems, from the illusion that
the quest is meaningful in conventional moral terms; transcen-
dence of his preconceptions can then be indicated by the bird of
despair which projects his feelings and vision out of himself and
which is for the first time a guide. When he can see beyond the
kinds of order he had presupposed, the tower which he sees becomes the quintessence of the disorder with which he had been
faced before but which he had refused to admit. A symbol in the
landscape can summarise the landscape when he looks out, not
in; the tower summarises all disorder by its darkness. Roland
now has something he can fight, and the discovery of lack of order
is itself an ordering.

I think we participate in this process of on-going experience,
and its variation is the strength of the poem. But even at this
point Browning could still go wrong – Roland could spell out
the moral of his experience, back away from it to give judgment.
We would then judge the judgment which is made, not the man
who makes it. But as in the others of the best monologues –
"Andrea del Sarto", "The Bishop Orders his Tomb", even
"Caliban upon Setebos" – Browning does no such thing. Roland
fails to understand that he has learned the truth of things, and so
blames himself for his obtuseness – "Dotard, a-dozing at the very
nonce, / After a life spent training for the sight!"[11] In the two
penultimate stanzas he flays himself for his stupidity, but we know
that it has not been stupidity at all. Roland has achieved a particular condition which finally lets him see what he sought, what
was there all the time, and what he could not see for his very
looking. But Roland never achieves articulate understanding –
all he knows at the end is that now he has a chance to fail. So
while we observe his pride at being able to blow the slug-horn,
we are not bothered by the pride as we are bothered, say, by the
posturing of the lover of "In a Gondola", or by the sense that
Norbert in "In a Balcony" may have used his consciousness of
moral choice to escape his moral duty.[12] Roland can in no way
gull himself or us when he does not even understand his action.

[11] "Childe Roland", 179-80.
[12] For an argument directly opposed to my implications on the playlet,
and summarising the controversy over its ambiguities, see E. E. Stoll,
"Browning's 'In a Balcony' ", *Modern Language Quarterly*, III (1942) pp. 407-15.

Because Browning keeps himself so rigorously out of the poem that he does not even give Roland's moralising (which might be taken for his own), and because Roland's attitude is made so clear and his confusion so convincing, we are left in no danger of ruining the poem in either of the two possible ways – we cannot claim, as we could with "Rabbi ben Ezra" or "My Last Duchess", that Browning is loading the poem, that he creates the character to prove a point of his own which we learn by applying the standards of an external morality; nor can we claim, as we could with "Count Gismond", that we do not observe the narrator's feelings clearly enough to distinguish his motive from his statement. We come to philosophic statement, as we must in anti-lyric, through understanding of the character's response to events, not through interpretation of the events themselves. And of course this kind of success is possible only through the techniques of anti-lyric, in which a created character need not understand the springs of his own action.

"Love Among the Ruins" presents the same pattern in its plot as does "Childe Roland", and was probably written on the day after it, as Browning claimed.[13] Here, as in "Childe Roland", a narrator at the end of a survey of a landscape finds his salvation in a concentration of will on one object which becomes summary and centre of the landscape. But where Roland's leap into action is in an exulting despair, the lover's in "Love Among the Ruins" is in an extinguishing and triumphant self-immolation, and at the end of his poem he moralises upon it. Roland and the lover both turn away from reflexion on their worlds to action in them, but

---

[13] William Clyde DeVane, *A Browning Handbook*, 2nd. edn., New York (1955) p. 212, accepts Mrs Orr's claim for the dating, and relegates the most important attack to a footnote. That attack, Johnstone Parr, "The Date of Composition of Browning's 'Love among the Ruins' ", *Philological Quarterly*, XXXII (1953) pp. 443-6, would put the poem no earlier than 1853. The theory has obtained critical support; see, for instance, the analytical entry by Francis G. Townsend in Austin Wright, "Victorian Bibliography for 1953", *Modern Philology*, LI (1954) p. 248. Yet DeVane's reluctance to forego at least the part of the dating which claims that "Childe Roland" and "Love among the Ruins" were written on subsequent days seems justified, since the two poems are so similar in setting and pattern. Erdman, p. 426, n. 14, points out that Parr's argument in another paper, "The Site and Ancient City of Browning's 'Love among the Ruins' ", *PMLA*, LXVIII (1953) pp. 128-37, "rather supports the accepted date" than Parr's own claim.

Roland's act (blowing the slug-horn) is a mediate goal on the way to one farther off which we cannot see, and so is summary of the process of the poem, not an Aristotelian end. The lover's act is, on the other hand, an embrace which is a final goal in itself, and so is in itself a moral comment which we must judge beyond the judgment of his character. Roland's final action is contained in his poem; the lover's is a gratuitous addition.

This distinction would not in itself damn "Love Among the Ruins", were it not that the moral of the action and the moralising reflexion which the narrator insists upon ("Love is best") seem, in fact, at odds. The narrator's shifting attitude simply does not lead to the conclusion that "Love is best", and so the worst of anti-lyric traps snaps shut – we cannot tell whether Browning intends us to take the narrator as right or wrong, as a spokesman for the poet with whose thought we are to agree, or as a deluded character like Roland who does not know what we know. The necessary signals for lyric or anti-lyric form are omitted, and to reach a final understanding we are forced to go outside the poem, to look to Browning's usual practice to tell us what Browning wanted us to think.

Clearly the trouble with "Love Among the Ruins" lies not merely in the fact that the narrator is a mediator between ourselves and the material he talks about. Subject matter in mediately narrated poems is only the medium for the poems' statements. "The Glove" is *about* Ronsard's sophisticated reaction to an equally sophisticated story; "Up at a Villa" is *about* the narrator's wistful longing for the city life he presents so vividly; "A Grammarian's Funeral" is *about* the disciple's fervour and its cause in his master's character. If we read any of these poems as imitations of attitudes, instead of imitations of character, we misread them, we miss the point. "Love Among the Ruins", on the other hand, seems *intended* to be about the contrast which dictates its structure, the contrast between old and new modes of life symbolised by characteristic settings. Its appropriate form is thus lyric, the form which allows concentration on the statement made rather than on the character who makes it. But the narrator is always before us; we observe a character different from ourselves who makes judgments different from those that we would make. So we judge him, as we judge Caliban or Andrea, to be wrong, and we read the poem, as we read all anti-lyrics, in terms of the tension established between the character and our expected responses. Yet, from our knowledge derived from other poems, we know that the anti-lyric reading is not what Browning intended. The failure of the poem is then a failure in basic strategy.

We may begin again with tone, which is the result of style and which in many cases signals us of intended form. Metrical recurrence in "Love Among the Ruins" creates precisely the opposite response from the very different kind of recurrence in "Childe Roland". We claimed for that poem that metre and stanza pattern distanced us, while rhythmic variation and run-on lines led to identification with the pressure of the knight's feeling. In "Love Among the Ruins", on the other hand, metre and pattern are self-sufficient, unopposed by varied shifts in rhythm. So the effect is of incantation, which tries to draw us in, to make us share the poem's attitude in sharing its dominating metre. As in Swinburne, the preponderance of weakly stressed syllables in the long lines, and the rigidity of the stress pattern in evenly alternated long and short lines, keep us involved in the pattern itself, not in its variations; we are always in danger of forgetting the possibility of variation and reading the poem as interminable sing-song. The only rhythm of the poem *is* its metre, and so we are drawn in, not out – to, not from, what the metre supports. And the very alternation of long and short lines, on the surface a clear variation, creates a sense of reverie in its unvarying repetition. The almost unvarying falling junctures at the ends of the long lines give the short lines which follow the quality of associative bursts, returns to and reflexions on the long lines. So the rhythm is modified in the direction, not of prose, but of association.[14] The evidence of rhythm, at least, indicates that as in all lyrics we overhear the meditation of the author.

The poem is usually read as lyric, and it is read as saying that the original inhabitants of the plain on which the ruins stand were destroyed by a commercially motivated lust for power. They took the wrong path, strove to dominate their environment by denying its natural character, loved hard sex, hard money, hard architecture, and so decayed. The narrator knows, however, and

[14] The terms and procedure of metrical analysis are derived from Northrop Frye, The *Well-Tempered Critic*, Bloomington (1963) pp. 75-80.

proves by juxtaposition in his poem, that perfect involvement in a relationship of true feeling is a better expression of sympathy with the environment than that reached by the aboriginals. He knows that his feeling for love is the way most in tune with nature, which approves in its very process solitary and subtle feeling, and disapproves in that process ambition, lust, and violence, by destroying their very traces.

So the narrator almost certainly does mean – but we must be very sure of the validity of his thought and of his character before we too can accept that love is best; as readers of anti-lyric, prepared for that form by the ambiguities of the narrator's relation to his poem, we must judge the quality of the narrator's feeling.

The principal symbol of the poem is the plain, the Campagna if it is indeed.[15] It is through his response to this symbol that we learn both the narrator's point and how we must evaluate it. The narrator treats the plain, like everything else in the poem, in two perspectives, past and present. In the past, the scenery was bounded by a wall "Bounding all", and within that wall were buildings, bridges, and above all, men. It was, in fact, a city "great and gay",[16] and it imposed its will through violence, planning "Peace or war",[17] and sending out armies to dominate others. The city was, in short, isolated, bounded by its wall, completely self-sufficient with its stock of "joy and woe"[18]; and yet, of course, its characteristic mode of action was not centripetal but centrifugal, since for its self-assertion this self-contained, self-conscious organism sent out armies from its centre of power.

In the present, the encircling wall is entirely lost, the earth has by historical process covered all, and not only the characteristically vertical architectural landmarks, but even trees, natural vertical frames of reference, are obliterated, so that it is only by the "rills / From the hills"[19] that we can tell features of the landscape apart "(else they run / Into one)".[20] Where there were men with joys and woes there are now only sheep. Where there were buildings there are now grasses. The plain has become featureless country, a land of possibility rather than achievement

---

[15] For the extensive scholarship on the landscape and its literary origins, see DeVane, pp. 212-3.

[16] "Love among the Ruins", 7.

[17] Op. cit., 12.

[18] Op. cit., 31.

[19] Op. cit., 15-16.

[20] Op. cit., 17-18.

– yet the being is not a becoming, for the characteristic time of day, the narrator makes plain, is evening, which quietly smiles to watch the "folding" of the sheep,[21] a drawing in to rest. Unlike the city of the past, the landscape now is boundless; not isolated and single but universal. Its very fluidity and formlessness is its point.

The characteristic landmark of the place is the tower at the city's centre, which is, like the landscape around it, seen from a double perspective in time and indeed occupies the poem's spatial centre, being described in the fourth of the poem's seven stanzas. This tower (or lesser spires imagistically equivalent) shot up in the past "like fires",[22] and was a "brazen pillar".[23] The tower "sublime" at the dead spatial centre of both poem and landscape (the description shifts to it at the forty-third line of the poem's eighty-four) is ringed by a burning ring made by the racing chariots which parallels nearer the heart of flame the wall bounding all. In the present, on the other hand, this phallically dominating and vaginally ringed tower has shrunk to a turret which was in the past only a basement, and even that turret is overgrown by the fertile land. Far from dominating, it seems only a referent. It fails to mar the flatness of the landscape, which despite the presence of the turret contrasts still with the verticality of the city.

With the characteristic landmark in its two avatars, set in the characteristic landscape in its two, go characteristic actions. In the past, the action was the looking out from the tower of the king. He could see "Far and wide",[24] but his looking is more importantly summarised in the observation of the closest of the rings of concentric circles – "the monarch and his minions and his dames / Viewed the games",[25] the chariot race. Now, in the same place where once the king looked out as "the charioteers caught soul / For the goal",[26] a girl "with eager eyes and yellow hair"[27] waits in perfect patience for the narrator. Unlike the king, involved in his act of watching chariots and city, she seems without life without the narrator, is "breathless, dumb".[28] When the narrator arrives, the appropriate modern act takes

[21] *Op. cit.*, 51.   [22] *Op. cit.*, 20.   [23] *Op. cit.*, 75.
[24] *Op. cit.*, 62.   [25] *Op. cit.*, 47-8.   [26] *Op. cit.*, 57-8.
[27] *Op. cit.*, 55.   [28] *Op. cit.*, 59.

place, paralleling the watching of the chariot race but reversing its imagistic tone, as the folding of the sheep parallels but reverses the sending out of armies. The action is opposed in every way to the king's active and centrifugal observation. The girl will look at the narrator, not out from the tower but in to another object on the ex-basement turret, and narrator and girl will "extinguish sight and speech / Each on each",[29] extinguishing as they do the city's flame. The capture of the landscape in the act of looking at the summary of the landscape, which was characteristic of the old days, has given way to the "embrace" of the eye[30] and the extinguishing of the landscape in the new. And, of course, the new landscape, gray, hill-less, without landmarks, is entirely appropriate to this centripetal action, while the old landscape, visual, vertical, architectural, carried the eye out and captured it in its flame. Nature, clearly, has brought about the change: nature, which takes revenge on verticality, on architecture, on the centrifugal movement, by its horizontals which allow the centripetal flow.

The ancient city was, of course, corrupt – gold built it, financed its wars, led to its decay. The consequence was lust, shame, the "blood that freezes, blood that burns".[31] And on the other hand the modern landscape *is* fertile, all grass and sheep, and the evening smiles at it for all that it is "undistinguished grey".[32] The narrator sees and presents the fires, the violence, the commerce, the lust. The good of these, his juxtapositions imply, are preserved in the fertility of the land, in the gold turned to yellow hair, in personal love which has supplanted the thinly veiled sadistic sexual power. The sexuality of the city and its public games has been changed to a personal sexuality, and the social sex of the burning ring around the tower, brutal, impersonal, and violent, has been replaced by the tender embrace of the lovers on the levelled turret.

We cannot disagree with the narrator, or find flaws in his motivation, when he claims that money is bad, and commerce bad, and armies bad, and violence bad. If we are to damn Caliban for his brutality, as I think we do, surely we can agree with this narrator in his damning of another, less obvious brutality.

[29] *Op. cit.*, 71-2.   [30] *Op. cit.*, 69.
[31] *Op. cit.*, 79.   [32] *Op. cit.*, 53.

But the alternative, when presented in the imagery which we have seen, is not, by the same token, so perfect and acceptable a resolution of the city's imbalances as the narrator would have us think. If the lovers put out the fire of the burning ring, they also extinguish sight and fire together. The landscape with its burning spires is no longer fiery and phallic, but it has become formless, "undistinguished grey" which "melts" rather than burns – indeed, it is the wasteland of the previous day's "Childe Roland", though in a different tonality. Armies going out to battle no doubt represent the evils of a violent and commercial imperialism, but sheep put in their pens in a smiling sunset go to an equal, though more peaceful, bondage which is equal death.

In short, though architecture and chariot-races may be sterile, still grass, formless grayness, and extinguished sight are not so fertile in their symbolic overtones as they are impotent. The fires which are extinguished with sight remind us that Freud finds the possession of sight an inevitable symbol of sexual potency.[33] It seems then that the achievement of the perfect love and perfect oneness which the narrator uses to contrast ancient and modern city and plain are all too closely linked for him with death, dissolution, formlessness, and impotence. The world of excitement, life, and money gives way to a world of passion, death, and self.

So it is not only decadence and violence which seem bad to the narrator, but, as his imagery shows, involvement in the world – his ideal is a formless grey of passion which is indistinguishable from death and isolation, a centripetal movement indeed. For us, watching him and trying as readers of lyric to accept his attitude, it seems entirely appropriate that the earth should bury the ancient city. But as possible readers of anti-lyric, made suspicious by the narrator's attitude which seems so different from our own, it seems to us too great a reversal of our values that the fertile love which is the characteristic action of the modern plain is also a kind of death. The narrator's final implicit claim

[33] See Norman N. Holland, "Freud and the Poet's Eye", *Literature and Psychology*, XI (1961) pp. 36-45, especially pp. 39-40, for the relevant references, and for the argument that Freud himself, like most men, valued sight as equivalent to sexual power. On this point see also Sandor Ferenczi, *Contributions to Psycho-Analysis*, tr. Ernest Jones, Boston (1916) pp. 228-33.

that he has proved that love is best strikes us like Caliban's stoning his twenty-first, and we reject it. We find suddenly that we have read the poem as anti-lyric, that we have judged this all too realised character as we have taken in his attitude.

The narrator's projected achievement, his vision of the good, is then oblivion in pleasure which relieves responsibility. Browning has created an extraordinarily realised narrator, only for us to judge him as we might any other of Browning's extraordinarily realised characters. We are not convinced of the superiority of his kind of love to the old city's lust. The city had vitality, shape, form, not just extinguishing feeling. If we take the poem as lyric, as a product of Browning the poet which Browning the thinker should stand by, we see that it deals with the same problem as does Tennyson's *Idylls of the King*, yet in its answer to the problem it stands the values of the *Idylls* on their heads. Tennyson's masterpiece presents the necessity for social action (even with its seeds of decay) for the achievement of a stable balance of sensuality and aggression; within his Camelot and Arthurian order both are all too transiently satisfied, yet the social world of Arthur mirrors the healthy individual mind. In "Love Among the Ruins", on the other hand, Browning seems to solve his guilt and ours by removing one element of the disturbing mixture, by saying that sex purged of aggression may be as peaceful and sweet as the folding of sheep in evening, and as safe. He sees that social action is dangerous, leads to the manifestation of aggression which he fears, and so he achieves his sensuality in an extinction which removes the cause of fear; the blind lover, after all, can do no grievous violence. Both poets then strive to resolve the conflict between instinctual components, but where Tennyson's poetic myth achieves a unification of feeling and action in the perfect city, Browning's achieves the extinction of the city itself in an extinguishing love.

This analysis of both the *Idylls* and "Love Among the Ruins" takes them as rhetorical paradigms of health, imitations of actions which demonstrate their authors' ideas of health in society and in the individual. To read them both this way implies that both are lyrics, that they can be compared directly because they ask the same kind of response of their audiences. Certainly the *Idylls* are lyric within our definition, and equally certainly "Love Among the Ruins" would be an entirely reputable lyric if it were not for the smoke-screen of the narrator. As in "Apparent Failure", which gives us no reason to assume a dramatic narrator, we should have a choice of agreeing or disagreeing with the attitude imitated. If we were sure that the poem were lyric, that Browning might be called to account for the attitude the poem creates and imitates, then we might criticise it as we have just done, analysing the implications of its attitudes. Or we might look to the poem for biographical judgment of Browning, seeing in it support for Betty Miller's contention that Browning wanted to escape from responsibility and to be coddled, that he wished to submerge personality rather than to fulfil it.[34] These two critical techniques would lead us to respectively literary and non-literary judgments, but in neither case could we complain of the poem's technique, no matter how much we might object to the attitude which the technique supports.

But these judgments are not the point of this paper. For the smoke-screen is there, and the obscurity which results prevents us from reaching the level of critical analysis which would allow us to evaluate the poem's attitude. We simply do not know whether Browning wishes us to take his poem as true version of philosophy, or to read it as the attitude of a no doubt flawed character like the many others he so brilliantly creates. We have, after all, a narrator whom we know not to be Browning: he is too fully realised, too firmly set in the scene of his action, too different in his responses from the bed-rock humanity which writers of lyric must count on to achieve their audiences' sympathies. The narrator is dramatic, and the poem is not an imitation of an attitude, but, as anti-lyrics are, an imitation of a character. And from this fact develops the irony which pulls us out of the poem and which by so pulling us makes us able to damn the poem's technique; we can finally synthesise this poem only on the biographical level, and that this is so is condemnation. Without knowledge of Browning's authorship we should say that the poem proved not that love is best, but that the idea of love may be used by a flawed character as an excuse for escape from responsibility, as a way of reducing the world to grey.

Yet we do know that Browning wrote the poem, and we feel

[34] *Robert Browning: A Portrait*, New York (1952).

that if he wanted us to read it as anti-lyric he should have let us know without a shadow of a doubt that his narrator is as dramatic as he seems. As in "My Last Duchess", "Count Gismond", and "In a Balcony", we find here that the poem's potential order is reduced to chaos by an unintentional ambiguity which is unresolvable because it seems intentional and because we know that Browning most characteristically employs it for his most striking effects in other, better poems. If we take the poem seriously, inspecting it closely, following its logic, analysing the character it seems to imitate, there is no way out of this dilemma and we are forced to read it as anti-lyric. But to do so would be to misread the poem. It really means to say that love is best, and it asks no ironic undercutting of its final breathless, sightless triumph. But while we read the poem aright, we judge it to be a failure, because the boundaries of lyric and anti-lyric forms have been so confused that we cannot take the poem itself seriously. We know, in Allen Tate's famous phrase, that it will not sustain our irony. The failure which Browning intended us to see as only apparent becomes for us true failure, *not* because love is not best, but because the narrator, whose character we see too plain, thinks it is for the wrong reasons. Instead of a lyric about love we have an anti-lyric about a narrator, and our inspection of him leads to our rejection of his ideas as we reject his character. In "Caliban upon Setebos" this response is what Browning intends. Here he does not, and the poem fails because its rhetoric is not under perfect control.

K. W. Gransden

THE USES OF PERSONAE

A curious feature of Browning's literary career is his attempt to dissociate himself from his personae; to distinguish those poems in which he used personae from those in which he did not; and to suggest that the latter were more valuable because truer to his own experience. I believe the distinction to be a false, or at least a misleading one; but an examination of it may throw some light on the poet's attitude to experience and to his art. The obvious starting-point is the epilogue to *Men and Women*, "One Word More". This poem is addressed openly to Elizabeth (as "Two in the Campagna" and "By the Fireside" are addressed to her covertly); yet the real addressee is the reader, who is obliged by the poet to be both eavesdropper and *voyeur*; for this is a public poem masquerading as private, just as the dramatic poems with which it is so insistently contrasted are private poems masquerading as public.

Elizabeth, like Pauline in Browning's earliest collected piece, is both the addressee and the subject of the poem: in precisely the sense, also, that Lucrezia, Andrea's wife, is the addressee and the subject of "Andrea del Sarto". In all these poems, the addressee is placed in relation with a larger theme, that of the poet's art. Just as Pauline is invited to "look on this lay I dedicate to thee", so Elizabeth is asked to "take these lines, look lovingly and nearly". But the false dissociation occurs immediately, when the poet claims that these lines are "lines I write the first time and the last time".

The situation of this supposedly "unique" poem recurs continually in Browning: the relationship between the artist, his wife, and his career. The dramatic poems, Browning claims, are "all men's"; *this* poem is "just" for Elizabeth. The dramatic poems are brain-children, this poem comes from the heart; it is what the poet "really" wants to say. The implication would appear to be that he did not really want to say the things he said in the dramatic poems; but the underlying distinction is that between aspiration or vision, and actual (imperfect) achievement; or, in the words of the note at the end of *Pauline* (itself a curious early attempt at dissociation from what is clearly a very personal poem) between "conception" and "execution". This distinction runs through all Browning's work. It is well expressed in "The Last Ride Together":

> What hand and brain went ever paired?
> What heart alike conceived and dared?
> What act proved all its thought had been?
> What will but felt the fleshly screen?[1]

The poet claims that only an inspired act of courage can bridge this gap: hence the frequency of the word "dare" in his work: "dared and done" occurs in both "Abt Vogler" and "La Saisiaz", and in "One Word More" we find:

> Out of my own self I dare to phrase it.[2]

The claim is that it needed more courage to write this personal poem than to write "Lippo" or "Andrea". It was harder, more valuable, to be a "man" than an "artist" because art could easily become mere technique as it did with Andrea, Rafael's arm is "wrong" but his painting has "soul" and is therefore right in a higher sense than Andrea's. Browning's problem (which he faced overtly and finally solved in *The Ring and the Book*) was to get the facts right while giving them a deeper significance. He was always being told he was too clever; and "One Word More" seems to be a conscious attempt to answer the charge with a display of sincerity yet without losing control (as Rossetti was felt to have done, and as Tennyson was afraid he had done in *In Memoriam*).

Browning argues that in order to speak "in his true person"

[1] "The Last Ride Together", 56-9.
[2] "One Word More", 193.

the artist will use an art that is alien to him – "nature that's an art to others". This desire is claimed to be "natural", but is not, since it is merely the desire to be another kind of artist. If we were really to suppose (in the examples offered in the poem) that Dante's picture was better than the *Commedia* or Rafael's sonnets better than his madonnas, we might accept the confident assertion,

> You and I would rather see that angel . . .
> Would we not? than read a fresh Inferno?[3]

But the point is that the picture would be technically inferior yet "better" because done *con amore*, and the knowing, conspiratorial assumption merely invites us to exchange the critic's role for the *voyeur*'s. The idea is that amateurs (Dante the painter, Browning the "private" poet) don't have the problems of professionals; we draw close to the paradox that it is better to do something "badly" for one's beloved than well for an indifferent public. Yet Browning clearly did not think "One Word More" was a worse poem than "Lippo", only a different kind of poem. But it is not even this, any more than Wagner's *Siegfried Idyll*, written for his wife, is a different kind of music from the music of the opera to which it is thematically related. And in fact, by introducing painters, poets, and Hebrew prophets into "One Word More", Browning relates the poem to the rest of his art, from which he pretends to be differentiating it.

Indeed, it is with the prophets that the real theme of the poem, hitherto concealed by literary red-herrings, begins to emerge: the Shelleyan dissatisfaction with achievement, what is called in *Pauline*

> the chasm
> 'Twixt what I am and all I fain would be.[4]

Or, as the poet puts it in "One Word More", the difference between "heaven's gift" and "earth's abatement". Divine aspiration is constantly eroded by the disappointments of experience. The mere exercising in public of the divine gift (art, poetry, Aaron smiting the rock) cheapens and prostitutes it. So the poems that are "all men's" are prostitute poems. They are "known" and yet not known; and I use the sexual metaphor deliberately.

---

[3] *Op. cit.*, 50, 53. [4] *Pauline*, 676-7.

Browning's ambivalent attitude to his personae is nowhere more revealing than in his attitude to his characters' wives; and for this purpose it hardly matters whether they are really faithless like Lucrezia (to whom Andrea still refers as "mine") or only thought to be by psychotics like the Duke in "My Last Duchess" or Count Guido. So "One Word More" strikes a familiar note when Browning says to Elizabeth,

Thus they see you, praise you, think they know you.[5]

He is anxious to show that "his" Elizabeth is not "their" (the world's) Elizabeth, the poet more popular than himself; any achievement (he argues) is bound to be misvalued by the ignorant. The Jews were not grateful to Aaron when he produced water: if you "of all men" can do it, it is nothing. The artist, disgusted by the false response, retreats into his private world with *his* Beatrice: not the world's, but the one whose existence must be proclaimed to the world in compensation for failure, for abilities first doubted and then, when proved, dismissed. Browning's self-concern seems to me very clear here, beneath the biblical rhetoric. And the curious use of "belike", in "desecrates, belike, the deed in doing", is also revealing. Browning suggests that what one finds oneself doing is not what one had planned to do. The public exacts the grand gesture, so this itself becomes suspect; it becomes a habit, an indulgence, equally bad for the creator and the public. Aaron liked producing water and was happy to go on doing it whether water was wanted or not: Browning here isolates the confidence-trick element in art.

So it is better to produce water (art) for one who really wants it than to offer salvation to a public that neither wants nor deserves it. The prophet is indeed without honour in his own country: the theme of exile (Dante, Israel) affected Browning strongly, and is intimately linked with his own self-exile with Elizabeth. When he returned to London after her death his literary fortunes looked up.

Thus for all its parade of dissociation, "One Word More" demands to be related to Browning's persona-poetry. Though he says it is a different *genre*, a private poetry instead of the sonorous rhetoric ("bronze", "fresco") of his public art, it in

[5] "One Word More", 190.

fact displays the very mannerisms it purports to be rejecting. The habit is, after all, too strong. Thus the tone of the biblical passages –

> Moses, Aaron, Nadab and Abihu
> Climbed and saw the very God, the Highest – [6]

is the tone of "Karshish":

> The very God! Think, Abib, dost thou think?[7]

And the unqualified rapture of "yourself my moon of poets" finds its far more probing and ironic counterpart in Andrea's

> . . . my moon, my everybody's moon,
> Which everybody looks on and calls his,
> And, I suppose, is looked on by in turn. . . .[8]

Thus the poem continually works against its own assumptions. Nothing, for instance, could be more cloyingly "literary" than the "old sweet mythos" about the other side of the moon (an idea actually used by Browning in "Pan and Luna"), offered in order to elucidate the difference between "his" and "everybody's" Elizabeth. This kind of conceit can work in metaphysical poetry –

> O more then Moone,
> Draw not up seas to drown me in thy spheare,[9]

because its very unconventionality is itself a convention. The poet is controlling his emotions through the persona of a learned wit; or one can say that the ironic mode is itself the persona: the poet wears the mask of his art. Browning's "let's pretend" is as sentimentally naked as the fairy-story game between Jimmy and Alison in John Osborne's *Look Back in Anger*: we are obliged to be *voyeurs* of reality, not spectators at a play.

It is also interesting that what the moon's lover sees – the "other side" – is what the biblical prophets saw: God. Their return to the poem at what is being offered as its most intimate and private moment is itself sufficient comment on what is

---

[6] *Op. cit.*, 174-5.   [7] *Op. cit.*, 304.
[8] "Andrea del Sarto", 29-31.
[9] Donne, "A Valediction: of Weeping", 19-20.

happening. Moreover, the God of the prophets who figures in the rapturous rhetorical climax of section XVI –

> When they ate and drank and saw God also![10]

– makes a disconcerting reappearance in the very next section as the God who must be thanked for giving everyone two soul-sides. Browning can only sustain his self-deception by ignoring so gross a tonal clash. We are hurried into accepting the proposition that the heaven of the prophet-heroes and the heaven of uxorious love are indistinguishable. The same claim is made in "The Statue and the Bust": the lovers in this poem *would* have seen God along with

> The soldier-saints who, row on row,
> Burn upward each to his point of bliss – [11]

if only they had dared to elope as their creator had done.

2

In an early letter to Elizabeth, Browning says –

> ... you *do* what I always wanted, hoped to do, and only seem now likely to do for the first time. You speak out, *you*, – I only make men and women speak – give you truth broken into prismatic hues, and fear the pure white light, even if it is in me, but I am going to try. ...[12]

The "pure white light" is the light of Shelleyan idealism. Elizabeth had been trying to wean Robert away from mythology, and in these early letters it is she who rejects "art" (using the term in the dismissive sense in which Robert uses it in "One Word More") and demands "let us all aspire rather to *Life*". She also writes of "meeting face to face and *without mask* the Humanity of the age".[13] Browning tries to reconcile a longing to write in "her" way with his own profounder need for personae.

---

[10] "One Word More", 179.
[11] "The Statue and the Bust", 223-4. The term "soldier-saint" is also used by Pompilia of her lover (*The Ring and the Book*, VII, 1786). Cf. also "Prospice".
[12] 13 Jan. 1845. See *Letters of Robert Browning and Elizabeth Barrett Barrett (1845-1846)*, New York and London (1899), I, p. 6.
[13] Letters o f20 Mar. and 27 Feb. 1845. *Op. cit.*, pp. 45, 32 (italics added).

The inspiration of Browning's personal love-poetry is the Shelley of *Epipsychidion*:

> Our breath shall intermix, our bosoms bound,
> And our veins beat together . . .
> We shall become the same, we shall be one. . . .[14]

The poet of "Two in the Campagna" longs for this union of souls (the use of the optative is characteristic):

> I would I could adopt your will,
>   See with your eyes and set my heart
> Beating by yours, . . .[15]

but this *"verweile doch . . ."* can only be realised in death (see, for instance, "Porphyria's Lover", "Cristina", "The Last Ride Together"). Even in the early autobiographical poem *Pauline*, the Shelleyan vision is being modulated into a more domesticated and uxorious bliss:

> Leave me not,
> Still sit by me with beating breast and hair
> Loosened, be watching earnest by my side,
> Turning my books or kissing me when I
> Look up . . .[16]

(Cf. "Porphyria's Lover": "and thus we sit together now"). The poet of *Pauline*, disenchanted with the Shelleyan ideal, turns back to a (still idealised) uxorious vision:

> I had been spared this shame, *if I had sat*
> *By thee for ever* from the first, in place
> Of my wild dreams of beauty and of good . . .[17]

The paradox of Browning's love poetry lies in the fact that only when he adopted personae could he really dramatise the marital situation in psychologically acceptable terms. In "One Word More" the marriage is beyond exploration, beyond surprise; "Not but what you know me!" cries the poet rapturously, and that is the weakness of the naive love-poetry: it can move forward

---

[14] Shelley, *Epipsychidion*, 565-6, 573.
[15] "Two in the Campagna", 41-3.
[16] *Pauline*, 925-9.   [17] *Op. cit.*, 28-30 (italics added).

only into a kind of situationless irresponsibility, a total escape from any real world. Compare the vision of Pauline sitting for ever beside her adored lover, with the ironic realism of "Andrea del Sarto":

> If you would sit thus by me every night
> I should work better, do you comprehend?
> I mean that I should earn more, give you more.[18]

Andrea is a good poem precisely because the persona cannot escape: he is trapped inside his own ironic awareness of the world's judgement.

> Let my hands frame your face in your hair's gold,[19]
> You beautiful Lucrezia that are mine!
> "Rafael did this, Andrea painted that;
> "The Roman's is the better when you pray,
> "But still the other's Virgin was his wife. . . ."[20]

In the word "mine" (the "Cousin" is waiting outside) we feel the intolerable irony of a possessive love. If your wife is "yours" she may also be all men's: it is the old obsession of the Duke or Porphyria's lover. Lucrezia is neither Virgin nor wife, though "the world" accepts her in both roles and thinks Andrea lucky to have her even though he is no Rafael. Only Andrea knows what he might have been: "Ah, but a man's reach should exceed his grasp." The poem, like *Pauline* and like many of Browning's most interesting poems, is a confession: a confession of failure. The world's "knowing" suggestion is that Lucrezia is compensation enough for any lack of spirituality in his art; the irony of the judgment lies in the fact that it is Andrea who quotes it.

And even the splendour of Andrea's final vision (in which the poet's own voice is clearly to be heard) –

> Four great walls in the New Jerusalem,
> Meted on each side by the angel's reed,

---

[18] "Andrea del Sarto", 205-7.

[19] Gold hair is often associated with sensuality in Browning: e.g. in "Porphyria's Lover", "A Toccata of Galuppi's", "Numpholeptos", 15 ("gold means love"). Cf. also a striking passage about the gold hair of the Titian Magdalen in Naples, in the letter referred to in n. 12 (above).

[20] "Andrea del Sarto", 175-9.

> For Leonard, Rafael, Agnolo and me
> To cover . . .

– is muted and diminished as the ironic realisation returns:

> . . . the three first without a wife,
> While I have mine. So – still they overcome
> Because there's still Lucrezia – as I choose.[21]

The last three words are significant. Through all his personae the poet makes a similar existential choice, by which he is self-condemned to remain in the world of reality. The character *is* his choice and his self-analysis becomes an act of judgment which subsumes, and is larger than, the world's judgment. The irony lies in the awareness. As Blougram says:

> For nothing can compensate his mistake
> On such a point, the man himself being judge:
> He cannot wed twice, nor twice lose his soul.[22]

The freedom of the existential choice is the freedom of being imprisoned inside the situation of the poem.

But when Browning writes about married life without using a viable structure of personae, he loses his psychological freedom. Thus if we turn from "Andrea" to "Any Wife to Any Husband", we find the same desires and obsessions struggling to operate; but now these are repressed because they are no longer submitted to the ironies of judgment. What is interesting about "Any Wife to Any Husband" is not the transcendental *naïveté* of lines like

> Say to thy Soul and Who may list beside,
> "Therefore she is immortally thy bride,
> "Chance cannot change my love nor time impair."[23]

but the curious fact that the poet adopts, as a kind of suppressed persona, the personality of the wife. So the language used of the husband belongs to the wife: by an odd transvestism the poet identifies masculine "experience" with feminine "purity":

> So, how thou wouldst be perfect, white and clean
> Outside as inside, . . .[24]

[21] *Op. cit.*, 261-6.   [22] "Bishop Blougram's Apology", 298-300.
[23] "Any Wife to Any Husband", 52-4.   [24] *Op. cit.*, 25-6.

The fantasy in this poem is that if the wife dies first (as Elizabeth did) the husband may have other women but that this will not matter since the uxorious relationship is eternal: compare the line in "Cristina": "She has lost me, I have gained her". Again, the language and tone relate to those of "Andrea", but the irony has gone and the situation is embarrassingly out of control:

> Love so, then, if thou wilt! Give all thou canst
> Away to the new faces . . .
> Recoin thyself and give it them to spend, –
> It all comes to the same thing at the end,
> Since mine thou wast, mine art and mine shalt be,
> Faithful or faithless, . . .[25]

The fantasy of a man in complete possession of a woman only when she is dead recurs frequently in Browning's work. How can one "know" a woman exclusively in a world in which women are desirable? The death-fantasies start as early as *Pauline*:

> . . . a Pauline from heights above,
> Stooping beneath me, looking up – one look
> As I might kill her and be loved the more.[26]

Fascinated by sexuality yet unable to deal with it openly amid the moral pressures of Victorian society, Browning turned away to situations in which he could act out his fantasies openly under the ironic control of personae. So we enter the "frankly" amoral world of sensationalism, of "mistresses with great smooth marbly limbs": a world in which the poet is free precisely because his personae are not. The Bishop of St Praxed's gleefully parades before a voyeuristic world – that is, the Victorian reader, represented in the poem by the bishop's illegitimate sons, now acknowledged – his relationship with the woman "men would have to be your mother once". The "frankness" is guaranteed, as it were, by the bishop's being at the point of death, so the confessional structure is both apt and ambivalent, being secular in a religious context. The bishop condemns himself, thus subsuming the world's judgment in his own; the poet can speak ambivalently through both judgments. The reader, entering the poem, can, therefore, feel both open dissociation (how immoral they were

[25] *Op. cit.*, 85-6, 91-4.   [26] *Pauline*, 900-2.

in the renaissance) and secret pleasure (I wish I had lived then: they got away with it).

So too, when Fra Lippo Lippi talks both "knowingly" and euphemistically about the Prior's "niece" there is a savouring of sexuality, a sense of being a bit of a dog, half boasting, half ashamed, of "manliness". Lippo matches the bishop's boast –

> As still he envied me, so fair she was![27]

with his –

> You should not take a fellow eight years old
> And make him swear to never kiss the girls.[28]

And the self-pity of the (at first sight) very different poem "The Lost Mistress" is touched with this same knowingness: the speaker is only half sorry that it is now someone else's turn: a man can easily regard unfaithfulness as a sort of feather in his cap, so that he can feel openly hurt yet covertly flattered.

> I will hold your hand but as long as all may,
> Or so very little longer![29]

3

In poems like "Andrea del Sarto", "My Last Duchess" or "Porphyria's Lover", we feel the shiver of being held prisoner in a situation in which the personae themselves have a paradoxical freedom. To the "world", represented by the envoy, the Duke is a charmer, a connoisseur, a good catch; but he stands self-revealed to the reader as a psychotic murderer with a characteristic obsession – the "unfaithfulness" of a wife who smiles too freely. The poem is the crossing of these two versions of the character. "Porphyria's Lover" is even more claustrophobic in its effect; by the end of the poem, all externality has ceased to exist, and we can relate only within the structure of the situation itself. In the final lines –

> And all night long we have not stirred,
> And yet God has not said a word![30]

[27] "Fra Lippo Lippi", 125.   [28] Op. cit., 224-5.
[29] "The Lost Mistress", 19-20.   [30] "Porphyria's Lover", 59-60.

we realise that the lover is insane yet what he did was inevitable
and therefore aesthetically "right". God is brought into the poem
as a *voyeur*, not as a critic.

Browning's readers were intended to feel that it was irrelevant
to condemn these characters as mad or wicked, yet they could not
feel quite sure about this, despite Browning's insistence in *Pauline*
that "illa non probo sed narro". This is clearly too simple a dis-
claimer, since the personae evidently provided the poet with a
means of handling "forbidden" situations, which would normally
have baffled him, and also with a series of structures in which his
own attitudes could operate, albeit disguised, more freely. Hence
the difficulty of making categorical distinctions between the
"man" and the "artist" and the poet's insistence on our doing
this. In "The Statue and the Bust", for instance, the narrator is
supposed to be a Florentine, but we need to hear the poet's own
voice in the epilogue, and are allowed to by the pun on Guelph in
the line about "the stamp of the very Guelph": this can refer both
to the Florentine and the British ruling dynasty. The main
characters are characteristically condemned for a failure to "dare",
and the well-known "you of the virtue" (which must be the
poet's own readers) serves just to differentiate the poet's own
sympathy here, as he demands,

> Let a man contend to the uttermost
> For his life's set prize, be it what it will![31]

The confessional nature of many of Browning's poems reminds
us that they often depend for their effect on the moment at which
the speaker is made to articulate. A common pattern is to create a
whole past out of a significant moment. Thus Gigadibs "did not
sit five minutes" after his colloquy with Blougram, of which the
one bit that stuck was the simile of life as a sea voyage: their discussion was a turning point. The poems are epiphanies, in the
sense of the term used by Joyce in *Stephen Hero* xxv, moments of
"exact focus", "sudden spiritual manifestations". The effectiveness of a confession like Andrea's or the Bishop's can most easily
be seen if placed alongside a bad poem actually called "Confessions", in which a dying man looks back on what appears to be a
rather trivial love affair. The poem is set in Browning's own day

---

[31] "The Statue and the Bust", 242-3.

(the details show this) and the speaker has none of the freedom of the renaissance personae:

> A girl: I know, sir, it's improper,
> My poor mind's out of tune.[32]

He wants to show that he has been a gay dog in his day, he wants us to feel that "they" (Edward Lear's "they") are wrong to condemn him; yet out of a fatal deference to convention, from which the poem fails to enact its escape, he has to pretend to be deranged; and as he pretends we are being nudged and winked at by the poet himself, who wants us to feel that he is on the speaker's side and that "improper" really means "manly". But the slender structure cannot take the weight of irony, and the idea that the affair was wrong but fun loses itself in a pathetic gloating; conviction falters. We are offered neither a transcendental act of courage nor the kind of tongue-in-cheek irony of Lippo ("I've grown a man no doubt, I've broken bounds").

In his transcendental poetry Browning makes an absolute claim for the act of sexual daring: it lies, indeed, at the heart of his personal philosophy: "the instant made eternity" is the characteristic formula by which he polarises experience; or, again, in "By The Fire-side":

> So, earth has gained by one man the more,
> And the gain of earth must be heaven's gain too.[33]

The self-dramatising imperative cuts through the tedious processes of logic (the intellectual equivalent of social convention): what is called in "By the Fire-side", in a typically dismissive phrase, "the obvious bliss", meaning the totality of ordinary experience. Browning is at his most characteristic when outsoaring the limits of ordinary achievement, and much of his charm lies in his power of convincing us of this through the leaping energy of his verse: indeed, I think he felt that the energy guaranteed the conviction; as Paracelsus says:

> What fairer seal
> Shall I require to my authentic mission
> Than this fierce energy?[34]

[32] "Confessions", 19-20.   [33] "By the Fireside", 261-2.
[34] Paracelsus, I, 333-5.

Many people, if asked to summarise Browning's "philosophy", would perhaps quote the tag about the "unlit lamp and the ungirt loin". Browning lacks the patience to examine the validity of action for its own sake, and so often makes claims for action which he cannot support. Achievement may, as in "One Word More", "lack a gracious somewhat", but it remains achievement none the less, and Browning has his full share of Victorian respect for it. Even the manic-depressive Andrea (who in his depressive moments realises what is wrong with his work and his life) can also boast:

> Some good son
> Paint my two hundred pictures – let him try![35]

and again:

> I do what many dream of, all their lives,
> – Dream? strive to do, and agonise to do,
> And fail in doing.[36]

And if one turns Andrea's achievement round one finds the Grammarian:

> Oh, if we draw a circle premature,
> Heedless of far gain,
> Greedy for quick returns of profit, sure
> Bad is our bargain![37]

The financial imagery here is typically Victorian (there is a good deal of it in *In Memoriam*).[38] It is easy to say that Andrea made a "bad" bargain and the Grammarian a "good" one ("for what shall it profit a man ..." is the text behind both poems), but Browning's attitude to both is profoundly ambivalent, and expresses itself through a dramatic structure in which the artist's choice and the world's judgment come into conflict. Browning's valuation of "the end in sight" might have clashed with the public's, but they would have agreed about the value of striving, and indeed would have felt that science proved striving to be man's nature; see, again, Paracelsus's reference to

[35] "Andrea del Sarto", 255-6. [36] *Op. cit.*, 69-71.
[37] "A Grammarian's Funeral", 97-100.
[38] See K. W. Gransden, *Tennyson's "In Memoriam"*, London (1964) p. 51.

this instinct striving
Because its nature is to strive. . . .[39]

There is an interesting discussion at the beginning of *Paracelsus* where the sage is asked if he is sure he can distinguish between his feeling that God has singled him out to "know", his desire to achieve knowledge, and his desire to gain a reputation for it. His answer is that, even if this is true, it makes no difference:

Be sure that God
Ne'er dooms to waste the strength he deigns impart![40]

which anticipates *In Memoriam*, where Tennyson feels that it would have been a waste of Hallam's life if God had not planned some link between this world and the next. So with the Grammarian: I think Browning would have felt that it did not matter if his goal seemed boring or dead because of the vision and energy which drove him on.[41] And if the tone of the close is ironic,

Leave him – still loftier than the world suspects,
Living and dying,[42]

the irony is, characteristically, at the expense of "the world", which rejects what it cannot comprehend.

4

The "world's" sneers at self-revelation, in the much discussed sonnet "House", again reveal the strength of Browning's anxieties about betrayal or prostitution through art. His own art had developed logically from Shelleyan myth (expressing dissatisfaction with the world's valuations through stock ambivalent figures like Prometheus who were either wicked or good according to your standpoint) to the personae, which imply that you are more likely to save yourself if you pretend your thoughts are "really" those of someone "dead and done with". But there was also a feeling that self-revelation was something expected of poets,

[39] *Paracelsus*, 1, 335-6.   [40] *Op. cit.*, 345-6.
[41] I do not entirely agree with Richard D. Altick's interesting article on this poem reprinted in *Robert Browning*, ed. Philip Drew, London (1966) pp. 199-211.
[42] "A Grammarian's Funeral", 147-8.

who were then attacked for it, so that the artist had always to be defending himself. In "House", the sonnet is taken as the stock autobiographical form – it does not seem to matter much whether the target is Rossetti or not – and the central image is of a house damaged by earthquake so that passers-by can gape at the owner's secrets: these are, inevitably, marital ones:

> "I doubt if he bathed before he dressed.
> A brasier? – the pagan, he burned perfumes!
> You see, it is proved, what the neighbours guessed:
> His wife and himself had separate rooms."[43]

Thus "half-Rome". The poem shows again how much pressure the public put on Victorian poets, forcing them to find their own version of the Petrarchan convention which kept Elizabethan sonnets "safe". What the persona offers to disguise is not the poet so much as his situation. (Thus in *Maud* it is the *situation* which we have to analyse, not the emotions; the latter are insistently revealing and naked, but the personae require them to be related to a "structure of situation" which was coming more and more to be the province of the novelist rather than the poet.) And it is as novels, or as the kind of epiphanic situation-sketches of Chekhov, that many of Browning's poems offer themselves.

In *The Ring and the Book* Browning claims that it is "the glory and good of Art" that it is the "one way possible / Of speaking truth" (XII, 842-4). You cannot speak truth to the individual, for he will not accept it: it will "turn to falsehood in the telling" (cf. "One Word More" and the perversions of achievement brought about by the falsifying response). We are at the beginning of that obsession with problems of communication in which our own art is still caught up.

The personae of the poem are related not only to each other, novelistically, and to the poet, but also to "the world" (which also appears in the poem, in the gossip sections, tedious precisely because they represent a baffled distaste for the complex, a search for "emphatic warrant"). And the various partial or loaded views, in which the main characters bend the situation to their own desires, are added up to produce a "world view" in another, and profounder sense. The poem thus becomes the world it addresses;

[43] "House", 25-8.

it subsumes its own criticism; nothing is left outside, therefore nothing is vulnerable. The epitome or paradigm of this scheme is the Pope's monologue, representing judgment, authority, discrimination of truth – thus magnificently generalising the whole structure. The Pope's opening remarks about his predecessors also establish a historical perspective through the past (the introduction by Browning himself has already established a perspective into the future, has fixed the poem as a "then-as-now" structure). The Pope looks back on a long tradition of fallible judgments: his present judgment is also offered in suspension to the future; his speech is the pivot on which the poem is tilted into the judgment of all men: we have even more evidence than the Pope, for we have the whole poem, while there are parts of it he cannot know. The gravity of the Pope's responsibility is also the poet's own burden, a last effort to see clearly the problems about truth which art has to solve. The Pope is, moreover, dying; he is passing through the crucial last moments of experience; neither he nor his creator will have such another chance:

> I have worn through this sombre wintry day,
> With winter in my soul beyond the world's.[44]

Not only *is* the Pope the world he symbolises and serves: he is also the moment at which he speaks. In the closing lines of his monologue he refers to an experience of awe in nature similar to that which, for Karshish, represents the significant moment of his own and the world's weariness, the "only possible" moment when he first met Lazarus and began, like the world itself, to enter a new order of awareness. The Pope, like Karshish, and like the reader, has "only" to decide,[45] and the ambivalences involved in judgment lie at the centre of the poem's complexity.

> All's a clear rede and no more riddle now.
> Truth, nowhere, lies yet everywhere in these –
> Not absolutely in a portion, yet
> Evolvible from the whole: evolved at last
> Painfully, held tenaciously by me.[46]

---

[44] *The Ring and the Book*, x, 212-3.
[45] Browning himself tells the reader that the Pope's is "the ultimate / Judgment save yours" (I, 1220).
[46] *Op. cit.*, x, 228-32.

In "Two in the Campagna" the poet in his persona of baffled lover – "just when I seemed about to learn" – says, speaking of the "tantalizing thought" that experience is transitory,

> Help me to hold it![47]

I think *The Ring and the Book* was Browning's great challenge to himself to produce, and to the world to accept, a sustained and fully realised set of relationships. The "impossible" truth of perfect love, "love without a limit", sought in vain in poems like "Two in the Campagna", is here reached and justified through the Pope's finding it in Pompilia

> . . . then as now
> Perfect in whiteness: stoop thou down, my child,
> Give one good moment to the poor old Pope
> Heart-sick at having all his world to blame. . . .[48]

Again the key-word is "world". If the Pope is the poem's pivot, Pompilia is its still centre. If perfect love can be established through her,

> Then is the tale true and God shows complete.[49]

Love, truth, and wholeness can be brought into relationship through the acting out (which now also becomes a re-enactment) of a situation which is both real and ideal.

Pompilia gives the poet's own view of marriage:

> In heaven we have the real and true and sure.[50]

She is waiting for her lover to be united to her in death. And the lover is a priest and thus represents the purity so curiously veiled elsewhere. In the great closing lines of Pompilia's monologue we find Browning's characteristic optative controlled and, as it were, guaranteed by the situation and structure of the poem:

> Could we by a wish
> Have what we will and get the future now,
> Would we wish aught done undone in the past?

[47] "Two in the Campagna", 11.
[48] *The Ring and the Book*, x, 1005-8.
[49] *Op. cit.*, 1372.
[50] *The Ring and the Book*, vii, 1826.

So, let him wait God's instant men call years;
Meantime hold hard by truth and his great soul,
Do out the duty! Through such souls alone
God stooping shows sufficient of His light
For us i' the dark to rise by. And I rise.[51]

The poem's elaborate time-perspectives are fully felt here. And the characters "rise" out of their immediate situation into a fully symbolic stature: Pompilia stooping to the Pope (servus servorum Dei) is God stooping to men.[52] At the same time, beneath the moral fervour, one feels that for Browning the fascination of the Pompilia-situation lies precisely in the fact that she is a woman under suspicion yet "innocent". It is that characteristic Victorian version of *courtly love* which Tennyson deals with in the *Idylls of the King*. Guinevere's marriage with Arthur survives betrayal, just as the marriage in "Any Wife to Any Husband" survives the fantasy-betrayal which the poet wants to be both permitted and forgiven. The tone of the following lines from "Guinevere" urges the parallel:

I cannot take thy hand; that too is flesh,
And in the flesh thou has sinn'd . . . .
Let no man dream but that I love thee still.
Perchance, and so thou purify thy soul,
And so thou lean on our fair father Christ,
Hereafter in that world where all are pure
We too may meet before high God, and thou
Wilt spring to me, and claim me thine, and know
I am thine husband. . . .[53]

Browning organised *The Ring and The Book* so as to allow himself dual entry into it, both through the central characters, who voice his own profoundest beliefs and desires; and in his own person. In the uneasy, jocular opening passage of the poem he is trying to establish a relationship both with his material and his coming involvement in it, and with his readers, who must be

[51] *Op. cit.*, 1838-45.
[52] Cf. "A Death in the Desert" (133): "such ever was love's way: to rise, it stoops".
[53] Tennyson, "Guinevere, 550-63.

equally involved, equally "in" the poem. I have been suggesting that this duality, here made overt, appears covertly in many of the persona-poems and, indeed, gives them their curious resonance and power: qualities which their recondite themes would not in themselves account for. Thus the point of that very fine poem "Karshish" lies in our being required to pretend, up to the very end, that we think Karshish does not believe Lazarus's story. This is what we are brought into the poem for; and this is why we are taken through every stage of a scientific incredulity which the poet himself relates to his own faith. "Thy pardon for this long and tedious case" says the persona: but Browning is nudging us into hearing the words in precisely the opposite sense. And the power of

> As if he saw again and heard again
> His sage that bade him "Rise" and he did rise.[54]

(supposed to be spoken by Karshish while still a sceptic) lies in the "as if": Karshish still thinks the idea of "the very God" absurd yet we need to feel that it is true now, so that an intense feeling of awe enters the lines before it ought to. This is a matter of time-perspectives: the crossing of two viewpoints (which in the great epilogue become one) creates the structure.

The tenacity of *The Ring and The Book* seems to be offered in answer to the charge that its author was not "serious" when he used personae: as for instance in "Master Hugues", a poem about a serious topic, the problem of getting difficult art accepted. Hugues's music is a clear analogy of the author's poetry, yet the best-known part of the piece is the joke-ending, with the colloquy breaking off, and the poet, still baffling, still baffled, throwing in his hand in mock-ironic despair at the "lingering misgiving", the "refusal" of truth.

So *The Ring and The Book*, vast and lofty though it is going to be, starts with the poet himself, half-uneasy as to how it will turn out this time, throwing the book into the air, pretending to be a journalist with a scoop, and addressing his public with the old wary ambivalence: "ye who like me not, / (God love you!)." I think the opening, with its rather laboured exegesis of the idea that "fancy with fact equals one fact the more", represents a

[54] "An Epistle of Karshish", 192-3.

defence-mechanism at work. Browning is deeply concerned to ensure that, this time, there will be no gap between the vision and the execution. The whole majestic concept, "as the artist had it in his brain", must be put over, and every care must be taken to prevent the falsifying response. Hence the image of the ring, the "perfect round" of "Abt Vogler", the ideal actualised. Yet the shaped work is still pure gold; that is, we are asked to care more because it is all true and the book is there to prove it; we are not going to be able to dismiss it as another huge fantasy. As Browning wrote himself into the poem, entered the situation as he reconstructed it, we find the *blocs* vanishing; the story offered material for the kind of engaged moral reflexion which Tennyson found in Malory, and one feels a kind of relief in this perverse, *recherché* poet as he settles down "to have to do with nothing but the true, / The good, the eternal".[55] At the end of the poem Browning felt, I think, that he had won his long battle not only with his own style and fantasies, but also with his public. His final claim is:

> But Art, – wherein man nowise speaks to men,
> Only to mankind, – Art may tell a truth
> Obliquely, do the thing shall breed the thought,
> Nor wrong the thought, missing the mediate word.
> So may you paint your picture, twice show truth,
> Beyond mere imagery on the wall, –
> So, note by note, bring music from your mind,
> Deeper than ever e'en Beethoven dived, –
> So write a book shall mean beyond the facts,
> Suffice the eye and save the soul beside.[56]

One sees again Browning's characteristic anxieties. The desire to "all-express" the original vision trembles on the edge of fulfilment; the "mediate" blocs and falsifications, the distorted achievement elicited by the false response – these are, with a new hope and confidence, replaced by this double claim for art, as charismatic and trustworthy. And the religious connotation is relevant, just as the prophets were relevant to Browning's feelings about his own career in "One Word More": this time the prophet will speak and his words will both "please" and "work". The

---

[55] *The Ring and the Book*, VI, 2089-90.   [56] *Op. cit.*, XII, 858-67.

reader is, this time, to be both totally involved in, and totally controlled by, the poet's vision. The "your" is all-inclusive: it is a formula for a "total" art, in which the reader's right response and consequent enlightenment is an integral part.

To Browning, as to Tennyson, the ultimate sum of fact, which was not yet ready to be added up, was the completeness of the whole structure of experience: and this included its "meaning", that is, our act of judgment on its meaning. In the persona of the dying evangelist, Browning, once again, enlists his modern readers' assent to an act of judgment on the processes of history. In *The Ring and The Book* the reader's assent to the poem as an act of judgment, a right reading, *is* the poem; without it, the poem will not work, for it will be merely an elaborate piece of sensationalism. If we value what Pompilia "stands for" we are accepting the poem, since we could not make a judgment without the poem: Browning's whole point is that the account of the trial in the book would not have done the trick.

Browning's reference to two kinds of truth – the immediate truth of (and to) fact, and a deeper truth beyond this – is itself characteristic of the age of Darwin and Strauss. As our knowledge increased, so we had to alter what we did with it (this is Tennyson's distinction between knowledge and wisdom). Browning's poem "Development" illustrates this preoccupation in terms of the relatively minor Homeric question: does it really make any difference if the *Iliad* turns out not to be factually true? The latest arguments (which are unlikely in any case to be the *last* arguments) do not jeopardise, perhaps rather increase, Homer's moral value. In a sense, the new ground broken by Victorian thinkers and scholars gave the artist a wider area of speculation to move in: all positions were still to play for, the fluctuations and relativity of knowledge threw into relief the quest for something beyond and beneath; the variables drew fresh attention to the value of the constants. "A Death in the Desert" makes the same point in the larger context of Christian revelation:

> "God's gift was that man should conceive of truth
> "And yearn to gain it, catching at mistake,
> "As midway help till he reach fact indeed."[57]

[57] "A Death in the Desert", 605-7.

"Fact" is that in which we can rest satisfied in the world of time. This poem, like so many of Browning's speculative poems, demands to be related to the parallel explorations of Tennyson, and reminds us that there is a large and important area of common ground on which the two poets meet. Out of this area of debate (often condemned as dull) spring the great flashes of lyrical and psychological insight, the validity of which depends on the hard work which made them possible. Both poets needed to argue out in their verse the great relevant issues of their time. Lines in "A Death in the Desert" like "man partly is and wholly hopes to be" are central to our understanding of Browning's search for a tenable theory of experience. The "copies" which are "replaced as time requires" and by which we are exhorted to "reach the type" represent Browning's reflexions on evolution and remind us of *In Memoriam*. Indeed, Browning anticipates Tennyson's poem in *Paracelsus* (1835); particularly in the passages in Part V on the fragmentation and ultimate wholeness of creation, the references to "types", to "narrow creeds of right and wrong" and to the "superior race":

> The heir of hopes too fair to turn out false,
> And man appears at last.[58]

Through the persona of a renaissance scientist Browning explores the philosophic hypotheses and aspirations of his own time.

So Browning takes fact in another sense: the truth about a situation, so far as time has revealed it; and the leap from this to "life" or inner truth is a leap through time and experience, a leap in the dark. After two hundred years, Pompilia is resubmitted to the world's judgement (St Joan in Shaw's play undergoes a similar "retrial"). In a poem like "A Toccata of Galuppi's", for all its lyrical concentration, the same process is at work. After a lapse of time, Galuppi's music, ignored by the people of Venice in his own day, begins to "work" again and the ghostly, ambivalent nature of the process give the poem its atmosphere. We feel some sympathy for the dead pleasure-loving Venetians who ignored Galuppi's art, just as we understand how Joan or Pompilia were treated in their own time. The double presence of the poet, as persona and commentator, and the double presence

[58] *Paracelsus*, v, 710-1.

of the reader, as judge in the original situation and as judge in the new perspective of time, are precisely what give the poems both dramatic urgency and moral significance.

Archibald A. Hill

"PIPPA'S SONG"

TWO ATTEMPTS AT STRUCTURAL CRITICISM[1]

> The year's at the spring
> And day's at the morn;
> Morning's at seven;
> The hill-side's dew-pearled;
> The lark's on the wing;
> The snail's on the thorn:
> God's in his heaven –
> All's right with the world![2]

John Crowe Ransom, in an able and important critical study, recently remarked of "Pippa's Song" that its last two lines were "a tag of identification so pointed as to be embarrassing". Thereafter he went on to justify the statement:

> She spends three lines dating the occasion very precisely. . . .
> Then come three details which constitute the concrete: the hillside, the lark, the snail. . . . And that would be the poem; except that she must conclude by putting in her theological Universal. . . .[3]

Ransom's approach is structural. He sees in the poem a pattern of two three-line groups followed by a two-line conclusion. He condemns the conclusion because it does not seem to be properly

[1] Reprinted from *University of Texas Studies in English*, xxxv (1956) pp. 51-6.
[2] *Pippa Passes*, 221-8.
[3] "The Concrete Universal, II", *Kenyon Review*, xvii (1955) p. 395.

related to the preceding material. It would appear that the units
with which he has operated are essentially semantic: units of time,
units of concrete experience, and a unit of abstract theological
universality. If the operating units are valid, his statement of the
structure and the resultant evaluation follow almost inevitably.

His units are not, however, the only ones that might be chosen.
In metrical structure the poem is remarkably rigid, each line being
ended by a terminal juncture, with no terminal junctures within
the lines. Each juncture-group has the grammatical form of a
sentence, with subject, verb, and complement. The lines of the
poem therefore invite the interpretation that they are the normal
first segments, since they are defined as units by their formal and
grammatical structure. Even at this stage, divergence from
Ransom's segmentation results. Ransom has taken the last two
lines as one unit, not two, because both are concerned with the
"theological Universal". To group them thus, he must disregard
the linguistic characteristics which mark line eight as separate
from line seven.

Yet the eight separate lines cannot be presumed to be unrelated.
A second task is therefore to search for and describe this relationship, since if the poem has a general pattern it must reside in its
parts and their relationship to each other and to the whole.
Because the parts are sentences, the relationships between them
belong to the study of stylistics (which deals with relationships
between sentences) rather than linguistics (which deals with
relationships within sentences). Typical stylistic relationships
show themselves in the repetition of formal patterns from one
sentence to the next.

The first three lines have the grammatical structure of noun,
copula, and prepositional phrase headed by a noun. Line four,
on the other hand, has the structure of noun, copula, and phrasal
modifier. Lines five, six, and seven repeat the structure of the
first three lines. Line eight has the structure found in line four:
noun, copula, and modifying phrase. There is therefore a formal
similarity between lines one, two, and three and lines five, six,
and seven, and a further similarity between line four and line
eight. In form, then, line eight is related to line four, rather than
primarily to line seven as Ransom stated. The formal similarity
between lines four and eight is backed by their linkage in rhyme.

The relationships so far stated have been arrived at by study of formal characteristics. Such a procedure is similar to that of linguistic analysis. It is true that the subject of analysis is here a printed text, in contrast to the oral material with which linguistics habitually operates. The difference is more apparent than real. Browning's punctuation, like that of English written composition generally, does not give a clear picture of the phonological structure. In analysis of any printed text it is necessary to read it aloud, so that thereafter it can be treated as a spoken utterance. The reading given to the poem is not to be defended as the necessarily right interpretation. It has been checked with several other speakers of English, and can therefore be described as a natural and possible rendering, however it may differ in detail from others.

If formal characteristics have been exhausted, the next step is consideration of lexical meanings. The content of line one, "The year's at the spring", can be stated in general terms. *Year* is a large unit of time, and *spring* is a unit contained within it. Many readers would agree that, in human terms, *spring* is the best of the contained units. The statement that *spring* is the best unit within the year is not forced by the structure of this line. It is a hypothesis to be tested by its results in analysis of the rest of the poem.

Line two, "And day's at the morn", also contains a larger unit of time and a contained unit, though the larger unit of this line is smaller than the larger unit of the first line. When sentences are stylistically linked by structure, it is to be expected that there will be analogies in meaning as well. If the hypothesis about line one is correct, it is reasonable to suppose that *morn* is also the best of the contained entities.

In line three, "Morning's at seven", there is once more a larger unit of time, and a contained unit. By stylistic implication, the contained unit is again the best of its group. There is, moreover, an additional fact which emerges from line three. *Morning* is a form exchangeable with *morn*, so that the contained unit of line two is the containing unit of line three. In stylistic relations, particularly those in the relatively permanent form of literature, spans of interpretation can spread backward as well as forward, and it is therefore possible to reinterpret the relationships in the earlier lines. The entities in the first three lines descend in a general order from larger to smaller. Yet it is possible that the pattern is even more precisely parallel and that *spring* and *day* are in the same relationship to each other as *morn* and *morning*. The point cannot be settled, since it is obvious that *spring* and *day* are not exchangeable, but the suggestion is certainly there. A reasonable reading might therefore assume that the structure of the poem has equated the two words. The first three lines can now be given in a schematic statement of the stylistic structure which emerges from lexical examination:

> Large A is at contained B (its best)
> Smaller B is at contained C (its best)
> Still smaller C is at contained D (its best).

In the grammatically different line four, "The hill-side's dew-pearled", *hill-side* can be defined as a part of the physical scene. In contrast to a unit like *world*, in line eight, it is a small and immediate part. The phrasal modifier, *dew-pearled*, indicates a state in which the hillside is certainly attractive. A generalised statement is "Little X is good Y". Line four, though related to line eight, is also related to the lines which precede. Carrying forward the hypothesis that the contained units are the best of the several groups, it is possible to see in the attractive state of the hillside a similar excellence: being dew-pearled is its best state. The formulaic statement should therefore be revised to "little X is good Y (its best)". Further relationships between the first three lines and line four are not explicitly indicated, but as stated earlier there is a change in grammatical form and content with line four. The tightly knit sequence of the first three lines is broken by a statement of a different sort, though one which is related to the preceding. In linguistic analysis, as in the everyday interpretation of speech, it is a sensible procedure to settle on the interpretation of highest probability and disregard all others. There is no reason why this technique should not be used here. The most probable interpretation of the meaning of such an incremental change is that the relationship is one of cause and result. *Post hoc ergo propter hoc* may not be good logic, but it is good probabilistic interpretation of stylistic sequences. A final statement of line four is then: "Therefore small X is Y (its best)".

Now that the lexical and stylistic pattern has been tentatively established, the rest of the poem can be more quickly described. Lines five, six, and seven move in general from small objects to large. The objects are living beings, and the prepositional phrases which follow the copulas are, by analogy from the content of the first four lines, the proper and best place for each of these beings. It is true that *wing* is not strictly a place in the same sense as *thorn* or *heaven*, but the minor difference is overridden by stylistic similarity to the surrounding sentences. The order from small to large is a reversal of the order in the first group of lines. Yet this ascending order is itself reversed by lines five and six, where *snail* is smaller than *lark*. The break has a startling result in that it brings the extremes of the scale, *snail* and *God*, into immediate juxtaposition. We can therefore represent lines five, six, and seven thus:

> Small E is on F (its best place)
> Smaller G is on H (its best place)
> Large I is in J (its best place).

Line eight is also readily describable. It is, like line four, a result – "therefore the large scene is at its best". The statement that the poem deals with best entities and states has up to this point been hypothesis – not contradicted at any point, but without confirmation. The last line furnishes explicit confirmation in the words "all's right". A final statement of the pattern of the poem is now: three analogically related descending statements and their result on a small scale, then three analogically related ascending statements and their results on a large scale. The surprise in structure is the departure from order which brings the smallest and largest entities of the second part into contiguity.

The analysis of this poem has been thus laboured only partly because of a desire to arrive at an interpretation, and not at all because of a fondness for elaboration. The attempt has been to work out an orderly critical procedure having a maximum of rigor at each step. The method should therefore be defined. It might at first seem to be linguistic, since linguistic data have been used at a number of points. Such a description would not be accurate. The method falls wholly within the area of the metalinguistic – those portions of the communication situation beyond the fields of phonology, morphology, and syntax. The linguistic data (phonology and grammar) were used as a tool for the first segmentation of the poem into components, in a fashion similar to the use of phonetic data for a preliminary segmenting of the sounds of speech into phonemic units.

I have elsewhere said that the whole of microliterary study belongs on the metalinguistic level, while microlinguistic data fall, as here, onto the preliterary level.[4] The parallel with linguistic analysis is made even closer by the fact that the preliminary (microlinguistic) units, once segmented out, were analysed for recurrent component parts, just as phonemic units are analysed for their recurrent components – the distinctive features. The result of this examination of preliterary segments and their components was a statement of the first level of microliterary structure, the grammatical similarities between the several sets of lines within the poem. As in linguistic analysis, analysis then moved to a level higher in the structural hierarchy, in this instance the lexical. Lexical examination resulted in further insight into stylistic relationships; from full exploitation of them the statement of the total pattern of the poem finally emerged. When such a pattern is reached it can be said that microliterary analysis breaks off. Any further statements of meaning are in the metaliterary sphere of correlation between the literary structure and known facts of patterned cultural behaviour and values. One such statement is worth making. Ransom has called the last two lines a well-schooled theological tag. Pippa breaks her strict analogical pattern to bring *snail* and *God* together. The juxtaposition does not correlate with the way we expect theologians to talk about God. It correlates, instead, with the way we expect children to talk of Him, in concrete and simple terms. Pippa's statement also correlates with our belief that simplicity like hers often contains insights somehow better than those found in the words of the most philosophically sophisticated. One is tempted to find, in the breaking of the pattern Browning has established for her, a sort of model of the cultural contradiction in our attitudes toward children. We treat them as not yet perfected human beings, yet we remember the Biblical "out of the mouths of babes and sucklings".

[4] "An Analysis of The Windhover, An Experiment in Structural Method" *PMLA*, LXX (1955) pp. 972-3.

It remains only to state the differences between Ransom's method and that used here. Ransom is structural in his approach, but uses semantically defined units without having worked through the formal linguistic differentia. His method is therefore similar to that of traditional grammar, where a formal word-class, such as nouns, is defined in terms of the semantic content of the class. In contrast, the analysis given here rests on one of the most basic assumptions in linguistics, that it is form which gives meaning and not meaning which gives form. Ransom's assumptions are commonly used by critics, those used here by linguists. Since the two sets of assumptions are correlated with differing kinds of activity, it is impractical to measure which set is the more reasonable. Fortunately the two analyses can be measured otherwise. They must be assumed to be significantly different, since one cannot be mechanically translated into the other. If different, both cannot be true; one must be more complete, more consistent, and more simple than the other. Evaluation may be left to the reader.

Park Honan

THE IRON STRING IN THE VICTORIAN LYRE

BROWNING'S LYRIC VERSIFICATION

I

Even though legions of Victorian reviewers and a number of modern critics have cavilled at Browning's "harshness", no one has stated the major objection to his lyric versification more compellingly (despite wit's exaggeration) than Oscar Wilde.

> There are moments when he [i.e., Browning] wounds us by monstrous music. Nay, if he can only get his music by breaking the strings of his lute, he breaks them, and they snap in discord, and no Athenian tettix, making melody from tremulous wings, lights on the ivory horn to make the movement perfect, or the interval less harsh. . . . If Shakespeare could sing with myriad lips, Browning could stammer through a thousand mouths. . . . The only man who can touch the hem of his garment is George Meredith. Meredith is a prose Browning, and so is Browning. He used poetry as a medium for writing in prose.[1]

The tettix (or cicada) witticism is the critically important one.

Even very good English lyres, from time to time, seem to snap strings and emit harsh chords. But when they do, there is a compensating cicada's "melody" or euphony in the movement to make the "interval less harsh". Yet when Browning deliber-

---

[1] "The Critic as Artist. A Dialogue", *The Complete Works of Oscar Wilde*, New York (1927) v, pp. 115-7.

ately breaks his lyre's seventh string, and is harsh, there is no compensating euphony whatever.

No cicada sings for him.[2]

Of course the passage amuses us because it seems damning and at least half true. Wilde locates a feature in Browning's versification that is new, even revolutionary, and yet he fails to suggest a principle that would lead us to search for aesthetic functions of tonal harshness. We are left with the scandalous image of a bad poet who forgot that prose is prose, verse verse. Wilde's Browning neither sings nor speaks – only stammers.

But Wilde, a pleasant lyricist himself, is in a bad position to appreciate stylistic experiments. In the eighties and nineties, a very deep reaction against early Victorian innovations in style has set in, so that one finds "smooth" traditional lyricists like Tennyson esteemed and "rough" experimental prosodists like Browning mainly admired despite their styles. The few scraps of Hopkins that get into print in Wilde's time cause no stir, and Hopkins and Browning alike influence prosody later. Significantly, Donne waits to be "rediscovered".

Even so, the principle that governs Browning's lyric versification and that Wilde misses does not come suddenly into being and then go quickly and completely out of fashion. It exists, rather subversively, in the sixteenth century. It can be felt behind some Metaphysical lyrics and with other "anti-Ciceronian" styles. While it does not impress itself very strongly on neo-classical poetry it does influence prose style in the rising genre of Pope's and Johnson's age, the novel. Later on it is implicit in the Wordsworthian revolution, and Coleridge – as we shall see – supports it in theory. After his *Paracelsus*, and indeed with his *Strafford*, a play that is at once crude, defective, and boldly new in style, Browning is consistently within limits its advocate.

This is the principle that is directly opposed to the elaborate decorum whereby each literary genre and sub-genre has its more or less fixed range of appropriate styles. The opposing principle insists that style should be determined primarily by the requirements of the literary subject. And Browning proceeds farther

[2] But a cricket sings for one of Browning's characters who has snapped a lyre's seventh string; see the lyric that follows "The Two Poets of Croisic" – and also, for the tettix, line 9 of "Pheidippides".

under its special influence, with lyric versification, than Donne,
Wordsworth, or other successful English lyricists had gone
before.

2

What is chiefly new with his prosody, so far as the style-subject
principle is concerned, is the method of compensation for
irregular rhythm and phonetic dissonance.

The English lyricist from Wyatt to Tennyson, whatever his
particular principles, has been at liberty to achieve some degree
of vigour and contrast in sound, and some degree of imitation or
sound-symbolism, by exploiting to various degrees the three
potentials of cacophony:

(A) metrical variation from an expected norm;
(B) phonetic difficulty (including harsh clusters, harsh or
    discordant verse-sequences of phonemes, and no asson-
    ance);
(C) syntactic breaks or punctuation-pauses within the line.

While each of these is properly a lyrical device, in its extreme each
one is strongly disruptive or anti-lyrical. Traditionally, the
English lyric genre has not tolerated noticeable degrees of (A),
(B), and (C) in one verse – and among good lyricists before
Browning, chiefly Donne, and perhaps most of all in his "Holy
Sonnets", will raise the question as to the exception:

> Th'hydroptique drunkard, and night-scouting thiefe,   9
> The itchy Lecher, and selfe tickling proud   10
> Have the remembrance of past joyes, for reliefe   11
> Of comming ills. To (poore) me is allow'd   12
> No ease. . . .[3]

But even in such a case, though Donne seems to veer as far from
Spenserian smoothness and towards cacophony as he ever does
in a short lyric, each verse effectively compensates for its own
harsh or disruptive features.

While in lines 9 and 10, there is definitely (B), there is little of
(A) – only single inversions – or little of (C) since the effects of

[3] Sonnet III, *The Complete Poetry and Selected Prose of John Donne*, ed. C. M.
Coffin, New York (1952) ll. 9-13.

the comma pauses are weak. And while (C) is prominent in line 12, (A) is not, nor is (B): "comming ills" and "me . . . allow'd" have a pleasant, transverse pattern of sound repetition – (m)(l): (m)(l) – that saves this line from phonetic difficulty.

As a good student of this subject in the Metaphysical lyric aptly observes, Donne's "harshness and discords are an absolute artistic necessity, reflecting the state of his soul and the world",[4] but lyrically he pursues *asperitas* only so far. Euphonic features compensate for dissonant or disruptive ones in each of his verses: very typically, (A)'s absence or presence in a line sets off (B)'s presence or absence, and though Donne sometimes strains against the limits of an established style-genre decorum, he does not violate it.

His famous "conversational" openings, as in

For Godsake hold your tongue, and let me love[5]

or

Now thou hast lov'd me one whole day[6]

are metrically but not *phonetically* audacious. They have (A), but not (B). Assonance, resonant sequences of vowel sounds, iterated and sometimes alliterated consonants – all compensate for daring stress sequences. If the style-subject principle is nearly at odds with the style-genre one in such cases, and can be felt, Donne's concern for "reflecting the state of his soul" does not lead him to a new prosody, nor does he ever veer so far towards unrelieved jolting in a line as the Elizabethan dramatist may:

Up – so. How is't? Feel you your legs? You stand.[7]

Lear's genre tolerates that extreme in sound, but "The Canonization's" does not.

We spend some time with Donne for our purposes not merely because we have Browning's repeated word of high esteem for him – esteem that does itself, perhaps, lead students of their lyrics to conclude that their prosodies are alike and that Browning is only trying (ineptly) to do what Donne did (superbly) – but

[4] See Arnold Stein, "Donne's Harshness and the Elizabethan Tradition", *Studies in Philology*, XLI (1944), p. 409.
[5] "The Canonization". [6] "Womans Constancy".
[7] *King Lear*, IV, vi, 65.

because Browning's prosody begins where Donne's leaves off. Their methods are not the same. Neither of the two style principles disappears with Browning but their precedence is inverted. Requirements of the lyric subject have priority in determining what his style will be like, rather than do the traditional and implicit requirements of the lyric genre. Prosodically what this means is that the verse need not compensate for its own irregular rhythm or phonetic difficulty if its tonal extremes contribute to expressive effects in the stanza or larger lyric structure. Aesthetically his practice seeks its justification in this: euphony or resonance is temporarily suspended not merely for the sake of surprise or variety, but always, when Browning is successful, for expressive intensity. Cacophony increases the relevance of rhythm and phonetic features to the lyric's manifest subject: the particular thoughts and feelings or vision of life that it presents.

Browning's lyric prosody, we should note too, accords with Coleridgean rather than Wordsworthian theory – and it is Coleridge, rather than Wordsworth, who suggests a critical standard to employ when we criticise the Browning lyric for its sound. It is true that Wordsworth's desire to extend the limits of poetic diction to include the "language of conversation in the middle and lower classes of society" is one that supports the style-subject principle.[8] In theory, Browning's diction is Wordsworthian. His own considerable extension of the range in poetic diction follows in the path of Wordsworth's precepts. But Wordsworth regards metre in all poetry merely as something pleasingly attendant or superadded to natural language, "a supernumerary charm", as M. H. Abrams justly puts it,[9] whereas Coleridge sees metre and sound as structural devices, integral parts of poems, and finds poetic value to lie "in the balance or reconciliation of opposite or discordant qualities".[10] Thus Coleridge anticipates Browning's actual use of metrically irregular, harsh verses with more resonant ones as components of expressive

---

[8] See the Advertisement to *Lyrical Ballads*, London (1798).

[9] See his excellent discussion of Coleridge on Wordsworth in *The Mirror and the Lamp: Romantic Theory and the Critical Tradition*, New York (1958) pp. 116-24, especially p. 117.

[10] See chapter xiv in *Biographia Literaria*, ed. J. Shawcross, Oxford (1907) II, p. 12.

structure. For Coleridge antithetic features in a poem are not only permissible but highly desirable, providing always that they are synthesised, and their imaginative synthesis is for him a prime criterion of poetic excellence.

Correspondingly, in Browning, the synthesis that should arise from the use of verses with extremely different meanings or styles is the test – and properly the only test – of the lyric's success. We cannot reasonably excerpt "beauties" (or even aesthetic "horrors") from a Browning lyric by holding up this or that verse for inspection. None of his verses in isolation absolutely reveals itself to be good or bad. And when prosody is governed by the style-subject principle, only the stanza's and in some cases only the whole poem's expressive structure will indicate the *tonal* felicity or failure of a verse.

3

Now let us turn to his shorter poems.

He writes primarily three kinds of lyrics. Since the road through Browning criticism is dotted with gorgeously schematic classificatory wrecks, one should be warned against attempting to classify much more finely. Distinctions between his three kinds – the character lyric, the musical lyric, and the lyric of dramatised thought and feeling – are not invariably firm and fast.

In Browning's typical character lyric, the subject is either a particularised dramatic speaker or an entity particularised through details or emblematic images so that it seems to have a limited essence or a character of its own. "The Laboratory" and "Soliloquy of the Spanish Cloister" are typical character lyrics. So are the two "Earth's Immortalities", with their ironic emblematic images for the characteristics of Fame and Love. Or "Sibrandus Schafnaburgensis" – with its details that offer a vision of nature's essence, or character, as it contrasts with human pedantry.

Let us see how rhythmic and phonetic elements figure in "Sibrandus". For obvious reasons this poem is unlike any of Wordsworth's nature lyrics. Its effervescence, the fascination for the insect world that it attests to, and the jaunty ridiculing of pedantry are all Browningesque – and yet no aspect of it is more typical than its versification.

Take the rollicking stanza 7:

> How did he like it when the live creatures
>   Tickled and toused and browsed him all over,
> And worm, slug, eft, with serious features,
>   Came in, each one, for his right of trover?
> – When the water-beetle with great blind deaf face
>   Made of her eggs the stately deposit,
> And the newt borrowed just so much of the preface
>   As tiled in the top of his black wife's closet?[11]

That is humorous and lively, apparently casual, but it is not careless. For one thing, the stanza's indented or even-numbered lines have features that are not paralleled in its odd-numbered four. The indented verses are fairly regular metrically with two and three-syllable feet. Primary stresses are arranged so as not to fall in juxtaposition (the spondee-effect is mainly avoided) so that with their regularity and some assonance and alliteration, these lines seem of a traditionally lyrical variety. E.g.:

> Tíckled and tóused and brówsed him a̋ll óver
>
> As tíled in the tóp of his bláck wi̋fe's clóset?[12]

But the odd-numbered verses have juxtaposed primary stresses that break up the duple-triple rhythm. These four verses are not phonetically smooth enough to compensate in a traditional manner for their own queer rhythm. They seem relatively harsh, distinctly and peculiarly Browningesque:

> And wórm, slúg, éft, with sérious féatures
>
> – When the wáter-béetle with gréat blínd déaf fáce[13]

What accounts for their style? Bunched stresses and some harshness very closely support the stanza's expressive structure. Nature is multitudinous, quickly scurrying and jumbled to the casual eye; but deliberate, methodical, purposeful to the selective eye that watches the individual detail. So through images that are increasingly particularised and alternate verse-movements

[11] "Sibrandus Schafnaburgensis", 49-56.
[12] *Op. cit.*, 50, 56.
[13] *Op. cit.*, 51, 53.

that seem on the one hand quick, easy, and expected, and on the
other, curious and slow, nature takes on a doubleness – or two
appearances of overall disorder and intricate order – that it has
in man's eye. Verse-style does not impose on the subject more
harmony or unity than it should have, and the whole effect is
subtle: even as the point of view in this stanza narrows, the
alternating quick and slow lines preserve an impression of nature's
two aspects. Style-genre limitations would not permit this
effect, but the style-subject principle does since it allows for a
method that synthesises in stanzas relatively harsh, metrically
irregular verses.

In character lyrics, all effects of tonal components depend on
the vividness, force, pertinence, and particularity of the *characterising* that is going on in stanzas. For example:

> At the meal we sit together:
>   *Salve tibi!* I must hear   10
> Wise talk of the kind of weather,
>   Sort of season, time of year: 12
> *Not a plenteous cork-crop: scarcely*
>   *Dare we hope oak-galls, I doubt:*   14
> *What's the Latin name for "parsley"?*
>   What's the Greek name for Swine's Snout?[14]   16

These verses characterise by contrasting a dramatised speaker
with his gentle-mannered foil (Brother Lawrence). As always in a
good Browning lyric, rhythms and sounds sharpen the pertinence
of details to the stanza's expressed subject. The most pertinent
verse, the last, seems even more abrupt and grating than it would
if the trochaic movement of lines 9-15 were not so regular. Its
harshness – indeed its coarse prosiness – emphasises a bitter,
richly perverse, comically bursting hatred suggested in its meaning
(surely with an intensity that equals that of other verses expressive
of strong feeling in English dramatic lyrics). Yet in reading
"Soliloquy of the Spanish Cloister" we are not troubled by the
harshness but rather delight in what line 16 so pungently reveals.
Its tonal anti-lyricism is perfectly synthesised in the stanza.

Contrast a notoriously cacophonous verse that fails because it
is not synthesised:

14 "Soliloquy of the Spanish Cloister", 9-16.

Poor vaunt of life indeed,   18
Were man but formed to feed
On joy, to solely seek and find and feast: 20
Such feasting ended, then
As sure an end to men;   22
Irks care the crop-full bird? Frets doubt the
maw-crammed beast?[15]

Verse 24 is not synthesised because the stanza's structure does not particularise a character, only an anti-FitzGeraldian idea, and a character is all that the cacophony in style relates to. Anti-FitzGeraldian *ideas* have no relation to the harsh texture. We may agree that "Rabbi Ben Ezra's" style is an appropriate one for a prophet whose tough old heart is afire and who shouts as he sings, but in this structure the prophet is only a shadowy entity since the imagery and sense of the six lines particularise no one. That is why the cacophony and abrupt break in the parisonic syntax of 24 will only jolt and glare no matter how often we are reminded by the well-intentioned critic that the style happens to suit Ben Ezra. The subject that governs the style must be vividly and forcefully depicted if anti-lyrical elements in the style are to become synthesised – that is, if they are to become *lyrical*.

Here is an even bolder prosodic experiment in a character lyric – the sonnet "Rawdon Brown" (1884) which Browning did not collect. I quote lines 2-11:

I needs must, just this once before I die,
Revisit England: *Anglus* Brown am I,
Although my heart's Venetian. Yes, old crony –
Venice and London – London's "Death the Bony"
Compared with Life – that's Venice! What a sky,
A sea, this morning! One last look! Good-by,
Cà Pesaro! No lion – I'm a coney
To weep! I'm dazzled; 't is that sun I view
Rippling the . . . the . . . *Cospetto*, Toni! Down
With carpet-bag, and off with valise-straps!

No one can say of this that the subject has not realistically determined the style. Furthermore, metrical disorder, syntactic

---

[15] "Rabbi ben Ezra", 19-24 (italics added).

disjointedness, and phonetic discords in these extremes are not out of place in style-subject poems. Browning's principle allows for this texture, and in some verse-paragraphs of "Mr. Sludge, 'The Medium' " one might show that a similar style is effectively used. The trouble here is that the subject is not depicted forcefully enough to justify the tonal harshness: style relates to chatter – not to character. All we are told about Brown, really, is that he loves Venice and will not leave.

But we always have strong impressions of the subject when character lyrics are successful. We do, for a final, brilliant example, in "The Laboratory", where rhythms and sounds and literal and symbolic sense together lay bare the heart of a grotesque daughter of the *ancien régime* – whether in her ghoulish chanting, in her impulsive energy felt through driving rhythms in stanzas expressing wonder and delight in all that is lethal, or in her anti-lyrical opening lines where the deliberate indefiniteness of the meter supports finely imaged symbols of her treachery and duplicity:

> Now that I, tying thy glass mask tightly,
> May gaze thro' these faint smokes curling whitely,
> As thou pliest thy trade in this devil's-smithy –
> Which is the poison to poison her, prithee?[16]

These instances of artistic success and failure remind one that Browning's prosodic principle is rigorously demanding. While it allows for immense range and sharp contrasts in the style of verses, it demands that the lyric structure depict its subject with the utmost relevance and intensity. When the structure fails to do this, we become aware of a failure in his tonal style.

4

There are fewer sheer failures among his musical lyrics. Browning *depicts* music with ingenuity and finds it everywhere – not only in the fugue or toccata or march or orchestrion's improvisation, but in the mind's reveries, in chanting, in the hoarsely shouted toasts of soldiers, or in the thud of hooves. Since in the musical lyric rhythms and sounds represent music, they are intended to be noticed, "heard" for themselves. Style is intrusive, patent, always bravura, forcing itself into the foreground. As Turner's pictures

[16] "The Laboratory", 1-4.

are visibly made out of paint and do not conceal their technique (the "visibility" of the paint is the mainstay of their technique), so Browning's musical lyrics are audibly made out of sounds.

Their subjects are music's occasions. When the occasion is insufficiently developed in an expressive structure, rhythms and sounds will seem monotonous no matter how ingeniously they are used. "Through the Metidja" is a flat failure:

> As I ride, as I ride,
> With a full heart for my guide,
> So its tide rocks my side,
> As I ride, as I ride,
> That, as I were double-eyed,
> He, in whom our Tribes confide,
> Is descried, ways untried
> As I ride, as I ride.[17]

But "How They Brought the Good News" is successful because its subject – a ride that is no more complex in its essential circumstances than the "Metidja's" – is developed in stanzas that express through their particularity a sense of immense urgency under disciplined control, so that one attends through the imagery to the prosodic music of the gallop:

> Not a word to each other; we kept the great pace
> Neck by neck, stride by stride, never changing our place;
> I turned in my saddle and made its girths tight,
> Then shortened each stirrup, and set the pique right,
> Rebuckled the cheek-strap, chained slacker the bit,
> Nor galloped less steadily Roland a whit.[18]

There is nothing anti-lyrical to be synthesised in "Good News" since nothing obstructs the powerful movement of its anapests. Punctuation pauses and heavy syllables (with vowels of considerable quantity and consonantal clusters of some difficulty) before the primary stresses, as in the first of these two feet,

$$\text{-strap, chained sláck} \mid \text{er the bít,}$$

only impart energy to the rhythm.

But while hoof-music of the gallop is appropriately rendered

[17] "Through the Metidja", 1-8.
[18] "How They Brought the Good News", 7-12.

in even rhythms, man's sophisticated instrumental music really is not. "It is more likely to be the harsh, rugged, dissonant poem", as Northrop Frye observes, "that will show in poetry the tension and the driving accented impetus of music",[19] and several of Browning's musical lyrics use anti-lyrical verses to imitate and depict that more complex, formal music. In this respect his prosodic principle gives him another advantage in realistic representation that the style-genre lyricist lacks.

His imitation of the fugue in "Master Hugues of Saxe-Gotha" is essentially humorous. "Hugues" parodies music. The occasion of the fugue-playing – a rather gaily ironic encounter between an organist and a defunct composer heard only through his fugue – is just sufficiently developed to sustain interest and synthesise dissonances through twenty-nine stanzas in which bravura verse-style performs imitative tricks:

> *Est fuga, volvitur rota!*
> On we drift: where looms the dim port?
> One, Two, Three, Four, Five, contribute their quota;
>   Something is gained, if one caught but the import –
> Show it us, Hugues of Saxe-Gotha![20]

The bravura quality of style is heightened in "A Toccata of Galuppi's" in the same way: the illusion that a dead composer is speaking in and through his music focuses attention on verse-sound as well as on verse-sense. But in the "Toccata", with great poignancy, the sense deepens. Galuppi's music has superficial qualities that are apparent, at first, even to the unaccustomed ear. So at first, rhythm is almost monotonously even in time and regular in stress:

> Oh Galuppi, Baldassaro, this is very sad to find!
> I can hardly misconceive you; it would prove me
>   deaf and blind;
> But although I take your meaning, 'tis with such
>   a heavy mind![21]

The rhythm is regular for six stanzas, which conjure up a conven-

---

[19] *Anatomy of Criticism: Four Essays*, New York (1966) p. 256.
[20] "Master Hugues of Saxe-Gotha", 86-90.
[21] "A Toccata of Galuppi's", 1-3.

tional scene of aimless hedonism in a midnight Venetian ball with Galuppi "stately at the clavichord". But this composer has something unconventional to say as well: it is heard by the well-attuned ear that can pick out qualities in conventional "sevenths" and "suspensions" – or by the ear that has become aware of variation and subtlety. In stanzas 7 and 8, we hear the music with this ear, alert to the message music gives through imitating and answering lovers' talk:

> What? Those lesser thirds so plaintive, sixths
> diminished, sigh on sigh,
> Told them something? Those suspensions, those
> solutions – "Must we die?"
> Those commiserating sevenths – "Life might last! we
> can but try!"
>
> "Were you happy?" – "Yes." – "And are you still
> as happy?" – "Yes. And you?"
> – "Then, more kisses!" – "Did *I* stop them, when
> a million seemed so few?"
> Hark, the dominant's persistence till it must be
> answered to!"[22]

Bravura style renders both the conventionality and subtlety of Galuppian music here. We attend at once to a prevailing "toccata" rhythm (established earlier) as well as to the magnified toccata-variations that contain the heart of the composer's message for Venice. Typically, the tonal style is effective not in being traditionally smooth but in being functional – intricately synthesised – in the expressive structure.

A fuller study of Browning's bravura styles would take into account lyrics as different as "Cavalier Tunes", "The Pied Piper", "Thamuris Marching", "Up at a Villa – Down in the City", "Holy-Cross Day", "The Heretic's Tragedy", and "A Grammarian's Funeral" – and several dramatic idyls, such as "Echetlos" (which, it is no surprise to learn from Colvin, Browning read with "his foot stamping vigorously in time"[23]) and "Pheidippides". All of these are musical even in their occasional harsh-

---

[22] *Op. cit.*, 19-24.
[23] Sir Sidney Colvin, "Some Personal Recollections", *Scribner's Magazine*, LXVII (1920) p. 79.

ness: sound supports sense in them, while sense heightens the
bravura appeal of sound's imitativeness.

5

Yet very disrupted and very smooth verses alike tend to be
missing in Browning lyrics that dramatise thought and feeling
not musically, and not to depict whole characters, but to emphasise psychological processes in their own right or for their
own dramatic appeal. "In a Year", typically of these, uses a
middle style – or one that avoids both cacophony and lyrical
melodiousness – to depict the process of a woman's reflecting on
a love-affair that is virtually over:

> Never any more,
>   While I live,
> Need I hope to see his face
>   As before.
> Once his love grown chill,
>   Mine may strive:
> Bitterly we re-embrace,
>   Single still.
> Was it something said,
>   Something done,
> Vexed him? was it touch of hand,
>   Turn of head?
> Strange! that very way
>   Love begun:
> I as little understand
>   Love's decay.
>
>   *   *   *
>
> That was all I meant,
>   – To be just,
> And the passion I had raised,
>   To content.
> Since he chose to change
>   Gold for dust,
> If I gave him what he praised
>   Was it strange?[24]

[24] "In a Year", 1-16, 49-56.

These structures depict a mind of delicacy and sensibility in the act of searching through its store of memory. Imagery is bare since feeling is quiescent. Short lines emphasise the lambency and rapidity of thought's process, and verse-rhythms are varied temporally to support the illusion of a mind conversing with itself. Although each stanza is made up of foreshortened double "quatrains" of 3, 2, 4, and 2 trochees, catalectic, correct to the syllable, phonetic contrasts constantly alter the tempo from verse to verse:

> Never any more   (is quick)
> Once his love grown chill   (is slow)
>
> While I live
> Mine may strive   (are relatively slow)
>
> As before
> Single still   (are quicker)

Assonance and consonance are present, but rather limitedly, since very much sound-repetition (the basis of melodiousness) would defeat the illusion of the mind in colloquy with itself; and it is just this "conversational" illusion that focuses attention on the mind's introspective, recollecting process – which is, indeed, suggestively given in the spare stanzas of "In a Year".

The *process* of the mind's reviewing emotional experience is really the subject of a great many if not all of Browning's lyrics that are concerned with love. When the subject is not such a process, but is dramatised romantic feeling itself, style can be extremely smooth and can even approximate the lyrical melodiousness of a Herrick. This is the case, for example, with the simple and atypically resonant "One Way of Love":

> All June I bound the rose in sheaves.
> Now, rose by rose, I strip the leaves
> And strew them where Pauline may pass.
> She will not turn aside? Alas!
> Let them lie. Suppose they die?
> The chance was they might take her eye.[25]

Certainly not very much more than the name of the disdainful young lady would indicate that Browning wrote that stanza.

[25] "One Way of Love", 1-6.

Thought is not important in it. Mildly (and conventionally) despairing feeling is.

But contrast tonal style in the more typically Browningesque "Two in the Campagna" – the first four verses of whose stanzas are in "One Way of Love's" metre:

> No. I yearn upward, touch you close,
> Then stand away. I kiss your cheek,
> Catch your soul's warmth, – I pluck the rose
> And love it more than tongue can speak –
> Then the good minute goes.[26]

The subject of this stanza is not a feeling, but is the process of a speaker's reflecting on his emotional experience. Thus slightly broken rhythms with somewhat reduced sound-repetition place emphasis on the act of observing what is felt, rather than on feeling itself:

> No ‖ I yearn upward ‖ touch you close
> Then stand away ‖ I kiss your cheek

A similar style is achieved in the iambic pentameter – the "speech" metre of dramas and dramatic monologues alike – of "Any Wife to Any Husband", which closes with these two conversational stanzas:

> And yet thou art the nobler of us two:
> What dare I dream of, that thou canst not do,
>   Outstripping my ten small steps with one stride?
> I'll say then, here's a trial and a task –
> Is it to bear? – if easy, I'll not ask:
>   Though love fail, I can trust on in thy pride.
>
> Pride? – when those eyes forestall the life behind
> The death I have to go through! – when I find,
>   Now that I want thy help most, all of thee!
> What did I fear? Thy love shall hold me fast
> Until the little minute's sleep is past
>   And I wake saved. – And yet it will not be![27]

Of course there is a "dissociation of sensibility" in both of the last poems, but the dissociation is exactly what Browning's "love

---

26 "Two in the Campagna", 46-50.
27 "Any Wife to Any Husband", 115-26.

lyrics" are so often about. What they frequently express or depict is thought that is slightly removed from feeling and in the act of contemplating it, and it is just for this reason that their lyricism is deliberately restrained. Their subjects dictate tonal styles that help to suggest either the silent conversation of the mind in contemplation of feeling, or overheard talk that reveals contemplated feeling. These lyrics dramatise psychological processes with a new realism that extends to their sounds, and indeed their methods have influenced the development of modern English versification.

6

In fact Browning's vigorously experimental lyric styles are only one indication – but an important one – of the general shift in the nineteenth century from a closed decorum of style and genre to an open decorum of style and subject. This shift is already under way in 1798, and it may be seen not only in the poetry of Wordsworth, Coleridge, Browning, Arnold, and Hopkins, but in the genre-crossing prose styles of Carlyle, Disraeli, Dickens, Ruskin, or Meredith, and even though the last quarter of the century witnesses more "purism" in poetic and prose styles than had prevailed in earlier decades, the open decorum becomes the norm very soon in our own century – the century of *Ulysses* and *The Waves*, of free verse and Hopkins' fame, and of radical stylistic experimentation. The genres still mean something to us, but they no longer rigidly limit literary styles, or even sharply divide verse from prose.

Browning's lyric prosody contributes vitally to this shift. He enlarges the tonal range of the English lyric by showing that lyrical effects are not intrinsically dependent on the harmony or isolated beauty of the individual line of verse but may arise from verses in which resonance is restrained to enhance illusions of conversation, or even from seemingly unpleasant, joltingly harsh, "prosy" verses if they are expressively synthesised. His modern aim is to suggest the particularity and complexity of actual experience, or (in "Pisgah-Sights'" terms) to bring

> Life there, outlying!
> Roughness and smoothness,
> Shine and defilement,

into the lyric by representing "life" as closely and realistically as technique will permit. His lyrics imitate life's sounds, and in so doing they prepare the way for bolder, later experiments in free verse and open rhythms, and for the end of the absolute dominance of versification based on a syllable-stress metric. For traditional harmony, Browning substitutes a difficult harmony that blends tonal extremes in the lyric, and that can contribute with unusual intensity to lyrical effects – as Ezra Pound of the *Cantos* and T. S. Eliot of the *Four Quartets* have recognised.[28]

[28] The reader is referred to the following critical studies of special interest in connexion with the subject of this essay in addition to those mentioned in the Select Bibliography: Harvey Gross, *Sound and Form in Modern Poetry: A Study of Prosody from Thomas Hardy to Robert Lowell*, Ann Arbor (1964); *The Structure of Verse: Modern Essays on Prosody*, ed. Harvey Gross, New York, (1966); Park Honan, "Matthew Arnold and Cacophony", *Victorian Poetry*, I (1963) pp. 115-22; W. K. Wimsatt, "On Scanning English Meters", *Michigan Quarterly Review*, v (1966) pp. 291-5.

Barbara Melchiori

DARK GOLD, or DEVIL'S DUNG[1]

"The love of money is the root of all evil." This text, the truth of which they never questioned, was a source of great distress to the Victorians. Their consciences were far from clear. To say that the Victorian age was an age of hypocrisy is begging the question: the need for hypocrisy arises when there is something to hide. It was an age, rather, of deep moral self-searching; men looked into their actions and found much of which they were ashamed, much that they sought to disguise. Many characters in the fiction of the time were obsessed with money, characters against whom both authors and readers could release their accumulated moral condemnation, censuring what they felt to be wrong in society, and in their own lives. The "good" characters either gave money away or sacrificed it to marry for love (whereupon it was frequently returned to them). But money, whether greedily grasped or nobly refused, was of paramount interest in Victorian fiction. Bulwer Lytton's play, *Money*, had a record run for the period, being given at the Haymarket for eighty consecutive nights. For money was pouring into the country, the great banks were building their palatial establishments – the banks which Butler in his satire of the era was to substitute for the churches as the centres of national worship. Wealth was in the air, it was visible in the building going on in London, in the increase of trade. As its importance grew, the fear of losing it became greater, and, at the same time, a feeling of guilt over its unequal distribution began to creep in. The more wealth was revered, the more poverty was feared and hated. The sense of guilt which came

[1] Reprinted from *Browning's Poetry of Reticence*, Edinburgh, Oliver & Boyd (1968) pp. 67-89.

with the possession of money was offset by the sentimental ideal-isation of the labourer in literature as "poor but honest". This was a common feature in novels at the time, although Trollope, at least, had the sense to see that poverty could have not only a narrowing but also a hardening influence, as in the parish of Hogglestock. Browning subscribed to the traditional view, not only in *Pippa Passes*, but also in the gate-keeper who refuses Guido's bribe in *The Ring and the Book*:

> Whose palm was horn through handling horses' hoofs
> And could not close upon my proffered gold![2]

Browning, whose subject-matter was so often drawn from the past and from other countries, might well have been expected to free himself more easily than the rest of his contemporaries from this preoccupation with money. But in fact he was obsessed by it beyond all measure. We have only to take two of his best-known poems and compare them with their Italian sources to see how the emphasis has shifted: "Andrea del Sarto" and *The Ring and the Book*.

1. Money in "Andrea del Sarto"

"Andrea del Sarto" was based on Vasari's *Le Vite de' Pittori* and Baldinucci's *Notizie de' Professori del Disegno*.[3] In the Italian histories Andrea's wife, Lucrezia, is accused not of greed but of bullying. Vasari, who was a pupil of Andrea's, and had lived in his house as an apprentice, writes with feeling on this point. The misappropriation of the loan from the French King is re-corded in the source-books, but not emphasised. Browning has developed the money question far beyond its original significance. The reason is probably not purely sociological. The money which passes from the husband's hand to the lover through the wife may be partly sexual in interpretation, for Browning was a fine instinctive psychologist. But what interests us here is that out of hints in the Italian art-historians and De Musset, Browning has made so much of the question of money, which is seen in Victorian terms. The "cousin", for whose whistle the wife is

---

[2] *The Ring and the Book*, XI, 1672-3.
[3] See William Clyde DeVane, *A Browning Handbook*, 2nd edn. New York (1955) pp. 244-8.

so restlessly waiting, has "gaming debts to pay". Anyone familiar with eighteenth-century and Victorian fiction will realise how much worse these seemed, how much more vicious, than other debts – for gaming was the squandering of money. It is true that in another detail Browning has one of his characteristic flashes of intolerance, and breaks away from accepted Victorian money-making morality. Meditating on the fact that he has allowed his parents to die of want, a detail suggested by Vasari – "And he made provision for her father and sisters; but not for his own parents, whom he never wished to see; so that in a short time they died in poverty" – Andrea tries first to put forward an unconvincing plea in self-excuse:

> They were born poor, lived poor, and poor they died:
> And I have laboured somewhat in my time
> And not been paid profusely.[4]

Then he pushes aside this hypocrisy, to exclaim:

> Some good son
> Paint my two hundred pictures – let him try! . . .[5]

arguing that his dedication to his art was of more value than filial virtue, and that art has nothing to do with moral conduct. Despite this, his sense of wrong-doing remains, and the thought that Lucrezia's infidelity is a punishment to him for having neglected his parents follows immediately:

> No doubt, there's something strikes a balance. Yes,
> You loved me quite enough, it seems to-night.[6]

It is the same idea of punishment conceived as payment that we find later in Browning's poem on the drowned men lying in the Paris Morgue.

This one short monologue, "Andrea del Sarto", which deals with subjects of such interest as the relations between a husband and an unfaithful wife, and investigates the whole question of the assessment of an artist's achievement, contains the following words connected with money, showing how the theme ran in an undercurrent through the whole poem: price, money, count, saves, dear, grasp, gain, profitless, given, give, gain, compensates,

---

[4] "Andrea del Sarto", 253-5.
[5] *Op. cit.*, 255-6.   [6] *Op. cit.*, 257-8.

award, golden, gold-chain, crown, reward, golden, gold, fortune,
earn, give, gold, gold, loans, debts, pay, buy, spend, worth, pay,
worth, pay, thirteen scudi, coin, want, poverty, riches, rich, poor,
poor, poor, paid.

2. Money in *The Ring and the Book*

This basic theme is to be found over and over again in Browning's
poetry. The well-known lyric "The Lost Leader" is completely
in this key. But it is in *The Ring and the Book* that we notice how
far this emphasis is exaggerated and abnormal. This long poem
is a detailed examination and presentation of the truth as it emerges
from a long law-suit, or rather a series of law-suits. And the facts
of the case are taken, with great accuracy of detail, from its
famous source, the Old Yellow Book, the volume which Browning picked up on a stall in Florence. But what has never been
sufficiently noted by the commentators, is that the whole emphasis
in Browning's version has been changed. In the source the crime
is conceived in Italian terms – the motive is Honour. Or it might
be more correct to state that the defence, including Guido himself,
stakes everything upon this plea – the one most likely then, as
now, to be regarded at least in the light of an extenuating circumstance by Italian justice.

Some mention of money is made in the Old Yellow Book, for
the facts of the case are those elaborated by Browning. There is
the question of the Comparini's need of a legal heir, there is the
wrangle over Pompilia's dowry, and her alleged theft from her
husband, and there is Pietro's will. But sums of money are mentioned on relatively few occasions – only the inventory of stolen
goods (all of which are valued in *scudi*) makes anything like a show.
Scudi are the only currency mentioned, with the exception of the
gratie paid for a lamb to show the parsimonious house-keeping at
Arezzo, of which Pietro and Violante complain so bitterly:

> For the food of all this tableful, the Franceschini bought on
> Saturday a sucking lamb, on which they spent, at most,
> twelve or fourteen gratie. Then Signora Beatrice cooked it
> and divided it out for the entire week. And the head of the
> lamb she divided up for a relish three times, and for the relish
> at other times she served separately the lights and intestines.[7]

[7] *The Old Yellow Book*, ed. Charles W. Hodell, Washington (1908) p. 41.

A sum of three hundred *scudi* is mentioned as the security or bail, under guarantee of which Pompilia is released to give birth to her child in the home of her foster-parents, where the murder takes place, and the sum bequeathed in Pietro's will is recorded. This, as far as the source-book is concerned, is the extent of the interest in money.

Not so in Browning. Even a casual reading of *The Ring and the Book* is enough to show how differently he viewed the question. To start with, we are told of his purchase of the Yellow Book itself:

> I found this book,
> Gave a *lira* for it, eightpence English just. . . .[8]

It is most significant that he not only should mention the Italian sum (a very small one), but should trouble to give the English translation, showing, not only his extreme accuracy over money matters, but also his pride in the trivial bargain he has achieved, which he does not intend his readers (unfamiliar perhaps with contemporary conversion tables) to miss. It lay he tells us, among

> A pile of brown-etched prints, two *crazie* each,[9]

a detail which seems insignificant enough, but to which he returns over three hundred lines later:

> The etcher of those prints, two *crazie* each. . . .[10]

It is, however, extremely significant for a fuller understanding of Browning and of his poem. For gold, money, coins, pour out of it on every page. Only Pompilia herself uses these words less often than the other characters, thereby suggesting her purity – for money throughout *The Ring and the Book* suggests soiling. Pompilia mentions money only to disown it:

> I no more own a coin than have an hour
> Free of observance,[11]

whereby the imagery seconds the argument for her chastity in that coins, for Browning, are the golden shower of Danae.

---

[8] *The Ring and the Book*, I, 38-9.   [9] *Op. cit.*, I, 66.
[10] *Op. cit.*, I, 370.   [11] *Op. cit.*, IV, 815-6.

That "coin" can have this meaning for Pompilia as well as for
Fifine is shown later in her confession –

Here, marriage was the coin, a dirty piece –[12]

while the idea of the sullying of chastity by gold goes back in
Browning as early as *Sordello*: "Shook off, as might a lily its gold
soil" and "soiled by its own loose gold-meal".[13]

Pompilia's confession apart, the rest of *The Ring and the Book* is
impregnated with gold. The Pope is in no way spared. He may
be economical, as indeed he is, for we are told, quite gratuitously,
at the beginning of the poem, of Pope Innocent, that

His own meal cost but five carlines a day,[14]

but he is involved to this small extent in the general corruption.

For money, and gold in so far as gold is used as money, is
regarded by Browning as fundamentally evil. The sociological
reasons I have already glanced at – a growing feeling that its
unequal distribution was wrong, the frame of mind which was
preparing the way for the economic doctrines of socialism and
communism. And Browning, who was married to Elizabeth
Barrett,[15] must have felt increasingly guilty on this count –
indeed Erdman[16] in an exciting study of "Childe Roland"
suggests that that poem contains suppressed guilt feelings over
the working conditions and economic hardships of the life of
industrial workers, linking it up with Elizabeth Barrett Browning's campaign against child labour.

[12] *Op. cit.*, VII, 407.
[13] Much the same words are used by W. S. Landor in his "Fiesole Idyl",
Imaginary Conversations and Poems, a Selection, ed. Havelock Ellis, London
(1933): ". . . the over-sacred cup / Of the pure lily hath between my hands /
Felt safe, unsoil'd, nor lost one grain of gold". Landor does not, however,
make the same point as Browning, that it is the gold itself which may soil
the lily.
[14] *The Ring and the Book*, I, 324.
[15] The best example of her attitude is to be found in her poems "The Cry
of the Children" and "The Cry of the Human", which contain lines such as
"The plague of gold strikes far and near", and "The curse of gold upon the
land / The lack of bread enforces."
[16] See David V. Erdman, "Browning's Industrial Nightmare", in
Philological Quarterly, XXXVI (1957) pp. 417-35.

3. Gold and the Roman Catholic Church

These doubts were strengthened by the Christian condemnation of money and gold. In the New Testament it is referred to as "filthy lucre", and the young Browning must often have heard sermons wherein the money-changers were cast out of the Temple. Moreover the Scarlet Woman of Revelations, who by Protestant interpretation represents the Church of Rome, must have left an indelible impression on the mind of the child:

> I will show unto thee the judgement of the great whore that sitteth upon many waters. . . . And the woman was arrayed in purple and scarlet colour, and decked with gold and precious stones and pearls, having a golden cup in her hand full of abominations and filthiness of her fornication.[17]

The gold cup in her hand is the communion cup or Grail; and for the abominations in it we need only recall:

> Had a spider found out the communion-cup. . . .[18]

The particular form taken by the "abomination" as a spider (a creature of which Browning was fond) is probably from *The Winter's Tale*: "I have drunk and seen the spider". In "A Forgiveness", instead, a barber's basin (which in medieval times may well have contained abominations) is changed into God's sacramental cup. It is difficult today to grasp the strength of the religious intolerance underlying this concept – to realise how much Protestants *hated* the Church of Rome. The evil seemed so insidious, the filth was to be found in the Communion cup itself.

This ambiguity in the Bible, whereby gold represented not only good but also the worst form of evil, may have encouraged Browning's own highly ambiguous use of the symbol.

4. Evil in Gold

In the introduction to *The Ring and the Book* Browning had used gold as a symbol for his art itself. Yet elsewhere he often uses it in its darker meanings. Gold, in the sense of money, was often for him a bribe or the reward of crime. Already in *Sordello* the Kaiser's gold is seen as an evil, and we have a situation fore-

---

[17] Revelations XVII, 1, 4.   [18] "Gold Hair", 104.

shadowing "The Bishop Orders his Tomb" with the children waiting greedily for their father's death (the situation Trollope touches upon with such subtle comprehension in *Barchester Towers*). In *Sordello* the father, like the dying Bishop of St Praxed's, is afraid of his children:

> I am sick too, old,
> Half-crazed I think; what good's the Kaiser's gold
> To such an one? God help me! for I catch
> My children's greedy sparkling eyes at watch....[19]

In *King Victor and King Charles* the gold is extorted, while in "The Laboratory" it is both the "gold oozings" of the poison and the gold to be "gorged" in reward. In "Instans Tyrannus" gold is used for temptation, while in "The Italian in England" it is offered for betrayal:

> the State
> Will give you gold – oh, gold so much! –
> If you betray me to their clutch.[20]

In "Andrea del Sarto", as we have seen, the gold is stolen, while in "Gold Hair" it is hoarded. This last poem alone would raise suspicions as to the normality of its writer's interest in gold. The morbid elements of this legend of Pornic are, to say the least, curious: there seems to have been something about this particular corner of France which set all Browning's neuroses on edge, some atmosphere to which he was peculiarly sensitive, for it is the setting of his much later poem *Fifine*.[21] In "A Death in the Desert" the value of gold to man is contrasted with that of fire, and a parallel drawn with the value of Christ:

> will he give up fire
> For gold or purple once he knows its worth?
> Could he give Christ up were His worth as plain?...[22]

in what may be an allusion to his betrayal by Judas – to which

[19] *Sordello*, ii, 873-6.
[20] "The Italian in England", 66-8.
[21] See Browning's letter to Elizabeth postmarked 5 Jan. 1846.
[22] "A Death in the Desert", 292-4. Here "these" are "half my subjects reserved by your skill".

Browning makes frequent references throughout his work, as the greatest evil wrought by money.

Gold is offered as a bribe by Guido in *The Ring and the Book*, Hervé Riel accuses the men of St Malo of being "bought by English gold", and in "Doctor –" a monarch tries to buy off death itself by bribing the Doctor:

> Be saved I will!
> Why else am I earth's foremost potentate?
> Add me to these and take as fee your fill
> Of gold – that point admits of no debate
> Between us: save me, as you can and must –
> Gold, till your gown's pouch cracks beneath the weight!
> This touched the Doctor.[23]

In this late poem, written when Browning was almost seventy, there is probably some personal consideration as he weighs the ultimate uselessness of gold, even while humorously noticing the doctor's greed. The greed inspired by gold is also the subject of "Cenciaja" where "blinded by so exorbitant a lust of gold" a youth sets out to kill the Marschesina Costanza, his widowed mother.[24] Gold inspires greed not only in this juvenile delinquent but also in the Roman Catholic Church, which Browning is ever-ready to censure. The "golden grist" of Monsieur Léonce Miranda's charity in *Red Cotton Night-Cap Country* pours steadily

> From mill to mouth of sack – held wide and close
> By Father of the Mission, Parish-priest,
> And Mother of the Convent, Nun I know,
> . . . in these same two years, expenditure
> At quiet Clairvaux rose to the amount
> Of Forty Thousand English Pounds. . . .[25]

[23] "Doctor –", 160-7. The source of this poem is probably to be found in the account of Louis XI's fear of death and attempt to bribe the doctors, given in the *Mémoires* of Philippe de Comines.

[24] A subsidiary source for this matricide may be found in Vidocq's museum "of knives and nails and hooks that have helped great murderers to their purposes". Browning describes his visit there in a letter to Elizabeth dated 1 Jul. 1845. He tells us "thus one little sort of dessert knife *did* only take *one* life. . . . 'But then' says Vidocq, 'it was the man's own mother's life, with fifty-two blows, and all for' (I think) 'fifteen francs she had got' ".

[25] *Red Cotton Night-Cap Country*, 3153-8.

The capital letters are Browning's own, clearly impressed by the enormity of the sum which seemed to him exorbitant and sadly misspent, in that a "trifle" went

> to supply the Virgin's crown
> With that stupendous jewel from New York.[26]

This theme of the ill-gotten wealth of the Catholic Church had always been popular with Protestants: it is perhaps best expressed in Hawthorne's *Marble Faun*, where the fascination and repulsion exerted by the combined sense of beauty and evil are very close to Browning's own. Henry James's *Roderick Hudson* catches something of the same atmosphere, but the sense of sin is best typified in the figure taken from Revelations: the whore of Babylon – a fitting symbol, not for the Church herself, but for the uneasy attraction she exerted over these Protestant writers. The Pope himself is allowed by Browning in *The Ring and the Book* to have doubts as to the utility of so much wealth, and to wonder, though only to wonder, whether it has not had a corrupting influence on one of his foremost prelates. Faced with the failure of the Archbishop of Arezzo to help Pompilia when she turned to him for advice in her distress, the Pope ponders:

> Have we misjudged here, over-armed our knight,
> Given gold and silk where plain hard steel serves best,
> Enfeebled whom we sought to fortify,
> Made an archbishop and undone a saint?[27]

The corrupting influence, as the Pope sees it, has been the gold.

5. "The Heretic's Tragedy"

In "The Heretic's Tragedy" the negative aspects of gold, both religious and sexual, come to a head in a forceful and somewhat frightening poem in which Browning concentrated all his major symbols. The nightmarish quality of the poem springs, I believe, not so much from the horror of the subject (the details of the burning of Jacques du Bourg-Molay at the stake in Paris in 1314), as in a strange distortion in the symbolism – for here many of

[26] *Op. cit.*, 3162-3.
[27] *The Ring and the Book*, x, 1467-70.

Browning's habitual symbols are seen, as it were, in reverse.[28] Instead of the bee of the flowercup image cluster (in which the associations of sex and gold are habitually linked together) we find John (as he calls Jacques)

> a-buzzing there,
> Hornet-prince of the mad wasps' hive,
> And clipt of his wings.[29]

And the honey, another symbol for sex and gold, has been degraded:

> Alack, there be roses and roses, John!
> Some, honied of taste like your leman's tongue. . . .[30]

The rose is the rose of Sharon, taking us back to the Song of Solomon, where the rose and lily are one:

> I am the rose of Sharon, and the lily of the valleys . . .
> And his fruit was sweet to my taste.[31]

So Browning's lily, which in the later poem *Fifine* was to become the symbol of the harlot, has already taken on some of these negative connotations with the association with the "leman's tongue". The climax comes in stanza ix, where the burning heretic takes the shape of a flower (rose + lily) to become

> . . . a coal-black giant flower of hell!

The "deliriously-drugged scent" of the flower in *Fifine* is here "a gust of sulphur". This detailed description of the burning man in terms of a flower is peculiarly horrible just because of the contrast it offers with the earlier connotations (already present in "Women and Roses", although they find their fullest expression in the later *Fifine*):

---

[28] Browning seems to have arrived at a literary technique comparable with the negative-print sequence which is fairly frequently introduced into modern films. But while the visual inversion is used (when it is used intelligently, as in *La Femme mariée*) to suggest alienation from the scene portrayed, this inversion of the symbols gives not only a sense of unreality, but of abnormality and horror.

[29] "The Heretic's Tragedy", 14-16.

[30] *Op. cit.*, 64-5.   [31] Song of Solomon II, 1-2.

> Lo, – petal on petal, fierce rays unclose;
>   Anther on anther, sharp spikes outstart;
> And with blood for dew, the bosom boils;
>   And a gust of sulphur is all its smell;
> And lo, he is horribly in the toils
>   Of a coal-black giant flower of hell![32]

This reference to Hell, the destination of the heretic, and the lurid imagery, remind us that Browning as a child, and a sensitive child, must have heard a number of Hell-fire sermons. These, however completely discounted later, must have remained as material for dreams and poetry. The burning-off at the wrists of Miranda's hands in *Red Cotton Night-Cap Country* is a further example of the use of the same background material. The crime of the heretic Jacques is twice equated with the crime of Judas:

> Jesus Christ – John had bought and sold,
>   Jesus Christ – John had eaten and drunk;
> To him, the Flesh meant silver and gold. . . .[33]

and

> the Person, he bought and sold again. . . .[34]

A great many meanings are entangled in the complex imagery of this poem. The burning flower is Sharon's rose, a figure of the Church, but it is also the Rosa Mundi named in the motto to the poem, thereby involving the whole world in the sin of Judas. The thirty pieces of silver have become, less specifically, "silver and gold", likewise extending the sin to all humanity. The Flesh is the body of Christ which to man "meant silver and gold" and for trafficking with this he is punished by the burning of Hell. The details of the pyre, with gallows, fork, and tumbrils, are a foretaste of the punishments of hell, emblems which are developed much more fully in Guido's second book in *The Ring and the Book*, where the torments of hell become dramatically present to the condemned man. At the same time here the burning of the heretic recalls details of the crucifixion, seen, as it were, in a distorting mirror:

[32] "The Heretic's Tragedy", 73-80.
[33] *Op. cit.*, 46-8.   [34] *Op. cit.*, 84.

> Then up they hoist me John in a chafe,
> Sling him fast like a hog to scorch,
> Spit in his face, then leap back safe,
> Sing "Laudes" and bid clap-to the torch,[35]

so that the heretic appears as an inverse personification of Christ.[36] Interwoven with the theme of the betrayal and crucifixion of Christ, involving the theme of gold, is the theme of sex, and the Puritan idea that this, too, carried with it the tortures and punishments of Hell. The burning man takes on the form of Browning's "sexual" flower emblem. The comment is unmistakable:

> What maketh heaven, That maketh hell.[37]

The fact that the rose is the rose of Sharon, the rose of the Song of Solomon, marks the association with sexual pleasure. But the root of the tree, with its roses, some "honied", some "bitter", grows, significantly, out of devil's dung:

> Their tree struck root in Devil's dung.[38]

Browning is not using the term "devil's dung" in the sense of the plant, asafoetida, but as a synonym for manure.[39] At the same time, the word carries the metaphorical meaning of gold and, by analogy, money. The tree striking root there reminds us that "the love of money is the root of all evil",[40] harking back to the buying and selling of Christ earlier in the poem. Freud has drawn attention to this association of gold or money with dung:

---

[35] *Op. cit.*, 32-5.

[36] The same pattern is visible in the description of the execution in *The Ring and the Book*, where, with the peasants hanging on either side, Guido is the inverted Christ figure: "To mount the scaffold steps, Guido was last / Here also, as atrociousest in crime. / We hardly noticed how the peasants died, / They dangled somehow soon to right and left . . .". *The Ring and the Book*, XII, 167-70.

[37] "The Heretics Tragedy", 81.   [38] *Op. cit.*, 67.

[39] Browning was to use "devils' dung" in the same sense many years later in *Red Cotton Night-Cap Country*, 1508: "the florist bedded thick / His primrose root in ruddle, bullocks' blood / Ochre and devils' dung for aught I know". Here the primrose is Clara de Millefleurs, the "rarity" raised in "social manure", and seen at this stage of the poem as a corrupting influence on the young Miranda.

[40] I Tim. VI, 10.

Wherever archaic modes of thought have predominated or persisted in the ancient civilisations, in myths, fairy tales and superstitions, in unconscious thinking, in dreams and in neuroses – money is brought into the most intimate relationship with dirt. We know that the gold which the devil gives his paramours turns to excrement after his departure. . . .[41]

The term "devil's dung" seemed to Browning peculiarly expressive of the evil at the root, an implication of extreme importance, for over and over again in his work gold has these overtones. We have already noted how gold pollen *soiled* the lily, how the pure Pompilia is less tainted by gold than the other characters of *The Ring and the Book*. Not only does she refer less to money, she also declares that she possesses none, implying not only her poverty, but also her purity.

In *Red Cotton Night-Cap Country* there is a long and amusing simile in which the Priest and Nun, carrying away Monsieur Léonce Miranda's money, are seen as carting manure. First they are compared to the Egyptian scarab which rolls dung, and then Browning presents

> the couple yonder, Father Priest
> And Mother Nun, who came and went and came,
> Beset this Clairvaux, trundled money-muck
> To midden and the main heap oft enough,
> But never bade unshut from sheathe the gauze
> Nor showed that, who would fly, must let fall filth,
> And warn "Your jewel, brother, is a blotch:
> Sister, your lace trails ordure . . .".[42]

The closeness of the relationship is evident in the above passage

[41] Sigmund Freud, *Complete Psychological Works*, London (1949) IX, 175.

[42] *Red Cotton Night-Cap Country*, 4131-8. A complex simile which would bear full psychoanalytical investigation is to be found in *The Ring and the Book*, VI, 668-82; Browning returns to it again in VI, 910-1. Here the soul of the liar issues from the body "By way of the ordure corner". A parallel is drawn with the scorpion issuing from the Madonna's mouth, and the same scorpion is referred to as a "blotch", linking it with the dung in the lines from *Red Cotton Night-Cap Country*. The elements of dung and painting are complicated here by reptile, birth, and death symbolism in a passage which challenges full interpretation, although the "argument" is clear enough.

of Browning, where the manure actually stands for the money. Sometimes, as in *The Ring and the Book*, the two are merely brought into contact:

> Grime is grace
> To whoso gropes amid the dung for gold. . . .[43]

Or in "Easter-Day":

> "The filthy shall be filthy still:
> Miser, there waits the gold for thee!"[44]

And in *Parleyings* "With Daniel Bartoli":

> Choose muck for gold?[45]

A similar connexion is made again in *The Ring and the Book* in the speech of the Fisc or lawyer for the defence:

> the lady there
> Was bound to proffer nothing short of love
> To the priest whose service was to save her. What?
> Shall she propose him lucre, dust o' the mine,
> Rubbish o' the rock, some diamond, muck-worms prize.[46]

There is a further subtlety in this passage, for the introduction of [filthy] lucre and muck-worms implies, without in any way stating, that the lawyer here is fouling Pompilia's fair name with his worldly argument that she should have committed adultery with the priest out of common gratitude. For while it is interesting to trace why, as a man, Browning was so often led to these images, it is even more so to realise the use that, as an artist, he makes of them. In *The Ring and the Book* Guido twice uses "muck" for "money":

> My dowry was derision, my gain-muck . . .[47]

and again:

> No better gift than sordid muck? Yes, Sirs![48]

where the ambiguity is quite deliberate, for besides implying

---

[43] *The Ring and the Book*, IX, 552-3.   [44] "Easter-Day", 713-4.
[45] "With Daniel Bartoli", 196.
[46] *The Ring and the Book*, IX, 509-13.
[47] *Op. cit.*, XI, 1215.   [48] *Op. cit.*, XI, 2182.

the worthlessness of money, there are further implications of the disgrace of Pompilia's shameful birth:

> The babe had been a find i' the filth-heap, Sir, . . .[49]

And:

> Daughter? Dirt
> O' the kennel! Dowry? Dust o' the street![50]

And the soiling of the family name:

> Another of the name shall keep displayed
> The flag with the ordure on it, brandish still
> The broken sword has served to stir a jakes?[51]

All these connotations underlie the use of "muck" in the first quotation. Perhaps Browning has escaped the accusation of coprophilia, to which lines such as these might well lay him open, chiefly because he does make poetry out of this, as out of other unlikely material. Another reason is the screen provided by the dramatic monologue. Were he to write in his own person, as Swift did, he could hardly have escaped censure, but the speaker is never Robert Browning, and is at times some evil-doer such as Guido or Sludge. But it was Browning who felt this sense of evil in money, who made this equation with dung and who transferred it to so many of his characters. Mr Sludge simply wallows in money – he refers to dimes, dollars, and V-notes with every breath. Fitly enough, it is to him that another coprophilic passage is attributed:

> And the cash that's God's sole solid in this world!
> Look at him! Try to be too bold, too gross
> For the master! Not you! He's the man for muck;
> Shovel it forth, full-splash, he'll smooth your brown
> Into artistic richness, never fear!
> Find him the crude stuff. . . .[52]

And he continues in the same vein, but with an even more surprising turn:

[49] *Op. cit.*, II, 558.   [50] *Op. cit.*, V, 772-3.
[51] *Op. cit.*, V, 1490-2.
[52] "Mr Sludge, 'The Medium' ", 753-8.

> That man would choose to see the whole world roll
> I' the slime o' the slough, so he might touch the tip
> Of his brush with what I call the best of browns –
> Tint ghost-tales, spirit-stories, past the power
> Of the outworn umber and bistre![53]

What is remarkable is that Browning is here sullying the very art of painting for which he had so great a respect. His suggestion that a painter might use "what I call the best of browns"[54] goes beyond the most daring of recent experiments and reaches back, we can only imagine, to some infantile fantasy. The idea is not exhausted here, for Browning touches on it again in *Red Cotton Night-Cap Country* where the full significance of the verb "daub" would probably go unnoticed if not read in conjunction with the Sludge passage above:

> And most of all resent that here town-dross
> He daubs with money-colour to deceive![55]

Painting, for Browning, often represented art in general, and just as he considers his own problems as a poet in his "painter" poems, so, too, "painting" is a cover for poetry. He seems here to be hinting at a basic question for him, the justification for the use of what Bagehot has defined as the "grotesque" in art.

Throughout his work Browning makes free use of words and compounds relating not only to "dung", but to "muck", "mire", "dirt", "filth", "ordure", and "manure". As we should expect, these words emerge most easily in his longer poems, where he was exerting least control. The shorter and more tightly-knit poems were subject to more conscious censorship. Nor were such terms by any means restricted to his evil characters. For instance, his contemporary Tennyson uses the word "muck" only

[53] *Op. cit.*, 768-72.

[54] Browning had already used this image, in a modified form, over ten years earlier, in a letter written to Elizabeth on 7 Jan. 1846, apropos of the colloquial language introduced into a poem by their friend Horne: "The Sailor Language is good in its way; but as wrongly used in Art as real clay and mud would be, if one plastered them in the foreground of a landscape in order to attain to so much truth – the true thing to endeavour is the making a golden colour which shall do every good in the power of the dirty brown."

[55] *Red Cotton Night-Cap Country*, 947-8.

three times, and then always in dialect poems: but Browning uses it in *Sordello*, "The Heretic's Tragedy", *Easter Day*, "Mr Sludge", *Aristophanes' Apology*, *The Ring and the Book*, *Red Cotton Night-Cap Country*, "Numpholeptos", *Parleyings* ("Bartoli"), "Ned Bratts", and *Strafford*.

In *Paracelsus*, an early poem in which Browning is much concerned with the task of the artist, Paracelsus states:

Ne'er shall boat of mine
Adventure forth for gold and apes at once.[56]

He wishes gold here to represent purity, art itself, and deliberately dissociates it from the apes, which represent filth, as is stated in an early play:

Though I warrant there is filth, red baboons.[57]

While for Shakespeare apes were associated with lechery, for Browning they were associated rather with dirt. The association is again a childish one, and it is curious to find Browning retaining it in his adult poetry. In *Colombe's Birthday* there is a styleme echoing the "gold and apes at once" in "gems and mire at once", where "gold" is replaced by "gems", and "apes" by "mire", showing how closely the two were inter-related.

The equation "money = dirt" is, after all, of universal application; and it is only in drawing the analogy so often and so thoroughly that Browning differs from many other writers. The extent of Browning's obsession with money can be substantiated by listing some of the varieties of currency which are specifically mentioned in his poems: crazie, cross, crown, dime, doit, dollar, drachma, ducat, farthing, florin, franc, half-penny, lira, louis, louis d'or, obol, paul, penny, penny-piece, pound, scudi, soldo, sous, talent, V-note, zechines. Browning's word-hoard was a formidable one, and nothing did he hoard more jealously than these coins – many of which are to be found time and again in his work. A perceptive passage of Edmund Wilson's in a study of Ben Jonson seems relevant in this connexion:

His learning [Jonson's] is a form of hoarding; and allied to it is his habit of collecting words. He liked to get up the special jargons of the various trades and professions and unload them

[56] *Paracelsus*, I, 650-1.   [57] "A Soul's Tragedy", II, 373.

in bulk on the public – sometimes with amusing results, as in
the case of the alchemical and astrological patter reeled off by
the crooks of *The Alchemist*, and even of the technique of
behaviour of the courtiers in *Cynthia's Revels*, but more often,
as with the list of cosmetics recommended by Wittipol in *The
Devil is an Ass* and, to my taste, with the legal Latin of the
divorce scene in *The Silent Woman*, providing some of his most
tedious moments. The point is that Ben Jonson depends on
the exhibition of stored-away knowledge to compel admiration by itself.[58]

How easily this judgment could be fitted to Browning! In his
lists of technical details he outdoes Jonson himself (whether he is
retailing varieties of Italian marble or juggling with variants of
"Hyacinthus"), and while the theatre must have exercised some
form of restraint on Jonson, no actor could have got through, or
audience sat through, the legal Latin which Browning poured in
a torrent of quibbles and puns into *The Ring and the Book*. And, as
we read the frequent food and cooking interpolations with
which Dominus Hyacinthus de Archangelis lards the speech he is
preparing –

> (May Gigia have remembered, nothing stings
> Fried liver out of its monotony
> Of richness, like a root of fennel, chopped
> Fine with the parsley: parsley-sprigs, I said –
> Was there need I should say "and fennel too"?
> But no, she cannot have been so obtuse!
> To our argument! The fennel will be chopped.) – [59]

we are reminded again of Wilson's definition of the "type" to
which Jonson belongs:

> They are likely to have a strong interest in food both from
> the deglutitionary and the excretory points of view; but the
> getting and laying by of money or of some other kind of
> possession which may or may not seem valuable to others is
> likely to substitute itself for the infantile preoccupation with
> the contents of the alimentary tract.[60]

[58] Edmund Wilson, *The Triple Thinkers*, Harmondsworth (1962) p. 246.
[59] *The Ring and the Book*, VIII, 543-9.
[60] Wilson, *The Triple Thinkers*, p. 246.

Edmund Wilson goes on to compare this trend in Jonson to James Joyce:

> Joyce, too, hoarded words and learning and attempted to impress his reader by unloading his accumulations; he, too, has his coprophilic side.[61]

Browning's word-hoarding is, I believe, of the same compulsive nature as that of Jonson and Joyce – and we can add another writer to the list in Thomas Carlyle. James Halliday has drawn attention to this in *Mr Carlyle – My Patient*, a book in which he examines Carlyle's neuroses.[62] This book has only a marginal interest for us, in that it is based mainly on biographical and medical details. But Betty Miller, in her study of Browning, shows, I think, considerable penetration in commenting on Browning's friendship for Carlyle. Seeking to explain Browning's admiration for Carlyle, she suggests:

> It was, perhaps, because he saw in Carlyle's attitude the mirror-image of his own that he felt so closely, so peculiarly bound to him.[63]

An attitude that was "the mirror image of his own". Now what Halliday demonstrates for Carlyle, and what Wilson demonstrates for Ben Jonson was that they fitted exactly into one of the Freudian psychological types, classified as anal-erotics, and of which Freud wrote:

> They are especially orderly, parsimonious and obstinate. . . . It is therefore plausible to suppose that these characteristic traits of orderliness, parsimony and obstinacy which are so often prominent in people who were formerly anal-erotics, are to be regarded as the first and most constant results of the sublimation of anal eroticism.[64]

There is no need to look far in Browning's biography to find

---

[61] *Op. cit.*, p. 259.
[62] James Halliday, *Mr Carlyle, My Patient: A Psychosomatic Biography*, London (1949).
[63] Betty Miller, *Robert Browning, a Portrait*, London (1952) p. 56.
[64] Freud, *Complete Psychological Works*, London (1953) IX, 169-71.

instances of these basic traits in his character. The standard biography by Hall Griffin and Minchin tells us:

> This extreme carefulness became a fixed habit, and pervaded his own expenditure after it had ceased to be necessary. He habitually rode in omnibuses and practised various small economies.[65]

This fits in with what he told us himself of his purchase of the Old Yellow Book for one lira, "eightpence English just". His obstinacy is well attested by his refusal to continue his university studies, and by the well-known story of his marriage. He wrote to Elizabeth on 26 Feb. 1845:

> For when did I once fail to get whatever I had set my heart upon? As I ask myself sometimes, with a strange fear.[66]

His parsimoniousness and orderliness can be seen together in a letter of his wife's which complains of his "morbid" horror of owing five shillings five days:

> I laugh insolently sometimes at Robert and his accounts, and his way of calculating for the days and weeks. . . . And *if* you were to see his little book, with our whole income accounted for to the uttermost farthing, week by week, and an overplus (yes, an overplus!) provided for casualties.[67]

In his poetry this horror of debt, moral as well as pecuniary, is shown in the grim comment of "Apparent Failure", where the poet stands in the Doric little morgue looking through a sheet of glass at the bodies of those suicides who had drowned themselves in the Seine: "One pays one's debt in such a case". Elizabeth herself attributed his fear of debt to early training, in that he was "descended from the blood of all the Puritans, and educated by the strictest of dissenters", but it seems probable that character combined with training and heredity. Fortunately for his art, Browning hoarded, not money, but words. Yet it is

[65] W. Hall Griffin and H. C. Minchin, *The Life of Robert Browning*, London (1938) p. 289.

[66] *Letters of Robert Browning and Elizabeth Barrett Barrett*, (*1845-1846*), New York and London (1899), I, p. 26.

[67] Quoted by Betty Miller, *op. cit.*, p. 142.

scarcely surprising that words conjuring with money should have been among those hoarded most jealously. Where another poet decorates his work with gems (which Browning used but sparingly, though he had a weakness for marbles), Browning adorned his work with ducats, drachmas, and doits. And everywhere and always, gold.

6. Conclusions

To break down the conclusions reached, for the sake of clarity, we are back with Browning's constant antithesis of good and evil. Gold is good in the Old Testament sense of what is of value, what is durable, what is pure. It is evil in the New Testament sense of filthy lucre – and was seen also by Browning as a characteristic of the Catholic Church, typified in the whore of Babylon. This Biblical duality (for the New Testament takes over also the *good* sense of gold from the Old) may have influenced Browning's own awareness of its ambiguity. Then gold is good in so far as it can be equated with sexual pleasure (as I have shown in the honey, pollen, egg-yolk, semen imagery), but is bad in so far as sex was regarded as wicked – "What maketh heaven, that maketh hell". Finally, it was good in so far as it represented excrement (good, that is, in the unconscious childish memory which comes to the surface with Browning when he treats of it as material for art and connects it with monkeys), but bad, above all, in this sense, too, as the first thing that the child was taught to abhor as filthy and vile, and which became mixed in this sense, too, with sin.

The conscious recognition of these ambiguities helps us, first of all, on the level of interpretation – often no mean task where Browning is concerned – for one passage can be read in the light cast by another. But more than this, it can aid us in the appreciation of the poems by showing not only what they meant but what they implied, and when the apparent meaning and the implication are at odds, then we have Browning at his most stimulating.

Poetry is more, much more, than a musical arrangement of words – it is the use of words in such a way as to evoke a wealth of echoes and associations. If the old definition of "memorable prose" were enlarged to mean, not only prose which can be memorised, but also prose which is full of memories, we begin to approach a definition. By tracing this one theme of gold (and its debased form, money) through Browning's work I have tried to show some of the associations it has had for him, to help us to realise consciously what his readers have already recognised unconsciously: the wide range of reference covered in the single word, and the ambiguities it holds.

F. E. L. *Priestley*

SOME ASPECTS OF
BROWNING'S IRONY

Everyone is familiar with the stories current in Browning's own time based upon the obscurity of his writing, and he himself shows an awareness of his reputation, sometimes rueful, sometimes impatient. The stories generally suggest that the sources of the obscurity are mainly, or even entirely, stylistic, and due to Browning's peculiar distortions of syntax and his habit of multiplying parentheses, asides, and abrupt disjunctions within a single contorted sentence-paragraph. One can sympathise with the complaints of his readers accustomed to the straightforward narrative verse of the earlier Romantics, and particularly with those who sought, in Browning's phrase, to make poetry "a substitute for a good cigar", and one can acknowledge that the syntax of a poem like *Sordello*, or parts of "A Death in the Desert", take a little patient sorting out. But our own generation, trained on Hopkins and a host of new Metaphysicals, and with a parcel of bright new critical theories to justify the use of the loom of language to weave patterns of Gordian knots, no longer find Browning's poetry difficult in this sense. We have long since broken much stiffer codes.

We are now able to recognise where the main problems of interpreting Browning lie. What is often most difficult to determine is Browning's attitude towards his subject, and the attitude he wishes his reader to adopt towards it. In *Sordello*, for example, the crucial questions are not those about the literal meanings of passages, but those about the meanings and implications of actions, judgments of characters, and so on. To know what one is expected to make of Eglamor and Naddo, of Sordello's abandonment of his attempt to create a new language for poetry, of his refusal of power, – to decide what the "one step" it was that Sordello refused to take which by Dante's time it was too late to take – these are far more crucial to an understanding of the poem and far more difficult to elucidate than any mere verbal difficulties. *Sordello* properly retains its reputation as the most obscure of Browning's poems because questions of this sort are in it more numerous and more problematic than in any other poem, partly from the absence of the kind of exposition which would guide the reader's interpretation (which may seem an eccentric comment on a poem so liberal with apparent expositions) and partly from the play of Browning's irony.

I use *Sordello* here as an example of the two quite different sources of problems in interpretation; I do not intend in this paper to make a frontal assault on that poem – having come to Browning's dark tower I shall insert a cork in the slughorn, and leave it for stronger lungs. What I do propose is to consider the general operation of irony in Browning's poetry, in its relation to the problem of interpretation. In this particular respect, *Sordello* differs from many other poems only in degree. In the discussion which follows, it will be obvious that I am often limiting my concern and my treatment very narrowly to "interpretation", and ignoring what are undoubtedly more important poetic concerns. I am fully aware of this; in abstracting and isolating single aspects of Browning's irony, and trying to investigate some main modes of its operation, I hope to throw some light, even if indirectly, upon what might be considered Browning's more strictly poetic procedures.

It is obvious, of course, that in many of his dramatic poems Browning uses irony of a familiar sort, and often in a relatively familiar and straightforward way which leaves us in no doubt as to his attitude, and consequently our own. In a monologue like "Andrea del Sarto", for example, we recognise easily the ironic play between Andrea's dream of what he might have been, of what, given a new chance, he might still be, and his resigned acceptance of what he takes to be his inescapable nature; also the irony of his alternating boasts of his powers and potentialities and his self-condemnation. In "The Bishop Orders his Tomb", we appreciate at perhaps an even simpler level the ironic juxtaposition of the professed Christian and the real pagan, of sensual gluttony preparing for death. In such poems, the irony is not only straightforward, but related simply and uniformly to the main structure of the poem, both as theme and as pattern of images. Consequently, these are poems with which critics are at ease, and no large disputes or areas of complexity surround their interpretations. "Fra Lippo Lippi" is almost of this sort, but not quite. If one compares it with "Andrea del Sarto", for example, which seems an obvious comparison, it is evident that in "Andrea" the relation of art to life is much more explicit; lines like the familiar "Ah, but a man's reach should exceed his grasp, / Or what's a heaven for?" leave the reader in no doubt that Andrea's art is a reflexion of his character, and that his character presents, by way of example, the poet's moral reflexion on life. In "Fra Lippo" this is not so explicit, and a reader could easily find a simple ironic contrast, something like that in "The Bishop Orders his Tomb", between the professed monk and the actual sensualist. This contrast is of course there, but it operates in a quite different and more complicated context. To begin with, Fra Lippo's sensuality is made a more innocent sort than the Bishop's, and we are given also insights, which undoubtedly we are meant to take seriously, into a genuinely religious side of his nature. Once we grasp that the poem is asserting "The value and significance of flesh", that "This world's no blot for us, Nor blank; / It means intensely, and means good", we recognise that the ironic contrast at the core of the poem is between the Prior's ascetic opposition of body and spirit, of worldly beauty and celestial truth, and Fra Lippo's (and Browning's) insistence on their close relation. The poem moves, in fact, from an opening which deliberately suggests and exploits one ironic pattern, and that perhaps the obvious and expected one, to a much more profound and serious one. This makes the structure of the poem itself ironic, in a sense not applicable to the other poem.

Another pair of poems inviting comparison is "Cleon" and "An Epistle of Karshish". And again the ironic pattern of the first is relatively simpler than that of the second. Cleon's recognition, in his epistle to Protus, of the one doctrine which would give meaning to temporal existence and to death, and his arrogant and contemptuous dismissal of the suggestion that Paul, "a mere barbarian Jew", might have "access to a secret shut from us", his refusal to enquire into Paul's teaching at first hand – "(as I gathered from a bystander) / Their doctrine could be held by no sane man" – and his consequent failure to discover that Paul's doctrine is identical with that which he sought, all establish a clear and obvious ironic pattern. The one theme in the poem not openly related to this primary irony is Cleon's assertion of the ultimate inferiority of art to life. This long passage, the most brilliant and moving in the poem, develops its irony from a contrast between Cleon's view of the nature of art and Browning's, which is not stated in this poem. It is relatively easy to recognise a fundamental irony in Cleon's doctrine: art imitates life and the joy and beauty of life, but the clear sight and apprehension embodied in the imitation are not the same thing as the actual experience in living:

> Because in my great epos I display
> How divers men young, strong, fair, wise, can act –
> Is this as though I acted? if I paint,
> Carve the young Phoebus, am I therefore young? . . .
> I can write love-odes: thy fair slave's an ode.[1]

The ironic theme of Keats' Grecian urn ode, the immortality of the imitation, the evanescence of the living reality, involves a contrast between art and life. But since the main ironic pattern of "Cleon" involves the contrast between the acceptance and the rejection of the Christian revelation, and its implications for the meaning of earthly existence, it becomes clear that more is implied here in the comments on art than Keats' kind of irony. We are expected to see an irony that Cleon himself does not see. He sees only too powerfully the irony of the permanence of art, but he does not see the irony of his own view of the nature of art, as he does not see the irony of his view of Paul and Christ. Readers who remember Browning's "Easter-Day" will also remember how in that poem (particularly in sections xxv and xxvi) art, equally with life, must receive its meaning from its relation to a higher eternal perfection. Art itself is an incomplete striving for the infinite beyond the finite. For Cleon, art is limited, as Browning saw all Greek (and, presumably, all pagan)

---

[1] "Cleon", 285-8, 296.

art to be limited, to "to-day's brief passion" ("Old Pictures in Florence"). Cleon's words, then, contain double irony: the irony of which he is aware, and the irony of which we are aware and he is not. The first irony is explicit in the poem, the second is not. Full understanding of the poem demands recognition of both ironies.

With "Karshish", the pattern is much more complicated. In the first place, the poem embodies two separate themes, not logically related to each other but both arising in Browning's mind from his conception of the Arab physician confronted by Lazarus. In fact, one could recognise three elements in the structure. The two themes I spoke of are of course the divinity of Christ, with which the poem ends, and the implications of Lazarus' behaviour after restoration to life. The third element, the development of the "character", Karshish, forms the warp of the poem into which the themes are woven as woof, if that is not too fanciful a way of putting it. Different patterns of irony are developed with each of the three elements. The simplest, and most conventional (conventional for Browning, that is, in terms of other poems) is the irony associated with the divinity of Christ, particularly at the end of the poem. This is like the irony of Cleon's rejection of Paul's teaching, with a difference. Cleon's "their doctrine could be held by no sane man" becomes here "The madman saith He said so: it is strange." The word "madman" hovers ironically between mere technical medical description and Cleon's contemptuous dismissal; the last phrase suggests that the dismissal need not be final. Throughout the poem, the ironic conflict between rejecting out of hand Lazarus' case and the thoughts it has provoked, and acknowledging the strange insistence by which they refuse to be rejected, provides a strong sense of drama and heightens curiosity about the ideas Karshish seems so reluctant to expose and so unable to free himself of. This continuous ironic conflict, established before any of the actual ideas are brought out into the open, serves as a unifying device in the structure of the poem. It is only as we come to Karshish's account of his actual meeting with Lazarus that the main themes emerge, and we recognise that Karshish's relation to the two themes is not a single simple one. The irony of his attraction-repulsion to the doctrine of the Incarnation (here expressed in

Browning's terms, familiar to readers of "Saul") is relatively simple. Not so his relation to Lazarus.

The theme presented through Karshish's account of his examination of Lazarus and interview with him dominates the centre of the poem (79-242). It is the theme, familiar in many of Browning's poems, of the necessity of human ignorance, or, in a perhaps less misleading phrasing, the function of the limitation of human knowledge. It is interesting to see how Browning develops it here. For the first part of the poem (1-78) our attention has been centred on Karshish, developed as a character, and on the novelty of using his point of view in what we recognise as a familiar setting in place and time. With the introduction of the actual case, soon explicitly identified as that of Lazarus, we find ourselves no longer watching Karshish, but watching Lazarus through Karshish's eyes, and no longer merely detached observers of a dramatic character, but highly interested participants in an examination which concerns us as well as Karshish. And we have certain expectations as to what Lazarus, who has had a glimpse of eternity, should be like – what he should do and say, or, if you prefer, what the poet should have him do and say. It is these expectations that Browning exploits for his irony. For we do not expect what we find: that enlightenment has detached Lazarus from life; that knowledge of the divine will has made him totally passive; that certainty of all values has given him a scale of values so remote from the ordinary human scale that he cannot relate them; that, in short, he can no longer communicate with humanity. Since we have assumed that the value of knowledge in life, and in the choices life presents, must mean that perfect and complete knowledge would be the ideal fitment for life, the irony of Lazarus' attitude strikes us very directly, and more powerfully than it is made to strike Karshish in the poem. The ironic paradox that full knowledge unfits for human life is thus made to suggest the corollary, that incomplete knowledge gives life meaning and activity. This irony operates directly between poet and reader.

At the same time, and in the same lines of the poem, another layer of irony operates through Karshish's view of Lazarus. For the Arab, the mundane scale of values is so obviously the right one that for him Lazarus "is witless of the size, the sum, / The value in proportion of all things." In Lazarus, "wonder and doubt come wrongly into play, / Preposterously, at cross purposes." Yet there obtrudes the thought that Lazarus "knows God's secret", that he sees God's will, "what it is, and why it is", the law of spiritual life known to him as that of earthly life. In these glimpses, the irony is cunningly reversed, for Karshish is made to offer this hypothesis of Lazarus' complete knowledge to explain his passiveness, understanding the truth of the situation before the reader. This prepares for the general ironic reversal, involving the reader, on which so much of the main theme depends. The reader, at first impressed by the quaint and obsolete bits of "scientific" lore by which Karshish sets such store (the reader is likely to overlook the inclusion of bits of accurate observation, like the association of alopicia and leprosy, or the value at that time, if it had been possible, of diagnosing fever by phlebotomy) has been tempted to feel patronising towards this "picker-up of learning's crumbs". Here is imperfect knowledge, or ignorance, with a vengeance. But the case of Lazarus, and particularly the confrontation of the aloof, passive Lazarus waiting for the release of death, and the eager, active, questing Karshish, pressing on through dangers and hardships in search of truth, and even the contrast between Lazarus, with his knowledge of divine things, and Karshish, with his musing utterance, "It is strange", – these must force on the reader the question, "Which is the true representative of humanity? Which is the type of myself?" So that finally, in Karshish, stumbling from error to fresh error, from partial truth to partial truth, the reader at last ironically recognises himself, and recognises too, Browning hopes, the necessity at last to decide, as Karshish must decide, whether he can accept the strange doctrine of the God who died for man.

In a good many of his poems, Browning adds a clue or indicator as a guide to the reader. This is often, as in the text quoted at the head of "Cleon", an indication of what might be called the primary pattern of irony. The opening indicators or clues are not always a sufficient guide to the reader, as "Caliban upon Setebos" illustrates. Here Browning supplies two clues, a sub-title and a text. Both are often ignored by the critics. The effectiveness of the sub-title, "Natural Theology in the Islands", depends on the

reader's knowledge of the technical meaning and history of the
term, "natural theology", and of Browning's views on theology.
Natural theology is the theology, or knowledge of God, arrived
at by the unaided natural reason, as opposed to revealed theology,
given to man in Revelation. Throughout the latter part of the
seventeenth century and much of the eighteenth, although
orthodox Christianity had recognised the existence and validity
(within limits) of natural theology, and had seen no clash between
it and Revelation, the Deist movement tended to place primary
importance on natural theology, and to use it as a criterion for
judging Revelation. The shift of emphasis is to be seen in two
famous works, Locke's *The Reasonableness of Christianity* (1695),
which takes, at least ostensibly, Revelation as the criterion in
demonstrating its harmony with reason, and Toland's *Christianity
not Mysterious* (1696), where reason becomes the criterion for
rejecting the "mysteries" of Christian orthodoxy. If the essential
truths of Christianity are seen as arrived at by the unaided reason,
it becomes a short step to suggest that religion has a merely
human origin – that all theology is natural theology in the sense
of man-made, and that there is nothing supernatural in it. This
is the force of Hume's *Natural History of Religion* (1757). In the
nineteenth century the assumptions of the "demythologising"
Higher Critics were essentially naturalistic; the criteria by which
they separated "fact" from "myth" were roughly the same as
Hume's, and they saw Christianity as a man-made system, developed by the accretion of myths around a few historical figures
and events. Browning's objections to their theories are elaborated
in "A Death in the Desert", but the sub-title of "Caliban" indicates a concern with the same general problem here. The text,
"Thou thoughtest that I was altogether such a one as thyself",
in effect sums up certain of the Higher Critics' theories: God is a
projection of man's own nature, wishes, aspirations, qualities.
It will be remembered that Thomas Hardy, in "A Plaint to Man"
uses this projection theory as a literal image, "thin as a phasm on
a lantern-slide . . . by none but its showman vivified". The text
also describes the whole process of Caliban's thinking about his
god, Setebos. This is indicated by the recurrent "So he".

It is clear from commentaries on the poem that Browning's
sign-posts have not made the way unmistakable. Many critics

seem unaware of the history of Deism and its close connexion with many elements of Higher Criticism, others take the text to indicate an attack on anthropomorphic conceptions of God, which it obviously is, and then point out that Browning knows that man must think in terms of his own notions. Few seem to recognise, first of all, that the "altogether" in the text is important, still less that Browning's view of Revelation must affect his view of natural theology. The text from Psalm 50 reads, "Thou thoughtest that I was altogether such an one as thyself: but I will reprove thee. . . ." The "altogether" suggests a view of God which is not only anthropomorphic, but exclusively so: it rules out the superhuman. Now, Browning in many poems insists that the doctrine of the Incarnation, the primary doctrine of Christianity, is known only through Revelation. This is abundantly clear in "Saul", where David ceases to be the poet and becomes the prophet to proclaim, "See the Christ stand!" It is clear too in "A Death in the Desert", where Browning has John repeat the lines about man's need of satisfaction to his questioning, "satisfaction God could give, / And did give, as ye have the written word." It is clear also in "Cleon" and in "Karshish", where the unaided reason fails to arrive at the notion of a God of love, willing to share man's suffering. Repeatedly Browning argues that the peculiarity of Christianity is that to the conception of an all-knowing and all-powerful God, it adds that of an all-loving God, embodied in Christ. And for him the very fact of its uniqueness argues its divine origin, its knowledge coming through Revelation, and not through natural reason. In Browning's view, the pre-Christian religions (with the exception of Judaism, with its prophecies of Christ, as illustrated in "Saul" and in the Psalms) arrived by unaided reason only at conceptions of a God of knowledge and power, not of love. This, then, is the limitation of natural theology, as distinguished from revealed theology. And this is the limitation of Caliban's. Nowhere in Caliban's speculations is there any sign of a God of Love.

Caliban in fact is made to range over most of the historic theology of pre-Christian times. He starts with cosmology, with the doctrine of creation that Plato's *Timaeus* was designed to counter, creation from envy. He includes a version of the *a priori* argument for the uniqueness of God, "He could not, Himself,

make a second self / To be His mate; as well have made Himself"
– Caliban's statement of the one self-caused necessary Being.
Caliban is a Voluntarist, not a Rationalist: his god is a god of
arbitrary will, exercising power through pure arbitrary choice.
As an orthodox Voluntarist, he holds that Right and Wrong,
Good and Evil, are not founded in the divine reason, but in the
divine will: his god does not will the good because it is good,
what he wills is good because he wills it. Setebos lies "Making
and marring clay at will," "such shows nor right nor wrong in
Him, / Nor kind, nor cruel: He is strong and Lord." (Those
unfamiliar with the theology of Voluntarism and Rationalism
will perhaps recall the secular version of Voluntarism in Hobbes'
political philosophy.) As a corollary to Voluntarism, Caliban
includes the doctrine of Election, or arbitrary choice: "Let
twenty pass, and stone the twenty-first, / Loving not, hating not,
just choosing so."

He then turns over a thought of "something over Setebos /
That made Him, or He, may be, found and fought, / Worsted,
drove off and did to nothing, perchance", and we recognise
echoes of Chronos, the Titans, and the Olympian gods. Then
the thought of the Quiet, "that feels nor joy nor grief, / Since
both derive from weakness in some way." Critics tend to seize
hopefully on Caliban's Quiet, as a sign that he is developing a
sounder theology.[2] But the Quiet is obviously very much like
the Epicurean conception of the gods, self-sufficient, careless of
mankind. It is difficult to believe that Browning saw in the Quiet
any hint of an approach to a God of Love. The final hope expressed by Caliban, that either the Quiet may catch and conquer
Setebos, "or likelier He / Decrepit may doze, doze, as good as
die" certainly shows no reaching towards a higher conception,
but only the wish to be free of a God of arbitrary power, to be
free of a religion of terror, not through the coming of a God of
Love, but through the death of the God of Power. Caliban, in
short, seeks the comforts of atheism, not of faith. (An interesting
parallel with "Caliban" is Tennyson's "Despair".) It will be
noted that Caliban's mother, Sycorax, is also a natural theologian,
and on two points differs from her son. She is a Zoroastrian, or

[2] Cf. Clarence Tracy, "Caliban Upon Setebos", *Studies in Philology*, xxxv
(1938) pp. 487-99.

Manichaean, and sees the Quiet and Setebos as Ormuzd and Ahriman, forces of Good and Evil. She also believes in eternal rewards and punishments of a material sort, with her god plaguing enemies and feasting friends. Caliban believes in no after-life. Through most of the poem, then, Caliban is arriving, through the use of his unaided reason, at a good many of the conclusions about God arrived at by pagans historically. But if he is presenting a history of natural religion, or even a natural history of religion (in Hume's sense, – but ironically, for Browning's purposes), the poet's intention is not historical, nor antiquarian. Still less is it to present a history of the "evolution" of religious ideas from lower to higher. Browning's views on the nature of truth and on the nature of revelation of it preclude this interpretation. And Caliban is not so much primitive man in the anthropological or popular "missing link" sense, as man reduced, for the poet's didactic purpose, to the purely natural. He is a barbarian not primarily in the cultural, but in the spiritual sense. What might seem to complicate the poem is that it includes doctrines that have historically been part of at least some branches of Christian thought. Some of the more extreme sects derived from Calvinism, for example, have held to a Voluntarism not much less extreme than Caliban's, and his doctrine of appeasement by sacrifice and by penance, expressed at the end of the poem, is related to a central orthodox doctrine of the Incarnation. It is perhaps significant that Browning seldom presents the Incarnation in terms of the Atonement. He does so in "Easter-Day" (section xxx) but this is a rare, if not unique, passage. He obviously comes more and more to connect the whole idea of the Atonement with the Old Testament doctrine of a powerful and jealous God, and to reject it as a man-made conception. Browning has his own kind of Higher Criticism; where the Germans reject the supernatural, he rejects the natural.

One part of the poem is much more complex than the rest. This is where Caliban returns to the subject of creation and cosmology, with a theory, again reminiscent of Classical thought, of this material world as an inferior imitation of the real, celestial world (lines 146 ff.). In describing the personal experience from which his theory is derived, Caliban reveals an unexpected degree of sophistication. He has himself created his own imitation of the little world of the island over which Prospero rules. In this "bauble" world he is of course an imitation Prospero, complete with an imitation book of magic, an imitation magic wand, and an imitation enchanter's robe. He has peopled this world with an "ounce sleeker than youngling mole" to represent Miranda, but shaping his own created world nearer to his heart's desire, "saith she is Miranda and my wife". Ariel is a crane, and to represent himself, Caliban has snared a "sea-beast, lumpish", which he has blinded and maimed, "A bitter heart that bides its time and bites."

This is a fascinating passage, and it will be noted that it has little relation to Caliban's theology, and also that it establishes an extremely complicated pattern of irony. The material world is an imitation of a real world; Prospero's world of the island is a microcosm in which Prospero exercises over Caliban, and indeed over all the inhabitants, mysterious, magical, and arbitrary powers not unlike those of Setebos; Caliban creates his own imitation of this microcosm. The self-hatred and self-contempt in his choice and treatment of the sea-beast to represent himself is a shrewd and moving piece of psychology. So also is the comment, "Plays thus at being Prosper in a way, / Taketh his mirth with make-believes." "In a way", indeed, and what an irony in the term "mirth". The whole little world Caliban creates, like the temple he describes building a few lines later, has all the ironic force of a bitter parody. That this irony is only connected, if at all, in very slight degree to the main theme leads us to a final consideration.

This is that "Caliban upon Setebos" might be Browning's most successful failure. If one forgets all about natural theology, the Higher Criticism, Darwin (who is surely totally irrelevant in any case) and other doctrinal matters, and remembers only *The Tempest*, what a brilliantly imaginative variation upon a theme by Shakespeare the poem is. But in this case, how inapplicable the guide-posts at the beginning become. It seems evident that in this poem, while the theme indicated in the sub-title and the text shaped the general line of argument and thought Caliban follows, in the detailed elaboration Browning's finest imaginative powers took over, or he was possessed by the spirit of Shakespeare.

This does not mean that the poem does not make its point

about natural theology; it does so very thoroughly to those who recognise the implications of the guides the poet provides. They will even notice that the poem in fact illustrates the reduction of the rational that takes place historically in Deism: Caliban's procedure is not strictly rational, it is a reduction of all reality to an analogy with his own sensory and emotional experience. But the fact remains that the fundamental irony suggested by the text at the opening, an irony dependent on a constant setting of Browning's theology against Caliban's, so that the reader ends by noticing the total absence of a doctrine of divine love, and, harking back to the sub-title, becomes aware that natural theology does not produce such a doctrine, – this sort of irony is not likely to suggest itself to the reader fascinated by the rich elaboration of Caliban's character. And if, as I believe, recognition of this irony and of the implications of the sub-title adds extra layers of meaning to the poem, I cannot bring myself to give great importance to this fact, since the greatness of the poem obviously lies in the imaginative gusto of its execution. In this it rather resembles Tennyson's "St Simeon Stylites". This, then, I take to be a case where Browning gave indicators to an ironic purpose, but the indicators have generally not functioned, and the poem succeeds without the primary irony.

I have written elsewhere on "Bishop Blougram's Apology", and will merely observe here that in this poem Browning includes an ironic indicator of deliberate ambiguity: "For Blougram, he believed, say, half he spoke", an ambiguity which has led to totally different interpretations of the poem. But at least the indicator ought to have served as a warning to the reader to expect ironies in the poem, and not to take it as a simple bit of psychological characterising. The irony in the poem is in fact pervasive and complex. I have also dealt elsewhere with *Paracelsus* and "La Saisiaz", which both offer complex patterns of irony, though for different reasons. Since "Christmas-Eve" in some respects combines the reasons, I turn to it next.

It is well known that "Christmas-Eve" was written at a crucial time in Browning's spiritual career, and that it records the most important decision of his religious life. It is rather startling, therefore, to find critics in general agreement that the great struggle was over the question of whether to attend a Nonconformist chapel, a Roman Catholic church, or lectures by the Higher Critics, or to choose between puritanism, ritualism, and intellectualism.

This interpretation I long ago found unsatisfactory. In the first place, "Christmas-Eve" as a title suggests to any reader of Browning, or ought to suggest, something of the depths of his preoccupation with the doctrine of the Incarnation. Moreover, De Vane was undoubtedly right in suggesting that Browning was unable to complete "Saul" until he had settled his own religious convictions.[3] The original, incomplete version of "Saul" (1845) left no doubt how the poem had to end. The deliberate placing of Saul in the posture of crucifixion, and the allusion to the king-serpent, obviously foreshadowed a conclusion in which the pattern would be completed by a prophecy of Christ. There would have been no point in this opening picture of Saul in his agony otherwise. But a poem thus begun and clearly planned from the start to have a Christian ending roughly the same, at least, as that it finally received is not really likely to be resumed upon a decision to attend chapel rather than turn Roman Catholic or Higher Critic. Nor is there any evidence that Browning was ever tempted by either of these last. In spite of Bishop Wiseman's review of "Bishop Blougram's Apology", Browning shows no sign of being strongly drawn towards Catholicism; it took him some effort to feel tolerant towards it. Nor did he like the Higher Criticism. The choice was hardly an urgent one if it was of these three, two of which he readily rejected.

Moreover, the incomplete "Saul" was published on 6 Nov. 1845, and reprinted in 1849. In 1845, as De Vane has pointed out,[4] Elizabeth Barrett's influence had brought Browning back "almost to his first position" of religious Nonconformism, restoring his "innate religiosity". Since he had begun "Saul" before this influence could have taken effect (he mentioned it to Elizabeth on 3 May 1845. – The subject of religion and religious worship comes up first in the letters of 2 Aug. and 4 Aug. 1845), it would perhaps seem that his mind had already turned to the subject of orthodox Christianity during the very beginning of their correspondence at the latest; her influence on his religious opinions did

---

[3] W. C. DeVane, *A Browning Handbook*, New York (1955) pp. 256-7.
[4] *Op. cit.*, p. 195.

not serve to bring him to complete "Saul" in this period, despite
Elizabeth's urgings (27 Aug. and 27 Oct. 1845). The often-
quoted letter of Elizabeth's of 15 Aug. 1846, and Browning's
reply of 17 August, which, as De Vane rightly says, "anticipate
the matter" of "Christmas-Eve",[5] would make it as certain as
possible that the choice usually considered to be at the core of the
poem was fully decided at this time. If this were so, it would be
difficult to explain first, why the same choice made three years
later allows Browning, as De Vane argues, to complete "Saul",
and secondly, why the severe spiritual crisis of 1849 can be resolved by the same decision as before. In the letters there is no
suggestion that the choice in 1846 is an agonised or even vitally
important one. The tone of the letters is serene and settled. It is
difficult to believe that the "dangerous physical and mental condition" of 1849,[6] or even the problem of the completion of "Saul",
resulted from a need to re-make a decision arrived at with so little
evidence of tumult in 1846.

   And it is important to note the limitation of the decision. In
both letters of 1846, Elizabeth's and Browning's, there is no
reference to specific Christian doctrines, to Christ and the meaning
of the Incarnation and Crucifixion – the closest approach is in
Elizabeth's rejection of Socinian and Unitarian worship as
throwing over "what is most beautiful in the Christian Doctrine".
Browning's reply does not pick up this remark, and seems to
reduce doctrine to "love God with all the heart, soul, and
strength". This suggests at most a commitment only to his
general view that Christianity adds to the concept of a God of
Power that of a God of Love, which he may take Elizabeth to
have meant. There is no sign of any doctrine of the nature and
significance of Christ. Another interesting note in his letter is his
comment on the "levity" of his writing: "This sort of levity only
exists because of the strong conviction, I do believe! There
seems no longer need of earnestness in assertion, or proof . . . so
it runs lightly over, like foam on the top of a wave." But the
"levity" in this letter is not the strained facetiousness and out-
rageous grotesquerie, mixed with intense earnestness, that we
find in "Christmas-Eve", and the correspondences in subject-
matter between the letters and the poem of three years later,

        [5] *Op. cit.*, p. 198.   [6] *Op. cit.*, p. 197.

when viewed along with the contrast of the serenity of the one and the agitation of the other, seem convincing evidence that the real subject of the poem does not lie in the common subject-matter. The simple decision which fully satisfied Browning in 1846 no longer suffices in 1849; its appearance in the poem must be ironic and ancillary rather than literal and central.

At this point it is useful to remember one of Browning's poetic habits. In *Paracelsus* the key to the whole meaning and to the pattern of ironies lies in the concluding great speech of Paracelsus and in his last words. In "La Saisiaz" the key to the whole poem lies in the conclusion. What does the conclusion of "Christmas-Eve" offer?

It offers, in the summing-up of section xxii, the important image of the cup and the water:

> Ha! Is God mocked, as he asks?
> Shall I take on me to change his tasks,
> And dare, dispatched to a river-head
> For a simple draught of the element,
> Neglect the thing for which he sent,
> And return with another thing instead? –
> Saying, "Because the water found
> "Welling up from underground,
> "Is mingled with the taints of earth, . . .
> "Therefore I turned from the oozings muddy,
> "And bring thee a chalice I found, instead. . . .
> "What matters the water? A hope I have nursed:
> "The waterless cup will quench my thirst."[7]

And further:

> . . . in the still recurring fear
> Lest myself, at unawares, be found,
> While attacking the choice of my neighbours round,
> With none of my own made – I choose here![8]

And finally:

> And refer myself to THEE, instead of him,
> Who head and heart alike discernest,

---

[7] "Christmas-Eve", 1278-86, 1290-1, 1294-5.
[8] *Op. cit.*, 1338-41.

Looking below light speech we utter,
When frothy spume and frequent sputter
Prove that the soul's depths boil in earnest!
May truth shine out, stand ever before us![9]

The first passage suggests that the speaker has, throughout the
poem, been concerned with the cup, rather than with the water.
This can surely mean only the form of worship, rather than the
divine truth it should contain. The last quotation emphasises the
depth of the turmoil reflected, as often in Browning, by a decep-
tively flippant style. It is the second passage that tends to support
the common interpretation, with its "I choose here", commonly
taken to mean "this chapel". But in the first place, this is surely
too literal a meaning. Browning did not, after all, henceforth
attend a little Zion Chapel. But is the choice he must make a
choice of a cup? or of water? He must make a choice not of
form but of faith; he must decide what Christmas Eve means to
him. And he cannot defer the choice. He must choose *here*, at
this point of space and time. What has he chosen?

Since this is a very personal poem, and records in some sense
Browning's progress through and emergence from a profound
spiritual crisis, it is wholly characteristic of the poet not to tell
us. As in that other deeply disturbed personal poem, "La Saisiaz",
he shies away from laying his heart bare. He merely indicates
some of the things he does *not* mean, and a few hints of his deeper
concern. We see some results of the struggle later in the theological affirmations of poems like "Saul" and "A Death in the
Desert"; we do not see the actual process of choice, and we are
deceived if we think that is what, in "Christmas-Eve", we are
watching. As in "La Saisiaz", we are permitted hints, but the
familiar defences are up.

This means that, in a sense, the whole poem is ironic. The
speaker is not Browning, but a persona whose relation to Browning is ironically uncertain; the style is ironically flippant for the
seriousness of the subject. Besides this, the attitudes expressed
are mainly ironic. There would, of course, be no point in writing
a poem of total concealment; the truth, or part of it, must, in
Blougram's phrase, be allowed to peep through. One notices,

[9] *Op. cit.*, 1349-54.

for example, that the style is not consistently flippant. One also notices, and should hardly fail to recognise the importance of, the figure of Christ himself.

It is significant that he appears after three sections (v, vi, vii) of what might seem irreproachable religious utterance followed by a valid mystical religious experience. The exposition of religious ideas (section v) is in familiar Browning terms, but it may be noted that it stops short of the full argument (as given in the completed "Saul" and in "Karshish"), since it includes no reference to Christ or the Incarnation. It is devout theist, rather than specifically Christian, in its theme. At first appearance the figure of Christ (section viii) is receding, "I saw the back of him, no more", and the speaker rushes to catch at the hem of Christ's garment, "the salvation of the vest". From this point on, the relation of the speaker to the figure of Christ is all-important. At each movement of the poem, the speaker diagnoses his own error, announces his repentance, and declares what lesson he has learned. As in *Paracelsus*, we must not take his assessments at face value. The speaker may be wrong in his diagnosis, or wrong in the conclusions he draws, or right for the wrong reasons. In *Paracelsus*, the criterion by which we can judge how far and in what sense Paracelsus' diagnoses of error and new "revelations" are ironic is supplied to us only at the end of the poem. In "Christmas-Eve", besides the "cup and water" passage, which similarly throws back light on all the speeches, we have the continuing criterion of Christ and the hem of his garment. In section ix Christ turns his face full on the speaker, and here for the first time the symbol of the cup is introduced. It is significant that in section viii the speaker has voiced a Christian affirmation, completing the theological pattern: "Thou art the love of God – above / His power, didst hear me place his love. . . ." It is this, presumably, which marks Browning's real and fundamental choice. The mystic experience of section vii, "I felt my brain / Glutted with the glory, . . . Until at length it burst asunder / And out of it bodily there streamed, / The too-much glory, as it seemed, / Passing from out me to the ground . . .", is echoed in section ix as Christ turns his face: "So lay I, saturate with brightness." The vision of Christ as the vision of the glory of God is clearly Browning's ecstatic recognition of Christ as God – his real choice of faith. But the speaker's comments are a mixture of truth and error, and section ix ends with a complacent sense of acceptance and of the superiority of the speaker's mode of worship. He is still thinking too much of the cup. His doubts return when he is left outside St Peter's, and again he confesses and diagnoses error, and again he is partly right, partly wrong. Sections xvi and xvii affirm, in Browning's own arguments, the crucial necessity of insisting on the divinity of Christ, and not reducing him to mere human moral teacher. The arguments are those elaborated later in "A Death in the Desert". But in section xix, the speaker again draws the wrong conclusions, as is evident from the storm that follows in the next section. He has let tolerance become "a mild indifferentism". The storm brings another passage of verse in which the tone takes on an earnestness that persuades us again that we have been allowed to draw close, as in sections vii and ix, to Browning's actual feelings and experience. And the theme, like that in "La Saisiaz", is the theme of incommunicability of faith and of choice: "It is but for myself I know. . . . I cannot bid / The world admit he stooped to heal / My soul, as if in a thunder-peal / Where one heard noise, and one saw flame, / I only knew he named my name. . . ." He is then lapped again in the folds of the robe, no longer merely holding the hem, "full-fraught / With warmth and wonder and delight, / God's mercy being infinite." It is not the choice of a form of worship that is involved here. As Browning was to write later, in "A Death in the Desert",

> I say, the acknowledgment of God in Christ
> Accepted by thy reason, solves for thee
> All questions in the earth and out of it. . . .[10]

The fundamental irony of the poem, revealed by the cup symbol, is that it appears to be pre-occupied with a choice of form. Man generally, as Browning recognises, has been pre-occupied with form of worship, and has neglected the worship. In his own day, the conflicts between Church and Dissent, and within the Church between Evangelicals and Broad Church, and between these and Tractarians, in quarrelling about forms and doctrines, seem to him to be neglecting the vital question each man must ask him-

[10] "A Death in the Desert", 474-6.

self, "What does Christ mean to me? and in my life?" This is the question Browning himself has asked, and his answer and his choice are suggested again in "Easter-Day": "I knew Him through the dread disguise / As the whole God within His eyes / Embraced me."

It will also be noted that on a strict examination, the extent to which even the surface-meaning concerns simply form of worship is not uniform. The most poetic lines in the visit to St Peter's are those describing the meaning of the moment of consecration (section x): "Earth breaks up, time drops away, / In flows heaven, with its new day / Of endless life. . . ." This passage is concerned, not with the ritual, but with the central meaning of the Incarnation. And the visit to the lecture-hall (sections xiv-xviii) is most directly concerned with arguing the need for accepting the divinity of Christ, rather than with modes of religious worship – with the *grounds* of worship rather than the method. Even the surface, then, is not simple, and it is further complicated by the ironic uncertainty the poet deliberately introduces about the central and most serious part of the poem: was the encounter with Christ and the journey with him a vision or merely a dream? Serious dream-visions for the presentation of the most sublime subjects are a regular convention in poetry and other religious literature, but Browning seems to be deliberately mocking the convention here. This, I would suggest, is the final irony.

In "Christmas-Eve", then, patterns of irony are pervasive and manifold. And their function is obviously very different from the simple kinds of irony we noted first in the dramatic monologues. We have moved from an irony that is open to the reader, a clear part of the aesthetic and dramatic structure, to one that seems to be deliberately opaque, from an irony that serves to clarify and emphasise the dramatic and thematic patterns to one that seems designed for concealment. The simple irony is made to play on the characters, objectively dramatised; this last complex irony plays on the reader and on the poet himself.

W. O. Raymond

BROWNING'S
"THE STATUE AND THE BUST"[1]

With the possible exception of *Fifine at the Fair*, there is no other poem of Browning whose ethics have provoked such controversy as "The Statue and the Bust". The two poems have frequently been linked both in hostile criticism and in eulogy. In the *Scottish Art Review* for December 1889, Mr Mortimer asserted that *Fifine at the Fair* and "The Statue and the Bust" showed that Browning "prescribes action at any price, even that of defying the restrictions of the moral law". Swinburne, on the other hand, enthusiastically admired both works. Lord Bryce has recorded how at a meeting of the Old Mortality Society in Swinburne's rooms at Oxford in 1858, the Pre-Raphaelite poet "repeated, or rather chanted, to his friends, a few of Browning's poems, in particular 'The Statue and the Bust', 'The Heretic's Tragedy', and 'Bishop Blougram's Apology'."[2] Again, shortly after the publication of *Fifine at the Fair*, Swinburne said, "This is far better than anything Browning has yet written. Here is his true province."[3]

In one respect, at least, the ethical problem involved in "The Statue and the Bust" was more disquieting to many of Browning's Victorian readers than that in *Fifine at the Fair*. In *Fifine*, Don Juan is the speaker throughout, and his defence of his immoral de-

[1] Reprinted from W. O. Raymond, *The Infinite Moment*, 2nd edn., Toronto (1965) pp. 214-23.

[2] Edmund Gosse, *Life of Algernon Charles Swinburne*, New York (1917) pp. 39-40.

[3] W. H. Griffin and H. C. Minchin, *The Life of Robert Browning*, 3rd edn., London (1938) p. 258.

linquencies could be interpreted as the utterances of a libertine casuist rather than the poet's own sentiments. But in "The Statue and the Bust", although Browning is relating an old legend, "this story . . . our townsmen tell", the comment is his own; and, moreover, in the last verses he defends his poem against the criticism which he foresees it will evoke and definitely states his personal convictions. This defence at once differentiates "The Statue and the Bust" from the so-called casuistical monologues of Browning, such as "Bishop Blougram's Apology", "Mr Sludge, 'The Medium' ", *Fifine at the Fair,* and *Prince Hohenstiel Schwangau.* If there is casuistry in the ethical thesis of "The Statue and the Bust" it is casuistry in which the poet himself is directly involved; it cannot be palmed off as the dramatic sentiments of any imaginary characters. What may be called the Epilogue to "The Statue and the Bust" is therefore of special importance. Although the dramatic disguise is very thin in many of Browning's monologues, it is seldom that he casts it off altogether and avowedly speaks in his own person.

In the body of the poem, the two lovers are criticised for the procrastination and infirmity of will which prevented them from eloping and gratifying their unlawful love. Does the poet then maintain that adultery may be laudable under certain circumstances? It is this charge which Browning strives to defend himself against in the Epilogue. At its outset he voices the foreseen adverse criticism.

> I hear you reproach, "But delay was best,
> For their end was a crime."[4]

The reference to adultery as a *crime* is in itself significant as an evidence that Browning does not condone it. He then proceeds with his defence. What he singles out and dwells upon is the weakness and cowardice of the lovers' procrastination and lack of resolution. Had they repented of their sinful passion and been deterred from eloping by moral considerations, he would have commended them. But they were deterred only through lack of courage and the fear of worldly consequences. Their sinful motives and desires, the lust of their hearts, remained unchanged.

---

[4] "The Statue and the Bust", 226-7.

Consequently the poet holds that they simply added to their original sin the vice of procrastination.

The method of Browning's argument in this poem may be illustrated by a comparison between it and the biblical parable of the Unjust Steward. After his dismissal from his position, the steward set about making friends for himself by dishonestly reducing the bills owed by his master's clients. Then we read: "And the Lord commended the unjust steward, because he had done wisely." Are we to assume that Christ's teaching was that the steward was to be praised on account of his dishonesty? It is clearly the energy, pains, and forethought of the steward in securing friends for himself after his dismissal which are singled out for commendation, abstracted, so to speak, from his dishonesty. His diligence and sagacity are contrasted with the slothfulness and ineptness of people whose ends are moral, but who are lukewarm, half-hearted, and negligent in their pursuit of these. "The children of this world are in their generation wiser than the children of light." What Browning says, in effect, in the concluding verses of "The Statue and the Bust" is that he has illustrated the weakness of procrastination, "the unlit lamp and the ungirt loin", through characters who were sinful rather than virtuous. Finally, in the last two lines of the poem, with a swift probing thrust, he rounds upon people who plume themselves upon their virtue but are slothful in pursuing it:

> You of the virtue (we issue join)
> How strive you? *De te, fabula!*[5]

Yet the ethical problem of the poem is not fully solved by Browning's concentration on the weakness of procrastination and infirmity of will. He has to defend his ethics on two grounds, the one specific, the other general.

In the first place he has maintained that the Duke and the Lady are as guilty in cherishing their unlawful love as they would have been had they committed the crime of adultery. He judges them by their motives, and in this respect we are reminded of Christ's words in the Sermon on the Mount: "But I say unto you, That whosoever looketh on a woman to lust after her hath committed adultery with her already in his heart." It is characteristic of

[5] *Op. cit.*, 249-50.

Browning that he lays such stress on inner motive, and that he should be primarily concerned with the soul of the individual rather than with the individual in his nexus of social relationships. Throughout his poetry the worth of the individual is estimated not by outward achievement, but by aim and motivation. Often, as in "A Grammarian's Funeral", he extols characters whose worldly accomplishment has amounted to little, in order to throw into relief the loftiness of their aspiration. As he writes in "Rabbi Ben Ezra":

> For thence, – a paradox
> Which comforts while it mocks, –
> Shall life succeed in that it seems to fail:
> What I aspired to be,
> And was not comforts me. . . .[6]

There is a sharp contrast between Browning's judgment of the Duke and the Lady and their position in the eyes of the law. From a legal point of view the secret love of the two would have escaped censure. The law, which is concerned with individuals as members of society, would not have condemned them until they had actually committed adultery. From an individualistic standpoint the poet is justified in regarding sin in motive as quite as culpable as sin in act. Yet it may be asked whether, since man is a social animal, it is entirely legitimate to abstract him from the society which helps largely to shape and mould him, and of which he is an organic part. Can an open violation of the restraints imposed by the standards, codes, even the conventions, of civilised society, the translation of sinful thought into act, fail to enhance individual guilt? As Berdoe puts it in his comment on "The Statue and the Bust": "If every woman flew to the arms of the man whom she liked better than her own husband, and if every governor of a city felt himself at liberty to steal another man's wife merely to complete and perfect the circle of his own delights, society would seem to be thrown back into barbarism."[7]

In the specific instance of "The Statue and the Bust", Browning has maintained that if motives are evil, it is better to act on these with vigour and resolution, than to be deterred by weakness of

[6] "Rabbi Ben Ezra", 37-41.

[7] Edward Berdoe, *The Browning Cyclopaedia*, 6th edn., London (1909) p. 519.

will and cowardice. It is, however, his generalisation of this into a universal standard of conduct which has provoked most hostile criticism:

> Stake your counter as boldly every whit,
> Venture as warily, use the same skill,
> Do your best, whether winning or losing it,
>
> If you choose to play! – is my principle.
> Let a man contend to the uttermost
> For his life's set prize, be it what it will![8]

It is clear that to the poet the most hopeless state of human nature is that of indifference and inaction. As Henry Jones has written: "It is under the guise of warfare that morality always presents itself to Browning."[9] The development of man's soul can be achieved only through conflict. Therefore, let truth and falsehood, good and evil grapple:

> No, when the fight begins within himself,
> A man's worth something. God stoops o'er his head,
> Satan looks up between his feet – both tug –
> He's left, himself, i' the middle: the soul wakes
> And grows. . . .[10]

In view of the supreme importance of the moral conflict, to evade it is, in a sense, the worst of sins. It is better, Browning holds, to act evilly than to lapse into atrophy of soul.

The situation in "The Statue and the Bust" is one of many illustrations in Browning's poetry of the importance he attaches to a climactic moment in the lives of individuals. In the "Epilogue" to *Dramatis Personae* he represents the spiritual powers of the universe as concentrating in some critical moment on the life of every man to challenge him to an all-important decision involving not merely temporal but eternal consequences. On a person's response or lack of response to this challenge his destiny depends. An individual at this crux is like a point of "central rock" in

[8] "The Statue and the Bust", 238-43.
[9] Henry Jones, *Browning as a Philosophical and Religious Teacher*, Glasgow (1892) p. 111.
[10] "Bishop Blougram's Apology", 693-7.

"Arctic seas" towards which all the waters converge for a moment before they "hasten off to play elsewhere". In "Cristina" Browning writes of moments

> When the spirit's true endowments
> Stand out plainly from its false ones,
> And apprise it if pursuing
> Or the right way or the wrong way,
> To its triumph or undoing.[11]

In the majority of instances this is what Browning calls "the good minute". His poems dealing with it fall into two classes. In the first, the good choice which the moment offers is made, and the result is beneficent. In the second, the good choice is missed or neglected, and the result is baneful. A fine example of the first class is the happy choice of the lovers in the beautiful semi-dramatic lyric "By the Fire-side". The heaven-sent opportunity of the "moment one, and infinite" is grasped, the positive decision made, and the fruitage is eternal.

> I am named and known by that moment's feat;
> There took my station and degree;
> So grew my own small life complete,
> As nature obtained her best of me –
> One born to love you, sweet![12]

Finally, in "By the Fire-side", as in "The Statue and the Bust", Browning generalises a specific incident in order to stress a general truth:

> How the world is made for each of us!
> How all we perceive and know in it
> Tends to some moment's product thus,
> When a soul declares itself – to wit,
> By its fruit, the thing it does![13]

"Dis Aliter Visum" and "Youth and Art" exemplify the second class of Browning's poems dealing with "the good minute", in which the failure to use its opportunities is disastrous. These poems are complementary to "By the Fire-side" in that they are

[11] "Cristina", 20-4.   [12] "By the Fire-side", 251-5.
[13] Op. cit., 241-5.

concerned with the destiny of potential lovers at a crucial moment of their lives, but contrasted in the results that ensue. Love is blasted by a failure, through weakness of will and worldly prudence, to act, and the lives of the lovers are irretrievably marred. As the woman in "Youth and Art" laments:

> Each life unfulfilled, you see;
>   It hangs still, patchy and scrappy:
> We have not sighed deep, laughed free,
>   Starved, feasted, despaired, – been happy. . . .
>
> This could but have happened once,
>   And we missed it, lost it for ever.[14]

Neither of these poems involves any ethical problem. It is indisputable that a failure to achieve a good end because of unworthy motives is morally wrong and culpable.

There are, however, in "The Statue and the Bust" and other poems of Browning, climactic moments of another order than that of "the good minute". In these, if the opportunities are embraced, the end is a crime not a virtue. Yet the poet holds that if a failure to grasp them is due only to infirmity of will, cowardice or procrastination, and not to any moral restraint, it would be better for the sinners to act with decision and energy, and commit the contemplated crime. As Dr Westcott writes of Browning's ethical teaching: "No room is left for indifference or neutrality. . . . A part must be taken and maintained. The spirit in which Luther said 'Pecca fortiter' finds in him powerful expression."[15]

In the poem "Before", the speaker maintains that even for the wrongdoer in a quarrel it would be preferable to fight the issue out in a duel rather than add cowardice to his guilt by avoiding it. Even in the event of his being the victor, there is more hope that remorse of conscience will ultimately redeem him than if he had shrunk from accepting the challenge:

> Better sin the whole sin, sure that God observes;
> Then go live his life out! Life will try his nerves. . . .
> And the price appears that pays for the misfeasance.[16]

---

[14] "Youth and Art", 61-4; 67-8.   [15] Jones, *Browning*, p. 118.
[16] "Before", 13-14: 24.

In "Too Late", where again the lives of a man and woman are ruined by a failure to avow love, the man declares that even violent action to take possession of "Edith" would have been worthier than his inaction:

> Why, better even have burst like a thief
> And borne you away to a rock for us two,
> In a moment's horror, bright, bloody, and brief. . . .[17]

In "The Worst of It", the sin of the woman in being false to her husband ultimately becomes the means of his redemption. In "The Lost Leader", the speaker maintains that it would be better for the leader, after his defection from the people's cause, to follow his wrongful course with energy and decision rather than to vacillate weakly and return to the party he has betrayed:

> Best fight on well, for we taught him – strike gallantly,
> Menace our heart ere we master his own. . . .[18]

In Browning's defence of his ethical standards in "The Statue and the Bust", the argument of the poems I have been considering is definitively summed up:

> Let a man contend to the uttermost
> For his life's set prize, be it what it will![19]

It is the poet's fervent stress on action, and above all on action as preferable to inaction, if the latter is due to unworthy motives, even when the end pursued is immoral, which has been assailed. At the same time there is a distrust, and indeed a dislike, of Browning's aggressive and unqualified emotional optimism, and a conviction of the inadequacy of his concept of evil. A portion of this criticism is, it seems to me, justifiable; but a larger portion has led to a grave misapprehension of his outlook on life and his ethical and spiritual tenets.

In his essay on "The Poetry of Barbarism", Santayana has declared that for Browning "the crude experience is the only end, the endless struggle the only ideal, and the perturbed 'Soul' the only organon of truth". Browning's temperament is such that for him "life is an adventure, not a discipline", and "the exercise

---

[17] "Too Late", 55-7.   [18] "The Lost Leader", 29-30.
[19] "The Statue and the Bust", 242-3.

of energy is the absolute good, irrespective of motives or of circumstances".[20] In similar vein, Professor Fairchild writes concerning Browning's poetry:

> At a time of deep uncertainty as to life's ultimate aim, the transference of value from the thing sought to the mere seeking provided a potent emotional lift. Since one did not know what the prize was, it was heartening to be assured that "The prize is in the process." The thing done, since it never *is* done, must be less important than the courage and vigor of the doing.[21]

It is undeniable that the militancy of Browning's temperament and the robustness of his optimism cause him to over-stress the value of action *per se*. The conquest of evil by discipline, self-control, and the restraints of reason is minimised. For him the crux of life is moral struggle, whose essence is not the overcoming of evil by self-denial or the avoidance of temptation but the overcoming of evil with good. Moreover, he welcomes the strenuousness of moral conflict. After paraphrasing the clause in the Lord's Prayer "Lead us not into temptation", the Pope in *The Ring and the Book* exclaims:

> Yea, but, O Thou whose servants are the bold,
> Lead such temptations by the head and hair,
> Reluctant dragons, up to who dares fight,
> That so he may do battle and have praise![22]

"The kingdom of heaven suffereth violence, and the violent take it by force"; and Browning has never more poignantly expressed his ideal of heroic moral achievement than when in utter scorn of the cowardice and procrastination of the Duke and the Lady in "The Statue and the Bust", he writes:

> Only they see not God, I know,
> Nor all that chivalry of his,
> The soldier-saints who, row on row,

[20] George Santayana, *Interpretations of Poetry and Religion*, New York (1924) pp. 212, 206.
[21] Hoxie Neale Fairchild, *Religious Trends in English Poetry*, IV, New York (1957) p. 154.
[22] *The Ring and the Book*, X, 1189-92.

> Burn upward each to his point of bliss –
> Since, the end of life being manifest,
> He had burned his way thro' the world to this.[23]

One cause of a biased and warped criticism of Browning's ethical and spiritual convictions has been, I believe, a concentration on his intellectual scepticism, especially in his so-called casuistical poems, and a neglect of his unswerving faith in the sovereign virtue of love. His gnosticism in the sphere of feeling and emotion, where the intuitions and revelations of the heart are concerned, is surely as much to be reckoned with as his rational agnosticism.

In order to evaluate the ethics of Browning in "The Statue and the Bust", it is necessary to consider his general concept of the nature of evil, and its function in the moral conflict. As an absolute idealist the poet believes that God is omnipotent and all-loving; and, as a corollary to this, he has, as Professor Jones puts it, "a conviction of the ultimate nothingness of evil, and of the complete victory of the good".[24] Yet how can such a faith be reconciled with the presence and power of evil on earth? Browning's attempt to solve this age-old problem has many facets; but his main argument is that the supreme purpose of God for man is the formation of his character; and that this can be achieved only through a moral struggle, centring on a choice between good and evil. "This dread machinery of sin and sorrow" must be designed to develop "the moral qualities of man" and "to make him love in turn and be beloved".[25] In this connexion, however, the poet's distrust of reason involves him in a difficulty. So far as knowledge is concerned, he maintains that every man is confined to his own subjective experience. He cannot be sure that this has any objective validity. Even though he himself is conscious of a moral law, he has no assurance, through knowledge, that the moral law of which he is aware corresponds with a moral law in the universe without, or is in harmony with the ultimate purposes of the Absolute. Such thorough-going scepticism might make it seem a matter of indifference whether an individual follows a

---

[23] "The Statue and the Bust", 220-5.
[24] Jones, *Browning*, p. 119.
[25] *The Ring and the Book*, x, 1375-81.

good or evil course. If man has no knowledge that his moral or immoral choice has any confirmation in objective reality, the only ethical value that remains lies in the qualities of energy and will evoked in the struggle. As the poet himself says, from the point of view of knowledge, "the prize is in the process". The justice of Santayana's criticism that for Browning "the exercise of energy is the absolute good, irrespective of motives or of circumstances" might seem to be confirmed.

Actually, however, this description of the tenor of Browning's poetry is far from being accurate. Lack of confirmation of its objective reality never makes the poet swerve from the conviction that man should act in accordance with the intuitions and promptings of his conscience which urge him to follow good rather than evil. These are, rationally, subjective, confined apparently to each individual's private experience, but they are an absolute for him. A man's ignorance of their ultimate worth the poet regards as part of his probation on earth. Even though he may not know until the Day of Judgment that they are in accord with divine reality, he must act in obedience to their guidance.

> Ask thy lone soul what laws are plain to thee, –
> Thee and no other, – stand or fall by them![26]

> . . . I do
> Discern and dare decree in consequence,
> Whatever prove the peril of mistake.[27]

> . . . Man's part
> Is plain – to send love forth, – astray, perhaps:
> No matter, he has done his part.[28]

> . . . I have one appeal –
> I feel, am what I feel, know what I feel;
> So much is truth to me.[29]

The poet's belief that he is a moral agent, even though this may be only a pious hope, is his

[26] "A Camel-Driver", 87-8.
[27] The Ring and the Book, 1250-2.
[28] "The Sun", 136-8.
[29] Sordello, VI, 439-41.

> . . . solid standing-place amid
> The wash and welter, whence all doubts are bid
> Back to the ledge they break against in foam.[30]

Like Kant, Browning holds that it is impossible to prove the
reality of the supersensible or the existence of God through
knowledge. But, again like Kant, the rational subjectivity of
man's experience is for him no warrant for disregarding the
intuitions of the moral consciousness. The choice of duty and
goodness which it enjoins is as much a "categorical imperative"
for the poet as it is for the philosopher.

Moreover, the moment Browning passes from the negations of
knowledge to the sphere of intuition and feeling, his intellectual
scepticism is replaced by emotional gnosticism.

> I trust in my own soul, that can perceive
> The outward and the inward, nature's good
> And God's. . . .[31]

Above all he bases his emotional gnosticism on the sovereign
virtue of love. Were knowledge all man's faculty he would be
compelled to confess that "the prize is in the process". The poet,
however, immediately adds, "But love is victory, the prize itself."
"God! Thou art Love! I build my faith on that!" Browning
wrote in *Paracelsus*, and this statement is the corner-stone of his
belief and spiritual conviction. It follows that, despite the
apparent contradiction between the testimonies of the heart and
the head, the loving purposes of God must be working themselves
out in the life of man and in the external universe.

> Is not God now i' the world His power first made?
> Is not His love at issue still with sin,
> Visibly when a wrong is done on earth?[32]

There is not, from the point of view of love, any gulf between subjective and objective, between the moral ideal in the heart of man
and its absolute reality in the nature of the being of God.

---

[30] "With Francis Furini", x, 509-11.
[31] *A Soul's Tragedy*, 1, 262-4.
[32] "A Death in the Desert", 211-3.

> Were knowledge all thy faculty, then God
> Must be ignored: love gains him by first leap.[33]

Consequently, in the light of Browning's concept of love, the worth of the moral conflict cannot be confined to the mere processes of subjective experience. Its motivation and its goal have an ethical and spiritual objective value and reality.

At this juncture, however, Browning has to grapple with the most perplexing and darkest aspect of the problem of evil. It is not difficult to comprehend that, since the development of the soul is dependent upon a moral struggle, the existence of evil is necessary in order that in combating it man's character may be shaped and God's purpose for him realised. But what can be said in the case of a sinner who makes the wrong choice and follows the path of evil? How can evil, in this connexion, be reconciled with the omnipotence and infinite love of God, or be regarded as subject to his power?

In dealing with this problem, Browning does not qualify the optimism of his absolute idealism. If God has absolute authority over evil as well as good, and if his purposes of infinite love cannot be thwarted by evil, then evil through being transmuted must be instrumental in the working out of his divine plan. There is no sin so vile, no evil so grim, as to be incapable of *ultimate* transmutation. As he writes:

> Of absolute and irretrievable
> And all-subduing black, – black's soul of black
> Beyond white's power to disintensify, –
> Of that I saw no sample. . . .[34]

For Browning, "all things ill" are not, as Milton regarded them, merely "slavish officers of vengeance" in the service of "the Supreme Good"; they are rather, through being finally transmuted, the slavish officers of God's love. Ultimately, since God is omnipotent as well as all-loving, every sinner, through remorse, repentance, atonement, and divine mercy, must be redeemed. Such a belief involves the rejection of the doctrine of eternal punishment. Confronted with an appalling aftermath of evil in

[33] "A Pillar at Sebzevar", 134-5.
[34] "A Bean-Stripe", 200-3.

the bodies of three suicides lying in the Paris morgue, Browning writes in "Apparent Failure":

> My own hope is, a sun will pierce
> The thickest cloud earth ever stretched;
> That, after Last, returns the First,
> Though a wide compass round be fetched;
> That what began best, can't end worst,
> Nor what God blessed once, prove accurst.[35]

It is in connexion with Browning's belief in evil as "stuff for transmuting" that his ethical standards in "The Statue and the Bust" must be evaluated. Whenever good and evil grapple there is no hesitation whatever in his praise of the choice of virtue and his condemnation of the choice of vice. This indeed is the very core of his moral credo. No other poet has been a more militant champion of virtue. In *The Ring and the Book* there is no measure in the contrast between his extolling of the good as represented in Pompilia and Caponsacchi and his denunciation of evil as represented in Guido. Yet, because he does regard evil as "stuff for transmuting", he holds that the shirking of the moral conflict is the worst sin of all.

If the will is alive, if a man acts with energy and courage even in pursuit of an evil end, there is hope for him. The poet believes that the punishment which sin entails, the prickings of conscience, the realisation on the part of the sinner that he is hopelessly contending against the will of God and is betraying his better nature, must, in conjunction with divine love and mercy, ultimately redeem him either on earth or in a life hereafter. But if a man's will is dead, if through inertness or cowardice he refuses to act at all, his passivity is a graver sin than that of an active evil-doer. Since he has shunned the moral conflict, no development of his soul is possible, not even through the transmuting of evil-doing.

> Let a man contend to the uttermost
> For his life's set prize, be it what it will![36]

To play a part in the moral struggle with will and decision is for

---

[35] "Apparent Failure", 58-63.
[36] "The Statue and the Bust", 242-3.

Browning the primary requirement of all. In *Christmas-Eve and Easter-Day* he rejoices that he can

> Be crossed and thwarted as a man,
> Not left in God's contempt apart,
> With ghastly smooth life, dead at heart,
> Tame in earth's paddock as her prize.[37]

In *The Ring and the Book*, the Pope denounces Pietro and Violante for their timidity and double-dealing in vacillating between right and wrong:

> ...Go!
> Never again elude the choice of tints!
> White shall not neutralize the black, nor good
> Compensate bad in man, absolve him so:
> Life's business being just the terrible choice.[38]

Browning's contempt for faint-heartedness and paralysis of will is, as Pigou notes, reminiscent of Dante's scorn for him "who made through cowardice the great refusal", and pines forever in the outskirts of the Inferno, "hateful to God and to his enemies".[39]

As has been stated, Browning believes that even a sinful course of action is ultimately transmuted to become an instrument for the realisation of the good ends of a God of infinite power and love. In "By the Fire-side" he maintains that hate as well as love may have a function in the development of individual souls, and consequently in the evolution of the human race:

> Be hate that fruit or love that fruit,
> It forwards the general deed of man,
> And each of the Many helps to recruit
> The life of the race by a general plan;
> Each living his own to boot.[40]

It must be acknowledged that the poet's argument here, and in kindred passages, skates perilously close to the verge of the pernicious casuistry of "Let us do evil that good may come". As a matter of fact it is twisted into such sophistry by Don Juan,

[37] "Easter Day", 1022-5. [38] *The Ring and the Book*, x, 1234-8.
[39] See A. C. Pigou, *Robert Browning as a Religious Teacher*, London (1931) p. 111.
[40] "By the Fire-side", 246-50.

Sludge the Medium, and other protagonists of Browning's casuistical poems. It must also be conceded that the poet's intellectual agnosticism beclouds, at times, his speculative thought on moral and spiritual problems. Yet the whole tenor and purport of his poetry, when he is voicing his own convictions, refute the assertion that for him "the exercise of energy is the absolute good, irrespective of motives or of circumstances". To maintain that evil by being transmuted is ultimately overruled by God for good, is very different from an acceptance of the casuistical precept "Let us do evil that good may come". In this respect Browning's belief may be compared with the Christian doctrine of the Atonement. Faith in the potency of the Atonement is in harmony with his conviction that evil is "stuff for transmuting", that no sinner is beyond the pale of final redemption: but it does not imply that evil *per se* is ever good, or that the following of it is ever justified. Browning would have echoed St Paul's impassioned protest, "Shall we continue in sin, that grace may abound? God forbid."

There is no other concept in Browning's ethics which has been more adversely criticised than his belief that evil is illusory. Yet there is an important element of truth in his contention. If evil and good are not coequal, evil cannot have the same degree of reality as good. Evil is rebellion, negation, imperfection, the consciousness of the gulf between man's moral ideal and his present state of being. Having served its end in the moral conflict it will be overthrown, since the purpose of a loving God for his universe must be the final and complete victory of goodness. The conviction that evil is relative rather than absolute has been nobly voiced by Milton:

> Yea, even that which Mischief meant most harm
> Shall in the happy trial prove most glory.
> But evil on itself shall back recoil,
> And mix no more with goodness, when at last
> Gathered like scum, and settled to itself,
> It shall be in eternal restless change,
> Self-fed and self-consumed. If this fail
> The pillared firmament is rottenness,
> And earth's base built on stubble. . . .[41]

[41] *Comus*, 591-9.

Milton's concept of the relativity of evil does not, however, imply that he regards it as *mere* semblance or illusion.

Unfortunately, Browning's representation of this aspect of evil is warped by his intellectual agnosticism. An extreme instance is his argument that although evil is an illusion, it is necessary for man to regard it as real in order to preserve the worth of the moral struggle. This would seem to make man's moral effort dependent on ignorance and delusion, or to hold, as Professor Jones writes, that "The world is a kind of moral gymnasium, crowded with phantoms, wherein by exercise man makes moral muscle."[42] As I have stated, the confusion of thought engendered by Browning's sceptical theory of knowledge seems to me responsible for much misunderstanding regarding his ethical standards. The poet exposes himself to this because he fails to realise that even from an absolute point of view evil has a relative degree of reality, and is not mere semblance and illusion.

There is also, I feel, on another ground, a residuum of truth in the hostile criticism of the poet's concept of evil. Often as Browning is preoccupied with the problem of evil, he never, even while condemning it, feels that loathing and horror of evil which characterises the prophets of the Old Testament. He does not, as *The Ring and the Book* is ample testimony, shut his eyes to it as Emerson did. One would hesitate to say of him, as it has been said of Milton contrasted with Dante, that in his representation of Hell "he never saw the damned". Yet the gulf between Dante's utter abhorrence of evil and Browning's reaction to it is wide.

The explanation lies in Browning's temperamental and emotional optimism. Its sources are both physical and psychical. A statement of Carlyle concerning the poet may be cited:

> But there's a great contrast between him and me. He seems very content with life, and takes much satisfaction in the world.
>
> It's a very strange and curious spectacle to behold a man in these days so confidently cheerful.[43]

As William James has written:

> In many persons, happiness is congenital and irreclaimable. "Cosmic emotion" inevitably takes in them the form

[42] Jones, *Browning*, p. 240.   [43] *Op. cit.*, p. 45.

of enthusiasm and freedom. . . . We find such persons in
every age, passionately flinging themselves upon their sense
of the goodness of life. . . .[44]

Such people are "animally happy", and spiritually their religion
is that of "healthy-mindedness". They know little of the divisions
of "the sick soul", or the agonising struggle of those who through
conversion must be "twice born" to achieve their ultimate
salvation.

Intellectually there is pessimism in Browning's attitude towards the world as it is. In "Reverie" and elsewhere he laments,

> Earth's good is with evil blent:
> Good struggles but evil reigns.[45]

Yet, the poet's emotional optimism is far more potent than his
intellectual pessimism. Psychologically this optimism is reflected
in the buoyancy and positiveness of his temperament, morally and
spiritually in his conviction that, since God is a being of infinite
love, the whole scheme and framework of his creation must be
flawlessly good from an absolute point of view, in which the
transient and illusory appearances of evil and discord are resolved
and transmuted into the eternal harmonies of God's all-loving
purposes. While it is somewhat arbitrary to wrench the lines in
Pippa's song from their dramatic context, ("God's in his heaven –
/ All's right with the world!") there can be no doubt that they
voice the poet's belief. So also do the lines in "At the 'Mermaid' ",
although dramatically attributed to Shakespeare:

> I find earth not gray but rosy,
> Heaven not grim but fair of hue.
> Do I stoop? I pluck a posy.
> Do I stand and stare? All's blue.[46]

Browning's representation of evil is conditioned by his optimism
and the militancy of his temperament and conflict-loving nature.
Evil is not in his eyes primarily horrible and loathsome, but
rather "stuff for transmuting". Like Roderick Dhu in Scott's

---

[44] William James, *The Varieties of Religious Experience*, New York (1920)
p. 79.
[45] "Reverie", 64-5.   [46] "At the Mermaid ", 93-6.

The Lady of the Lake he confronts it with eagerness, "and that stern joy which warriors feel in foemen worthy of their steel". As "stuff for transmuting" he must even show that "there is a soul of goodness in things evil". There is nothing in the world which

> But touched aright, prompt yields each particle its tongue
> Of elemental flame, – no matter whence flame sprung
> From gums and spice, or else from straw and rottenness,
> So long as soul has power to make them burn. . . .[47]

It cannot be denied that such tenets do tend to stress the worth of the moral struggle *per se* rather than the black-and-white opposition of its elements, sin as Dante saw it in its loathsomeness and virtue in its crystalline purity.

Yet this distinction is only relatively valid, and often more theoretical than actual. As I have pointed out, no speculative doubts regarding the confirmation in objective reality of his subjective experiences prevent Browning from deeming it imperative that he should be loyal to the guidance of his conscience. For him the choice between good and evil is an all-important decision. He takes his stand for virtue along with "the famous ones of old" who, in the "Epilogue" to *Ferishtah's Fancies*, his imagination pictures "thronging through the cloud-rift" as witnesses of his own moral conflict. They are an evidence to him that his choice of good rather than evil, so far from being a matter of indifference, has supreme value and significance.

> "Was it for mere fool's play, make-believe and mumming,
> So we battled it like men, not boylike sulked or whined?
> Each of us heard clang God's 'Come!' and each was coming:
> Soldiers all, to forward-face, not sneaks to lag behind?"[48]

Despite the approach to casuistry and the confusion of thought in which Browning is frequently befogged through his nescient theory of knowledge and distrust of reason, there is no real ground for the assertion that he is indifferent to ethical ends, or that for him "the exercise of energy is the absolute good, irrespective of motives or of circumstances". His belief that, if God

---

[47] *Fifine at the Fair*, 828-31.
[48] "Epilogue", *Ferishtah's Fancies*, 13-16.

is omnipotent and all-loving, evil must finally be transmuted,
by no means implies that he is blind to the moral distinction between good and evil, or in any way counsels "Let us do evil that
good may come."

Above all, when Browning turns from the evidence of the
head to that of the heart in what has been called "the richest vein
of pure ore" in his poetry, his view of the nature and function of
love, he attains a certainty of good which convinces him of its
objective as well as subjective validity. "But love is victory, the
prize itself." Who can doubt that in the noble utterance of the
Pope in *The Ring and the Book* the poet is attesting his own assurance:

I

Put no such dreadful question to myself,
Within whose circle of experience burns
The central truth, Power, Wisdom, Goodness, – God:
I must outlive a thing ere know it dead: . . . .

So, never I miss footing in the maze,
No, – I have light nor fear the dark at all.[49]

[49] *The Ring and the Book*, x, 1631-5, 1659-60.

George M. Ridenour

BROWNING'S MUSIC POEMS: FANCY AND FACT[1]

Browning is one of Shelley's main heirs in the nineteenth century. As a boy he had worshipped Shelley, who is the most obvious single influence in both *Pauline* (pub. 1833) and *Paracelsus* (pub. 1835), his earliest published works. He grew uneasy about the relationship later, but he never stopped being, in important ways, a poet in the tradition of Shelley. One of the enduring likenesses between them is the way both use their strong sense of the weakness of language in developing the meaning of poems. Shelley uses it most fully in *Epipsychidion*, where it serves a vision of the inadequacy of all human satisfactions. His solution is to set up a number of more or less satisfactory terms, calling attention to the fact that no one of them will do, and that they all together "do" only in special ways. This corresponds in language to the tendency to resist restrictions on personal relationships that appears in the Shelleyan "harem". The solution in both cases can be awkward, but in the case of language, at any rate, the awkwardness is part of the meaning.

Browning remained more susceptible to the harem notion than he liked to admit, and he played with it (to reject it) in *Fifine at the Fair*.[2] The problem of language is, to a large extent, the problem of *Sordello* (pub. 1840), but it was first integrated into the meaning of a whole work in *The Ring and the Book* (pub. 1868-69).[3] Here

[1] Reprinted from *PMLA*, LXXVIII (1963) pp. 369-77.
[2] *Fifine* may be to some extent an answer to *Epipsychidion*. Cf. H. C. Duffin, *Amphibian: a Reconsideration of Browning*, London (1956) p. 243.
[3] There are interesting brief comments on this subject in Park Honan's *Browning's Characters*, New Haven (1961) pp. 36-7, 142.

Shelley's technique of "varied approximation",[4] as a means of defeating the limits of language, is expanded into the well-known system of different points of view defining and judging the same act. As the problem grew more acute with advancing age, Browning tended to think of the relation between language and reality as increasingly indirect, so that if language is to be serviceable for capturing an ever more uncertain reality, it must itself be increasingly elaborated. And so we have the intricately circular arguments of *La Saisiaz* (pub. 1878) or some of *Ferishtah's Fancies* (pub. 1884), "talking about", "circumscribing" a reality that cannot, in words, be got at directly (cf. the "ring" of *The Ring and the Book*). It is the use of argument for non-argumentative ends that makes some of these poems almost as interesting as they are irritating – more, in any case, than "mere grey argument". It is apt to be argument against the possibility of conclusive argument, carried on, like Asia's conversation with Demogorgon in *Prometheus Unbound*, to suggest ways of framing answers by making us see why certain ways are inadequate. The questions are in a sense the wrong questions, but it is important to ask them, and they must be answered carefully, if only to discover that the answer we get is defined by the way the question is asked. For the point is to understand the meaning of the different questions and answers, which correspond on the rational level to the multiplication of symbolic and social units already mentioned as characteristic of both poets.

Both Shelley and Browning present refined strategies for fixing these multiplicities without distorting them, structures which will allow us to consider them in themselves and as a part of a unified view of reality. Browning finds the analogy of music especially helpful for this purpose. He is particularly struck, for example, by what seems to him the speed with which one musical style succeeds another.[5] But while styles in music change so that it is hard for one age to feel what earlier ages had felt about particular works, this very weakness, as is usual for Browning, is perceived as a source of strength. It is the price music pays for

[4] Milton Wilson, *Shelley's Later Poetry*, New York (1959) p. 224.

[5] This point was first developed by William C. DeVane, in his *Browning's Parleyings*, New Haven (1927) esp. pp. 257-9. The whole section on "Charles Avison" should be consulted.

having got such a firm grasp on central human realities in the
first place. What appears, therefore, with a sophisticated understanding of the history of music, is a series of more or less discrete
modes, each in its own terms presenting a version of vital human
concerns, each adequate for its own time, and each still valuable
to an imaginative listener.

Even these quick generalisations will suggest something of the
range of Browning's poems on music. There are two main
questions: the relation between the chaos of experience and our
shapings of it (always, at any time), and the relation between the
fixed form of the shapings and the flow of time to which they are
in turn subject (historically). The most authoritative presentation
of these matters is found in the late parleying "With Charles
Avison" (from the *Parleyings With Certain People of Importance in their
Day*, pub. 1887). The other more specialised (and better) poems
may usefully be discussed on the basis of the parleying.

Browning begins with a long and vigorously developed image
to tell us what art, very practically, does. It responds to the needs
of our state of chill and confinement, expressed by the March
day on which the poet, confined to the house, looks out into his
bleak garden. Nature itself offers him suddenly a vision of colour
and vitality; a finch ("blackcap") appears against the cold brick
of the garden wall, where the hard winter has torn away the vines.
The finch has come from some distance to get just the piece of
cloth that had held the ivy against the wall, and which now hangs
loose:

> Was not the fine wool's self within his range
> – Filchings on every fence? But no: the need
> Was of this rag of manufacture, spoiled
> By art, and yet by nature near unsoiled,
> New-suited to what scheming finch would breed
> In comfort, this uncomfortable March.[6]

We appreciate the vigour of the description and its range of
evocation, playing with various kinds of relation between nature
and art. The passage, however, is not only effective in itself, but
also serves to arouse a train of association that grows into the
argument of the poem. Furthermore, the opening description

[6] "With Charles Avison", 31-6.

(as in "Tintern Abbey", "Mont Blanc", or *La Saisiaz*) will continue to give metaphoric support to the rest of the poem, which will be developed largely in terms of concept.

There is no need here to follow the movement of the argument in detail. It is enough to notice that the poet, having defined the problems of the relation between, on the one hand, amorphous reality and fixed form, and, on the other, between the fixed forms and the flow of time, takes them up alternately, allowing them to comment on each other. The solution is developed non-conceptually, out of the word "march".

March means, as we have seen, first of all the month – cold, harsh, "uncomfortable", but which leads to spring:

> Truths escape
> Time's insufficient garniture: they fade,
> They fall – those sheathings now grown sere, whose aid
> Was infinite to truth they wrapped, saved fine
> And free through March frost: May dews crystalline
> Nourish truth merely, – does June boast the fruit
> As – not new vesture merely but, to boot,
> Novel creation? Soon shall fade and fall
> Myth after myth – the husk-like lies I call
> New truth's corolla-safeguard: Autumn comes,
> So much the better![7]

Even as thought of the month of March had earlier led the poet to the memory of the musical composition ("Avison's Grand March"), so now the thought of March leads on to May and June, and the thought that May and June lead on again to autumn is not dismaying because the progression defined is that of coherent progression, like a march:

> Therefore – bang the drums,
> Blow the trumps, Avison! March-motive? that's
> Truth which endures resetting. Sharps and flats,
> Lavish at need, shall dance athwart thy score
> When ophicleide and bombardon's uproar
> Mate the approaching trample, even now

[7] *Op. cit.*, 371-81.

Big in the distance – or my ears deceive –
Of federated England, fitly weave
March-music for the Future![8]

Marching is seen as universal, both in the natural world and in man, who must always be marching somewhere, for something. And this is why it is so suitable a matter for art. "March-motive? that's / Truth which endures resetting" – in, for example, "Avison's Grand March", with which the poem ends.

A march, as a work of art, is a shape that follows the contours of its material with especial closeness, progressive, but formally coherent. It has the further quality of embodying human aspirations so as not only to conform to them, but also to lead them, to inspire the development of the impulse it shapes. "Man's / The cause our music champions."[9] All good marches are manifestations of this one impulse to march. Their truth is a function of their excellence as marches. This is the truth of music, and it is a type of the truth of art in general.[10] That the point can be made more clearly and effectively in terms of music is one of the reasons why Browning wrote his music poems.

The other music poems are more intensive explorations of separate aspects of the parleying. Browning had already, for example, made use of the notion of marching in the exciting "Thamuris Marching" (a fragment included in *Aristophanes' Apology*, pub. 1875). Since it is not well-known, I give the whole:

Thamuris marching, – lyre and song of Thrace –
(Perpend the first, the worst of woes that were
Allotted lyre and song, ye poet-race!)

Thamuris from Oichalia, feasted there
By kingly Eurutos of late, now bound
For Dorion at the uprise broad and bare

[8] *Op. cit.*, 381-9.
[9] *Op. cit.*, 405-6.
[10] Cf. Browning's discussion of "Art's response / To earth's despair" in the parleying "With Christopher Smart" (52-3). (I do not think it has been pointed out that the Chapel image, of which the lines quoted are a part, has its source in Byron's stanzas on St Peter's and the Vatican in *Childe Harold* iv, 155-63).

Of Mount Pangaios (ore with earth enwound
Glittered beneath his footstep) – marching gay
And glad, Thessalia through, came, robed and crowned,

From triumph on to triumph, mid a ray
Of early morn, – came, saw and knew the spot
Assigned him for his worst of woes, that day.

Baiura – happier while its name was not –
Met him, but nowise menaced; slipt aside,
Obsequious river, to pursue its lot

Of solacing the valley – say, some wide
Thick busy human cluster, house and home,
Embanked for peace, or thrift that thanks the tide.

Thamuris, marching, laughed "Each flake of foam"
(As sparklingly the ripple raced him by)
"Mocks slower clouds adrift in the blue dome!"

For Autumn was the season; red the sky
Held morn's conclusive signet of the sun
To break the mists up, bid them blaze and die.

Morn had the mastery as, one by one
All pomps produced themselves along the tract
From earth's far ending to near heaven begun.

Was there a ravaged tree? it laughed compact
With gold, a leaf-ball crisp, high-brandished now
Tempting to onset frost which late attacked.

Was there a wizened shrub, a starveling bough,
A fleecy thistle filched from by the wind,
A weed, Pan's trampling hoof would disallow?

Each, with a glory and a rapture twined
About it, joined the rush of air and light
And force: the world was of one joyous mind.

Say not the birds flew! they forebore their right –
Swam, revelling onward in the roll of things.
Say not the beasts' mirth bounded! that was flight –

How could the creatures leap, no lift of wings?
Such earth's community of purpose, such
The ease of earth's fulfilled imaginings, –

So did the near and far appear to touch
I' the moment's transport, – that an interchange
Of function, far with near, seemed scarce too much;

And had the rooted plant aspired to range
With the snake's license, while the insect yearned
To glow fixed as the flower, it were not strange –

No more than if the fluttery tree-top turned
To actual music, sang itself aloft;
Or if the wind, impassioned chantress, earned

The right to soar embodied in some soft
Fine form all fit for cloud-companionship,
And, blissful, once touch beauty chased so oft.

Thamuris, marching, let no fancy slip
Born of the fiery transport; lyre and song
Were his, to smite with hand and launch from lip –

Peerless recorded, since the list grew long
Of poets (saith Homeros) free to stand
Pedestalled mid the Muses' temple-throng,

A statued service, laurelled, lyre in hand,
(Ay, for we see them) – Thamuris of Thrace
Predominating foremost of the band.

Therefore the morn-ray that enriched his face,
If it gave lambent chill, took flame again
From flush of pride; he saw, he knew the place.

What wind arrived with all the rhythms from plain,
Hill, dale, and that rough wildwood interspersed?
Compounding these to one consummate strain,

It reached him, music; but his own outburst
Of victory concluded the account,
And that grew song which was mere music erst.

"Be my Parnassos, thou Pangaian mount!
And turn thee, river, nameless hitherto!
Famed shalt thou vie with famed Pieria's fount!

"Here I await the end of this ado:
Which wins – Earth's poet or the Heavenly Muse." . . .[11]

The march of Thamuris is a triumphal progress, and the word suggests the pride that led him to boast that he could defeat the Muse in a song-contest. Aristophanes' point in singing the song is just this, that Euripides was a Thamuris, whose aspiration as poet was presumptuously high. Marching has in the poem a further dimension, however, in that it stresses the action of the poet in encountering a natural world whose beauty he will enhance and on which he will confer significance. He goes to it, proceeds through it, and imposes himself upon it – all "marching".

This is a much more active form of imagination than is defined in the parleying, where (as in *The Ring and the Book*) the poet is diffident about claiming a genuinely creative function for poetry. From this point of view, "Thamuris Marching" recalls "Abt Vogler" and, to some extent, "Amphibian" (the prologue to *Fifine at the Fair*). And the dramatic use in *Aristophanes' Apology* relieves him of full responsibility. But here again, as in the other "march", the work of art is continuous with, shares the structure of, its material. And again the material is thought of as inviting artistic shaping – here by the splendour with which the dawn (Browning's regular symbol of transformation, entering into new dimensions of experience) creates a unity of heaven and earth, quite naturally, so that the poet's purpose is in a sense anticipated. He has only to take up and complete what has been so splendidly begun:

Such earth's community of purpose, such
The ease of earth's fulfilled imaginings, –

So did the near and far appear to touch
I' the moment's transport.

The poet gives two gifts, life and meaning. To the morning

[11] *Aristophanes' Apology*, 5188-264.

chill he gives "flame again / From flush of pride", and to the sounds of the morning he gives new status:

> It reached him, music; but his own outburst
> Of victory concluded the account,
> And that grew song which was mere music erst.

The placing of song above "mere music" is striking, and the poem anticipates Wallace Stevens' "Idea of Order at Key West". But Browning is more vigorous, more elegant, and less eccentric. He is also less confident of the creative role of any art, and he puts this most radical statement he ever ventured in the mouth of a figure whom his own revered Euripides (in the *Rhesus*) had implicitly reproached with hubris. He is more comfortable with Charles Avison, but he makes great poetry with Thamuris. There is undoubtedly evidence of uncertainty in Browning's attitude towards poetry. It is most generous to suppose that he is trying to be fair to the whole of his experience of what poetry can and cannot do.

Both the parleying "With Charles Avison" and "Thamuris Marching" deal in their different ways with one of Browning's most pervasive concerns, the relation between what he often called "fancy and fact". In the parleying, as Browning explains in the opening lines, it is the fact of the appearance of the bird, in those circumstances, that "led [his] fancy forth". But with regard to the poem's treatment of content and form, which is fancy and which fact? Feeling is more real than any expression of it, since expressions suffer from the very formality that enables them to serve as expression. They are swept away and constantly replaced. But at the same time the superstructure is directly definable in a way in which the thing defined is not. The apportionment of fancy and fact in "Thamuris" is especially delicate, and depends largely on its setting in the larger poem. It will be seen that music can be very helpful with the special problems of this poem, since the high degree of indeterminateness inherent in the most intricately developed musical forms may seem to give music a unique closeness to reality, while these same characteristics tend also to remove it from reality, making it seem remote, ethereal, fanciful. The consequence of this is that music can serve both as unformed fact (as in "Thamuris") and as forming fancy (as in the parleying), and in this manner help the poet to deal with the problems created by this division, or even to see it as not finally a division.

The relation of fancy to fact is handled most thoroughly in the *Asolando* volume (pub. 1889), which bears the sub-title: *Fancies and Facts*. And one of the most authoritative poems in the collection is the one that deals with the issue in terms of music: "Flute Music: with an Accompaniment". The flute music is heard from a distance, and the accompaniment is the conversation a man and a woman hold, discussing it. This is one of the occasions in which Browning reverses his more usual apportionment, and makes the woman the representative of the realistic or scientific viewpoint, the man of the imaginative. The sound of the flute suggests a love song to him, presenting a carefully defined nuance of love:

> Never, to my knowledge,
> Yet has pedantry enacted
>   That, in Cupid's College,
> Just this variation
> Of the old, old yearning
> Should by plain speech have salvation,
>   Yield new men new learning.[12]

But she explains that it is really a clerk in a neighbouring house, who is learnng to play the flute during his lunch-hour. He repeats the exercise over and over again, and his bad playing receives form and beauty from distance and fancy:

> Unexpectedness enhances
>   What your ear's auxiliar
> – Fancy – finds suggestive.[13]

The situation here is much more problematic than in "Thamuris Marching". Here there is natural enhancement of sound that is already a bungling attempt at coherence: in patterns of tone and rhythm. But the player is incompetent, and even if he mastered the instrument, says the woman, he would have nothing to say –

[12] "Flute Music, With an Accompaniment", 17-24.
[13] *Op. cit.*, 79-81.

only "tunes once bright now dusky – / Meant to cool thy porridge."

But in a sense the man hears what the flutist is really trying to say, the *kind* of statement he would make if he could (though he no doubt doesn't know it), the kind of statement one learns to play the flute to make. In any case, what the man hears is the truth of the playing – the central human aspiration ("the old old yearning") that art exists to embody (as in the "march" of the parleying). That is one of the senses in which he hears truly.

The other sense is harder to put. The man compares his experience in interpreting the sounds of the flute with his experience of the woman's love. Had he read the signs correctly? He had had suspicions, but intervening distance caused them to disappear, and, as with the song, distance had selected the elements of harmony and pattern. He is talking partly about perspective, which allows one to see things in true proportion – the deceits, in this case, which are accidents of the relationship:

> Distance – ash-tops aiding,
> Reconciled scraps else contrarious,
> Brightened stuff fast fading.[14]

But he has a more radical criticism to make of her position:

> Is not outside seeming
> Real as substance inside?
> Both are facts, so leave me dreaming.[15]

Not only are the discordant elements in an important sense less real than the perceived harmony, but the appearance (we recall the parleying) is at least as real as the substance. The reality particularly of a human relationship is never wholly reducible to any of its motives, as understood by either person. Appearances are realities, and are part of the experienced being of the person or thing, the woman or the song. And implicitly here the woman is the song. Or rather, the flute music as accompanied by the structuring commentary of the man and the woman all together make up the song, a fact which is a joke on the woman. It is a

---

[14] *Op. cit.*, 170-2.
[15] *Op. cit.*, 185-7.

song played on a flute: light, witty, playful (cf. "Peter Quince at the Clavier", where the title refers to the mode as much as to the content). But it is Browning's most accomplished use of music to show what can be said. (This does not make it the best of the music poems, the one that offers the richest possibilities of experience. That is no doubt "A Toccata of Galuppi's".)

The three poems we have been considering are all from the last decade and a half of the poet's life. They were taken up first because their more explicit and more elaborate treatment of themes common to the music poems as a whole makes them particularly helpful when thinking about earlier poems that are very oblique. The last three poems to be considered are from Browning's great middle period, two from *Men and Women* (pub. 1855) and one from *Dramatis Personae* (pub. 1864). All pose interesting problems.

The main difficulty of "A Toccata of Galuppi's" is the temptation to ask the wrong questions, or to require the wrong kind of answer. But our experience with later music poems, especially "Flute Music", should help us here. For again the mode is one of grace and elegance (an eighteenth-century clavichord piece), but made, like the flute-music, to produce a song to some extent in contrast with the instrument and its appropriate technique. Like the woman in the later poem, Galuppi is drawn into an understanding which is greater than his own, in some ways hostile to his own, but of which he is a necessary part: and all without his knowledge.

The point of departure is the notion, treated in detail in the parleying "With Charles Avison", that styles of music embody the spirit of the culture that produced them, and that this culture is especially approachable through its music. The Englishman who has expected to find Galuppi's music conforming to his sentimental notions of eighteenth-century Venice is surprised to find it embodying quite a different aspect of the Rococo: clear and elegant, to be sure, but ironic, witty, destructive.[16] Galuppi's music suggests one quality of the eighteenth century, its skeptical rationalism, commenting cynically on some of its more winning illusions. It is a split in the mind of the century, and, like the man and woman of "Flute Music", the two parts comment on each

[16] Cf. DeVane, *Handbook*, New York (1955) p. 221.

other.[17] Neither, however, annihilates the other, nor is there genuine synthesis, outside the imaginative form that lets us consider them together.

The split is thought of as one expression of a permanent division, found both in the speaker of the poem, an idealistic Englishman of the nineteenth century, interested in science (a "Victorian"), and in the poet, who sets facts against fancies to define a new harmony, of a sort, in his poem. Cynicism of Galuppi's sort is strictly unanswerable, and the poet must match his sophistication in moving him in the direction of a larger vision. By himself, as a Victorian might say, he is "soul-withering", and the emphasis of the poem is on this quality. But the meaning of the poem is not wholly Galuppi's meaning. For in a sense his music, in its style, supports the values he deprecates. The Venetians are right in enjoying it; it is "their kind" of music. Galuppi for the persons in the salon is a superior entertainer (Haydn in livery), and they for him are material for his wit. The social manner on both sides is stylish and vicious, the ferocities of caste, sex, and reason moving as elegantly in the song as in the salon. It is this aristocratic style of the period that both keeps the two parties from understanding each other and holds them together for us as complementary. They are both true for us in different ways, as the "sentiment" of the speaker is true, in its witness to the point of there being a Venice in the first place. These truths are part of the poem's truth as expressed in a structure that rather strictly controls our investigation of its contents. As we move through the poem's system of perspectives, only certain questions can be asked, they can be answered only in certain ways, and the answers do not wholly coincide. We have heard this before.

The contents of "Abt Vogler", however, are largely new to us. Here, uniquely in Browning, we have the high Romantic doctrine of the artist as creator. The composer has been "extemporizing upon the musical instrument of his invention":

[17] Since writing this I have been struck by the similarity in conception of Alain Resnais' film "Last Year at Marienbad". Resnais develops a similar opposition in Baroque art between the illusionistic palace interior (German) and the geometrical French garden, both real and unreal, in different ways.

176   GEORGE M. RIDENOUR

> Would that the structure brave, the manifold music I build,
>   Bidding my organ obey, calling its keys to their work,
> Claiming each slave of the sound, at a touch, as when
>   Solomon willed
>   Armies of angels that soar, legions of demons that lurk,
> Man, brute, reptile, fly, – alien of end and of aim,
>   Adverse, each from the other heaven-high, hell-deep re-
>   moved, –
> Should rush into sight at once as he named the ineffable
>   Name,
>   And pile him a palace straight, to pleasure the princess he
>   loved!
>
> Would it might tarry like his, the beautiful building of mine,
>   This which my keys in a crowd pressed and importuned
>   to raise!
> Ah, one and all, how they helped, would dispart now and
>   now combine,
>   Zealous to hasten the work, heighten their master his
>   praise!
> And one would bury his brow with a blind plunge down to
>   hell,
>   Burrow awhile and build, broad on the roots of things,
> Then up again swim into sight, having based me my
>   palace well,
>   Founded it, fearless of flame, flat on the nether springs.[18]

The emphatic amorality of the building is striking. It is based
on hell, and built by demons equally with angels, which is a good
deal more than acknowledging the existence of evil, making it
"part of the picture", or even making use of it. From this point
of view it reminds us of "Kubla Khan". The creator himself is
something of a conjurer, and so a bit suspicious. But this is not
to be stressed. Emphasis falls on the artist's belief that his upward
movement, towards "heaven", is met by a movement from heaven
to him (a "natural" heaven, we observe):

> Nature in turn conceived, obeying an impulse as I;
> And the emulous heaven yearned down, made effort to reach
>   the earth,

[18] "Abt Vogler", 1-16.

As the earth had done her best, in my passion to scale the
    sky:
Novel splendours burst forth, grew familiar and dwelt with
    mine,
Not a point nor peak but found and fixed its wandering
    star;
Meteor-moons, balls of blaze: and they did not pale nor pine,
    For earth had attained to heaven, there was no more near
    nor far.[19]

This union coincides with the integration of the poet himself
("For I was made perfect too"), of which it is both cause and
result. That coincidence produces the "thought" in which three
sounds become "not a fourth sound, but a star".[20] It is to express
the wonder of this experience that he is led to affirm the existence
of a total unfailing structure built by an absolute creator,[21] in
which his own partial and transient creation participates:

Therefore to whom turn I but to thee, the ineffable Name?
Builder and maker, thou, of houses not made with hands!
What, have fear of change from thee who art ever the same?[22]

It is this affirmation that makes it possible for him to live on the
ordinary level of "the C Major of this life".

Everyone is struck by the split between the brilliantly realised
opening and the tamer moralisings that follow. The song breaks
in the middle, unlike the flute-song and the toccata, whose contrasts are fully assimilated. But the poem may be less conventionally pious than it looks, since our knowledge of the absolute
creator is by analogy with human creation, and this is very in-
clusive, as we have seen. And the note of pride is remarkable.
It is almost arrogance in the seventh stanza, where (correspond-
ing to the "holy dread" of "Kubla Khan") we are required to

[19] *Op. cit.*, 28-32.

[20] See the discussion by C. Willard Smith, *Browning's Star-Imagery*, Princeton (1941) pp. 182-7. Smith finds more humility in the poem than I can
make out.

[21] As Mrs Orr puts it: "The effect was incommensurate with the cause;
they had nothing in common with each other". *Handbook*, London (1907)
p. 245.

[22] "Abt Vogler", 65-7.

"bow the head" at the wonder of his creation. The final acceptance suggests the mood found later in Joyce's *Portrait*: "I will be patient and proud, and soberly acquiesce." In so far as it is piety, it is a piety rather notably removed from moral concerns. Julia Wedgwood accused Browning of this about this time, and he agreed.[23] The divisions here are no more complex than those we have been examining, but they are more radical, and the instrument of integration is weaker. It is not clear, however, that Browning claims more than he supports, though he may be claiming something different from it.[24]

The most troublesome division, however, and Browning's characteristic ways of approaching it may perhaps be seen most suggestively in a poem in which the whole is only intimated. But the study we have made of the other music poems should help us catch the intimation. This is "Master Hugues of Saxe-Gotha", where the poet as musician makes his attempt at understanding the music of the composer into an organizing element in his music as poet. It is not this time a march, but a fugue: "*Est fuga, volvitur rota.*" As such it does not necessarily contradict the later vision of marching, but the emphasis is very different.

The main points made about the fugue are its dryness and its formal perfection. Nothing much seems to be said, but this little is elaborately developed; the work has great internal consistency. This is what fascinates the organist. The problem is one of making a connexion between this splendidly articulated structure and any kind of human truth. Has the truth been lost by the

[23] *Robert Browning and Julia Wedgwood* (letters), ed. Richard Curle, New York (1937) pp. 29-34. The relevant letters are from July 1864. "Abt Vogler", to which they seem to refer, had appeared late in May of that year.
[24] Coleridge composes the contradictory materials of "Kubla Khan" into a song that makes no claim to be anything else. It is the poet, by virtue of his special integration, who can form such wholes (last six lines). In "Christabel" the fragmentation and morbidity of the poem's world are harmonised and purified by the grace and purity of its music, as Bard Bracy speaks of purifying the wood with his song (560-3). But these are special cases even for Coleridge. The distinction between what a poet writes and what he thinks he is writing is a real one, but it does not always mean the same thing. With Browning it would be unwise to suppose that we can always penetrate directly to what he is saying and ignore what he thinks he is saying. He may be more unorthodox than he thought, but that he thought he was not is sometimes part of what he is saying.

passing of time? Perhaps. Is this an expression of Master Hugues's world view?

> Is it your moral of Life?
>   Such a web, simple and subtle,
>   Weave we on earth here in impotent strife,
>   Backward and forward each throwing his shuttle,
>   Death ending all with a knife?[25]

Perhaps again – more ominously.

The poet associates the fugue with "tradition", beneath which truth is concealed as the cobwebs conceal the gilding of the church roof. The cobwebs have to be brushed aside to get at the gold we can just see traces of. And all the time it is getting darker in the church as the candle begins to burn low.

> While in the roof, if I'm right there,
>   ... Lo you, the wick in the socket!
> Hello, you sacristan, show us a light there!
>   Down it dips, gone like a rocket.
> What, you want, do you, to come unawares,
> Sweeping the church up for first morning-prayers,
> And find a poor devil has ended his cares
>   At the foot of your rotten-runged rat-riddled stairs?
> Do I carry the moon in my pocket?[26]

The wit of the last line is consistent with the winning manner of the speaker throughout, at once earnest and playful. But it is also strangely exciting, coming here as it does, suddenly. The suggestion must be made carefully, but we are surely allowed to feel at least an allusion to the "epistemological", the manner of dispersing the darkness and perceiving the truth "golden o'er us". For if the light is not in our pocket we may have to stay in the dark. The Pope of *The Ring and the Book* finds illumination in an understanding of his own inability to see:

> So, never I miss footing in the maze,
> No, – I have light nor fear the dark at all.[27]

Such pervasive illumination is the ideal. But it is not the usual experience, as Browning depicts it, and even for the Pope com-

---

[25] "Master Hugues of Saxe-Gotha", 106-10.
[26] *Op. cit.*, 141-9.   [27] *The Ring and the Book*, x, 1659-60.

plicated mental strategies are necessary to support this simplicity of vision. Truth for Browning is ordinarily thought of as something that occasionally happens: in a flash of light, as it were. It is perceived now and again, in moments, but these are the moments that matter. This is Browning's equivalent of the Wordsworthian spots of time, Keats's moments of highest intensity, Joyce's epiphanies, and so on.[28] The truth perceived is one of unity and significance, and the problem is to get it into words. The image of a "web" corresponds to Browning's image of the way art catches reality in the parleying "With Charles Avison",[29] and with his own practice in the late discursive poems. And while none of this quite tells us whether Master Hugues's web of music catches or covers reality (it would do the second if it did the first), or whether the poet-organist has "the calm within and the light around / Which makes night day", it may help us understand what question is being asked.

Each of the music poems, in different ways, manifests a concern with two kinds of experience and two kinds of poetry. There are first of all, as we have just observed, moments of immediate apprehension of truth, cutting through the webs that surround it. The limitation of this kind is that it is entirely personal. One person apprehends the truth of another, or of a reality perceived as ultimately personal. This is not communicable directly, except *in* such moments, and these are undependable. The webs are more reliable, but less intense. They are largely ways of supporting values achieved in moments of high realisation.[30] These are

[28] The experience is found in Shelley, but his version is harder to label. See Benziger (below, n. 30).

[29]   Each Art a-strain
            Would stay the apparition, – nor in vain:
            The Poet's word-mesh, Painter's sure and swift
            Colour-and-line-throw . . .
            . . . .
                                                Outdo
            Both of them, Music! Dredging deeper yet,
            Drag into day, – by sound, thy master-net, –
            The abysmal bottom-growth. . . .
                                    (217-20, 234-7).

[30] In the chapter on Browning in his *Images of Eternity* (Carbondale, 1962) p. 184, James Benziger calls attention to the poet's own speculations in this regard in his drama "Luria".

roughly the lyric and discursive poles that Browning constantly manipulates, speaking more or less directly or through his various men and women. He often suspends passages of circular argumentation between two moments of lyricism, as in *Fifine at the Fair* or *La Saisiaz*.[31] In *Ferishtah's Fancies* he ends each section of thinly dramatised discourse with a sharp little lyric. In *Asolando* he uses both modes of presenting an experienced reality which is neither simply fancy nor fact. The two are united with especial elegance in "Flute Music: with an Accompaniment", as we have seen. In music, of course, the conflict between conceptual elaboration and lyric intensity can be overcome in a way hard to parallel in words. That is a main reason why Browning, who felt such a strong need for co-ordinating these fundamental impulses, wrote the poems we have been considering. It is one of the ways in which music is used to deal with some of the questions raised in terms of it.

But along with the values inherent in the poems in themselves, as leading to truth, they make interesting suggestions about the sense in which other of Browning's poems may be thought of as true. The most obvious problem is that posed by *The Ring and the Book*, which so insists on its fidelity to the truth of its source in the records of a Roman murder case of the late seventeenth-century. Now we have already been struck by Browning's interest in forms as such, in musical shapes, such as marches (forward) or fugues (in a circle), with the suggestion that these shapes correspond to permanent human realities which are never completely realised in life, and which must constantly assume new content in order to preserve the old meaning. In the same way, but more tentatively, I suggested that the song of the flute-player did in a sense, intrinsically, as a flute-song, have something of the meaning attributed to it by the man, whether the flute-player was aware of the fact or not. It is something of that sort, I think, that

[31] Pompilia speaks in this manner of herself:

> I am held up, amid the nothingness,
> By one or two truths only – thence I hang,
> And there I live, – the rest is death or dream,
> All but those points of my support.
>
> (vii, 603-6).

The arguments of the lawyers, similarly, are "suspended" between the visions of Pompilia and the Pope.

Browning saw in the story in the Old Yellow Book. He felt that his version of the case was not only identical with the truth of the source, but truer, and one meaning of this may be that in the poem the situation is for the first time released into its inherent (human) meaning, comes fully to mean what it "would" mean all along. The shape of the experience, only partially realised in circumstance, defined from the beginning in the stories of Perseus and St George, already embodied in the enacted myth of Robert Browning and Elizabeth Barrett,[32] is allowed to show itself in its true shape as a form of "the old, old yearning". The fugue is countered by the ring, as a sign not of futility, but of the completeness to which the crude fact itself, the ore, corresponds only as potentiality. Fact is fanciful in spite of itself and fancy is not content until it finds itself embodied in fact. Both are true, but they are not true in the same way. And they are "truer" together. The poem includes both truths in its own truth, and presumably becomes truer as it becomes a better poem, as the test for the truth of the march was its excellence as a march.

Browning found, then, that the multiplicities of experience could be caught in webs of music or myth. So when his imagination was caught by the working out of beauty and purpose in a repulsive and morally perplexed murder story he could easily conceive it in terms of the "fancy" he had been brought up with, as fact, of a divine Nativity under unlikely circumstances. That is what he sees "really happening" in the story, the substance of all stories of divine acts among men:

> [The] repetition of the miracle,
> The divine instance of self-sacrifice
> That never ends and aye begins for man.[33]

Whatever his views on the birth in the manger as an historical fact, and it is clear they were not always the same, Browning was certain of the truth of the fancy: God is born of human flesh.

---

[32] See William C. DeVane, "The Virgin and the Dragon", *Yale Review*, XXXVII (1947) pp. 33-46.

[33] *The Ring and the Book*, x, 1656-8. The difference in context demonstrates the pervasiveness of the notion. For comment on Browning's principle of "repetition of the miracle" see William O. Raymond, *The Infinite Moment*, Toronto (1950) 2nd edn. (1965) pp. 37-8, 47-8.

Not *was* (though perhaps so), but is – certainly. Though the miracle is symbolised by the "virgin-birth" of Pompilia's child (Browning takes advantage of the fact that the murder occurred during the Christmas season),[34] the important birth is in the lovers themselves:

> Metamorphosis the immeasureable
> Of human clay to divine gold.[35]

But it is strictly the whole poem that is an epiphany of the divine in the human, out of opposition. It is another version, in terms of myth, of the comprehensions presented by the marches, fugues, flute-songs, toccatas, and improvisations of the music poems. Music and myth alike move towards the conclusion of *The Ring and the Book*, developing (as in this essay) the relations between fancy and fact:

> But Art, – wherein man nowise speaks to men,
> Only to mankind, – Art may tell a truth
> Obliquely, do the thing shall breed the thought,
> Nor wrong the thought, missing the mediate word.
> So may you paint your picture, twice show truth,
> Beyond mere imagery on the wall, –
> *So, note by note, bring music from your mind,*
> *Deeper than ever e'en Beethoven dived, –*
> *So write a book shall mean beyond the facts,*
> *Suffice the eye and save the soul beside.*[36]

[34]   My babe nor was, nor is, nor yet shall be
         Count Guido Franceschini's child at all –
         Only his mother's, born of love not hate!
                    (vii, 1762-64)
         I never realized God's birth before –
         How He grew likest God in being born.
         This time I felt like Mary, had my babe
         Lying a little on my breast like hers.
                    (vii, 1690-93)

[35] *The Ring and the Book*, x, 1616-7.
[36] *Op. cit.*, xii, 858-67 (italics added).

G. *Robert Stange*

BROWNING AND MODERN POETRY[1]

"Uberhaupt," said Ezra Pound, "ich stamm aus Browning. Pourquoi nier son père?"[2] The language of this statement leaves something to be desired, but the literary debt it acknowledges is of great importance. For whatever may be our judgment of the achievement of Mr Pound we must accept the truth that many modern poets stem from *him*. His acceptance of Browning as poetic father defines a significant connexion between the verse of our contemporaries and that of the great Victorians.

In the minds of the readers of our century Browning's image has – not precisely lived, but – lingered in two quite separate guises, one as unfortunate and misleading as the other. The younger readers of poetry tend to think of him as a long-winded, knotted, and gritty versifier whose language is hardly worth penetrating. Older readers, however, remember the caricatures of the philosophical poet celebrated by the Bacchantes of the Browning Clubs or the boyish enthusiasts who called themselves the T.B.I.Y.T.B.'s ("the best is yet to be"). To recognise Browning as a germinating figure of serious modern poetry is frankly to rescue his image from his most clamant admirers, to refurbish it, and enshrine it in the modern pantheon.

It was probably necessary for the growth of our literature that modernist critics should reject Browning. Now, however, we have grown beyond that need; we can afford to see what spirit and intelligence the old man had, and can take pleasure in discovering that his influence was working all the time, shaping

---

[1] Reprinted from *The Pacific Spectator*, VIII (1954) pp. 218-28.
[2] Letter of May, 1928, to René Taupin. See *The Letters of Ezra Pound 1907-1941*, ed. D. D. Paige, New York (1950) p. 218.

the achievement of even the most rebellious of his artist sons.

A realisation of what elements of Browning's art have fructified in modern poetry and what aspects of his thought and practice have been rejected can clarify our knowledge of the literature of the last hundred years. The complete subject could only be realised in a long study; I intend here merely to suggest how one would begin to examine Browning's influence on the twentieth century. The natural point of departure is in the work of Ezra Pound; he has been the most assertive admirer of Browning and, in spite of his idiosyncrasies, has had a greater effect than any other contemporary on such poets as Eliot, Yeats, and the Imagists. Pound and Eliot are the two who seem to me most representative of the modern movement; a brief look at their poems and critical statements can give a fair notion of the viability of Browning's poetic achievement.

It is necessary to begin with some dangerous generalisations about the poetry of our time. Let us agree first that the distinguished English and American poets of this century have been concerned with technique to an unusual extent; they have continually examined and theorised upon the instruments and resources of their craft. In respect to technique modern poetry displays three main characteristics. The leading poets emphasise the necessity of a dramatic treatment, with the objectification that that term implies; Pound sought the novelist's method of dispassionate presentation; Eliot spoke notoriously of his "objective correlative" to a personal emotion; Yeats laboured to create a poetic mask, to write poetry that was "hard and cold as the dawn".

Another striking technical quality of modern verse is its simplicity of diction. Pound said that his apprenticeship was an attempt "to find and use modern speech". And as Eliot put it, the influences to which both he and Pound responded were those which insisted upon "the importance of *verse as speech*". In their manifesto the Imagists too demanded the language of common speech and the *exact* rather than the decorative word. This search for simplicity and naturalness does not carry over, as the average reader would be quick to point out, to total poetic expression. In creating a structure of thought and imagery – and this would be a third notable characteristic – most modern poets try to achieve extreme economy, to use an elliptical method which

leaves the task of supplying transitions to the reader himself. This
technique is familiar to anyone who knows Eliot or Pound or
the later Yeats, but it has been most neatly described by an older
poet who lectured a puzzled reader as follows:

> I *know* that I don't make out my conception by my lan-
> guage. . . . You would have me paint it all plain out, which
> can't be; but by various artifices I try to make shift with
> touches and bits of outlines which *succeed* if they bear the
> conception from me to you. You ought, I think, to keep
> pace with the thought tripping from ledge to ledge of my
> "glaciers", as you call them; not stand poking your alpen-
> stock into the holes and demonstrating that no foot could
> have stood there; suppose it sprang over there?[3]

The impatient poet who speaks here is Robert Browning; his
chastened reader is John Ruskin.

Each of these salient characteristics of modern verse is at the
heart of Browning's contribution to English poetry. The
growth of his poetic powers from his first published work,
Pauline: A Fragment of a Confession, on up to *Men and Women*, to
their culmination in *The Ring and the Book*, might almost be described as the achievement of a dramatic method in poetry. It
could be said that in developing the form of the dramatic monologue Browning performed in his own career the kind of re-
direction of poetic interest that, repeated by twentieth-century
poets, was defined as a revolution in taste. The hero of the young
Browning was Shelley, whom he apostrophised as the "Sun-
treader" and defined as the model of the subjective poet. In his
Essay on Shelley Browning remarked that the subjective poet does
not "deal with the doings of men (the result of which dealing,
in its pure form . . . is what we call dramatic poetry)", but that
his study is himself, and he selects as subjects those silent scenes
"in which he can best hear the beating of his individual heart".[4]

The weakness of *Pauline* is precisely in the tender attention the
poet pays to the beating of his own heart. As Browning matured

[3] W. G. Collingwood, *The Life and Work of John Ruskin*, London (1893)
I, p. 200.
    [4] Robert Browning, *An Essay on Percy Bysshe Shelley*, ed. Harden, published
for the Shelley Society, London (1888) p. 14.

he advanced toward dramatic – what he called *objective* – poetry, and though he never lost his admiration for Shelley, he was increasingly influenced by the later Shakespeare and by Donne. Certainly the soliloquies of Shakespeare and the dramatic poems of Donne are the two main sources of the monologue form displayed in such poems as "My Last Duchess", "The Bishop Orders His Tomb", and "Andrea del Sarto".

In Shakespeare's soliloquies Browning found the technique of concise revelation through speech. Particularly in the later plays the soliloquies are in sharp contrast to the lengthy self-analyses and lyrical effusions which mark Browning's earliest poetry. A good example of Shakespeare's method is Edmund's soliloquy in Act I, scene 2, of *King Lear*. (*Lear* was Browning's favourite Shakespearean play.) Edmund reveals himself unwittingly, not through statement, but through the connotations of his language:

Thou, Nature, art my goodess. To thy law
My services are bound. Wherefore should I
Stand in the plague of custom, and permit
The curiosity of nations to deprive me,
For that I am some twelve or fourteen moonshines
Lag of a brother? Why bastard? wherefore base?
When my dimensions are as well compact,
My mind as generous, and my shape as true
As honest madam's issue?

The character speaks the truth as he sees it; the dramatist's method of exposure is indirect, ironic. Only by penetrating the tone of speech and attitude, the rhythm of the language, the casuistic use of words (as, for example, Nature) do we perceive Edmund's villainy. This is the technique of objectification, the command of the nuances of revelatory language, that Browning learned from Shakespeare, and that modern poets were to learn from both masters.

The Shakespearean soliloquy, however, involves no suggested interlocutor, no precise localisation of scene or time. The character is perceived within a known plot situation, but there is no emphasis on realistic historical moment, on nation, or milieu; these specifying features Browning supplied in creating his compressed form of drama. Some of the characteristics of the nine-

teenth-century dramatic monologue can, however, be found in
the poetry of Donne. The dramatic poems of *Songs and Sonnets*
and some of the elegies are set in a particular time and place, and
in addition to the speaker, one or more subsidiary characters are
suggested who help to define the situation or to reveal a conflict
of attitudes. Browning, as well as his modern successors, might
also have learned from Donne the use of natural speech rhythms,
of idiomatic language, of concentration on psychological complexity and strong feeling. The moment in these poems of
Donne's is usually one of crisis. Browning frequently followed
Donne in conceiving a dramatic monologue as a passionate outburst that consummates a long train of action, in beginning his
poems with shocking abruptness, in revealing the details of his
setting so indirectly that the reader cannot perceive it as a whole
until he has finished reading the poem.

Browning's continued and clearly expressed admiration for
Donne should interest a generation that believes Donne was
"discovered" in the twentieth century. Browning was attracted
to Shakespearean and metaphysical poetry because he found in it
those very features which were to excite the poets of our time.
He, like

> Donne, I suppose, was such another
> Who found no substitute for sense,
> To seize and clutch and penetrate.[5]

The description is T. S. Eliot's.

But a general interest in dramatic poetry, and the particular
achievement of a monologue form flexible enough to accommo-
date a wide range of psychological and historical interests, are
obviously the bases of Browning's appeal to modern poets. The
dramatic monologue, it can justly be said, has become the
dominant form of twentieth-century poetry. And it has become
so, not accidentally, but as a result of Browning's practice.

Pound was particularly influential in drawing the attention of
his co-workers to Browning's poetry. His most explicit statement is an early poem that is not as well known as it should be.
Pound's title is taken from Browning – "Mesmerism" – and his

[5] T. S. Eliot, "Whispers of Immortality", *Collected Poems 1909-1935*,
London (1936) p. 53.

epigraph is a line from that poem, "And a cat's in the waterbutt".

Aye you're a man that! ye old mesmerizer
Tyin' your meanin' in seventy swadelin's,
One must of needs be a hang'd early riser
To catch you at worm turning. Holy Odd's bodykins!

"Cat's i' the water-butt!" Thought's in your verse-barrel,
Tell us this thing rather, then we'll believe you,
You, Master Bob Browning, spite your apparel
Jump to your sense and give praise as we'd lief do.

You wheeze as a head-cold long-tonsilled Calliope,
But God! What a sight you ha' got o' our in'ards,
Mad as a hatter but surely no Myope,
Broad as all ocean and leanin' mankin'ards.

Heart that was big as the bowels of Vesuvius,
Words that were wing'd as her sparks in eruption,
Eagled and thundered as Jupiter Pluvius,
Sound in your wind past all signs o' corruption.

Here's to you, Old Hippety-hop o' the accents,
True to the Truth's sake and crafty dissector,
You grabbed at the gold sure; had no need to pack cents
Into your versicles.
            Clear sight's elector![6]

It is a tribute Browning might have liked.

As this poem suggests, Pound immersed himself in the idiom of Browning, though he was aware of the dangers of imitation. In a letter of 1916 he complained, "The hell is that one catches Browning's manner and mannerisms. At least I've suffered the disease."[7] But he continued to regard Browning as a poetic model: "Above all, I stem from Browning. Why deny one's father?" He defined his programme for the reform of English poetry as having two aims: the first, which he claimed to have derived from Browning, was the elimination from poetry of all superfluous language; the second was based on Flaubert's ideal of the *mot juste*, and of *presentation ou constatation* – a procedure

---

[6] Ezra Pound, "Mesmerism", *Personae*, New York (1926) p. 13.
[7] Letter of 27 Jul. 1916, to Iris Barry. See *The Letters of Ezra Pound*, p. 90.

which is related to the practice of dramatic poetry. Pound's frequent advice to struggling poets was to read *Sordello* (something that Browning's most devoted contemporaries rarely did), and in the *ABC of Reading* Pound quoted at length from that poem, commenting:

> There is here a certain lucidity of sound that I think you will find with difficulty elsewhere in English. . . . It will be seen that the author is telling you something, not merely making a noise. . . . The "beauty" is not applied ornament, but makes the mental image more definite.[8]

Early in his career Pound seems to have set out to school himself in objectivity – an exercise for which the dramatic monologue was well suited. Some of the early poems are evident imitations of Browning or variations on his themes: "Fifine", "Paracelsus in Excelsus", "Scriptor Ignotus (Ferrara 1715)". Though the more interesting of the early monologues are in Pound's own poetic language, he uses the form much as Browning did. His dramatic poems are sometimes the means of objectifying his speculations on the nature of art, and almost always attempts to apprehend the spirit of a past age through a created character. In succession to Browning's magnificent gallery of portraits Pound presents his lovers and troubadours, "Marvoil", "Pierre Vidal Old"; in "Sestina: Altaforte" it is Bertrans de Born who speaks, and in "Famam Librosque Cano" a Browningesque unpopular poet. "Cino" may stand as an example of Pound's early monologues. It is set in the "Italian Campagna 1309, the open road", and begins:

> Bah! I have sung women in three cities,
> But it is all the same;
> And I will sing of the sun.
>
> Lips, words, and you snare them,
> Dreams, words, and they are as jewels,
> Strange spells of old deity,
> Ravens, nights, allurement:
> And they are not;
> Having become the souls of song.[9]

[8] Ezra Pound, *A B C of Reading*, London (1934) p. 180.
[9] "Cino", 1-9.

The most complete realisation of the possibilities of Browning's method is to be found in one of Pound's major poems, "Near Périgord", which was published in *Lustra*, 1916. The poem is again a revelation both of a Provençal poet and of his age. As in Browning's Renaissance studies we find a suggested auditor, an objective tone, startling leaps of thought, strange juxtapositions of ideas or images, even a fascination with varying approaches to the same set of facts, with the blurred distinction between "truth" and fiction. "Near Périgord" differs from Browning's monologues chiefly in its melodic quality. Pound attempted to capture the rhythms of early Provençal poetry. One of his poetic aims was "to resurrect the art of the lyric, I mean [he said] words to be sung". But even in respect to melody he was willing to regard Browning as a worthy model. He believed that no true lyrics had been written in English since the time of Waller and Campion, except by Browning.

The subject of Browning's influence on Pound's *Cantos* can hardly be discussed without lengthy exegesis of the work itself. One might begin an investigation by observing that the *Cantos* have been interpreted as an enormous dramatic monologue. The flux and reflux of this complicated work can be regarded as a series of extraordinarily compressed self-revelations delivered by a host of historical personages – a kind of many-voiced monologue. Certainly the ghost of Browning hovers over the poem. He is specifically invoked in the opening lines of the second canto:

> Hang it all, Robert Browning,
> There can be but one "Sordello."
> But Sordello and my Sordello?
> Lo Sordels si fo di Mantovana.
> So-shu churned in the sea.[10]

Pound's most thorough critic, Mr Hugh Kenner, has explained these lines as suggesting "the artist's struggle to bring form (Browning's *Sordello*, Pound's *Cantos*) out of flux (the *Sordello* documents, the sea)".[11] So-shu, it has been explained, was an emperor who created order by building roads.

Readers who are not convinced by this stated similarity of aim

[10] Pound, Canto II, *Selected Poems*, New York (1949) p. 98.
[11] Hugh Kenner, *The Poetry of Ezra Pound*, London (1951) p. 318.

might at least agree that the *Cantos* resemble *Sordello* both in their obscurity and in the critical reception accorded them – a correspondence that is not meaningless in considering the relations of these two technical innovators to the poetry of their times.

In the case of Eliot, Browning's influence is more difficult to discover. It is not unjust to say of T. S. Eliot that the denial of his Victorian fathers is one of his chief poetic gestures. While the form and texture of his verse continually remind us of Browning, Tennyson, and even Swinburne, he has insisted on rarer and stranger poetic debts, recalling chiefly his transactions with the metaphysicals and Laforgue. In a famous passage in his essay on "The Metaphysical Poets" Eliot denied to Tennyson and Browning the "unification of sensibility" which was the glory of metaphysical poetry. And in a recent statement he announced that there was no American or English poet who "could have been of use to a beginner in 1908. . . . Browning was more of a hindrance than a help, for he had gone some way, but not far enough, in discovering a contemporary idiom."

These opinions reflect Eliot's later poetic development. The influence of Browning, and the acknowledgment of it, belong to the poetry up through the period of *The Waste Land*. In an unpublished lecture on the late nineteenth-century background of modern poetry (written presumably in the early 'thirties) Eliot spoke of Browning as the only poet of that period "to devise a way of speech which might be useful for others", to teach the possibility of using "non-poetic material", and to reassert "the relation of poetry to speech".

In the essay "Donne in Our Time", published in 1931, Eliot made a connexion which students might well have pursued. Rejecting the "school of Donne" as leading to a blind alley, he asserted that

> For the technique of verse, and for its adaptability to purposes, Donne has closer affinity to Browning, to Laforgue and to Corbière. The place of Browning in this group is obscured by several accidents: by the fact that he is often tediously longwinded, that he is far less a wit and ironist, and perhaps more than anything by the fact that his knowledge of the particular human heart is adulterated by an

optimism which has proved offensive to our time, though a later age may succeed in ignoring it.[12]

Eliot concludes by remarking that "the verse method, in all these four men, is similar: either dramatic monologue or dramatic dialogue."

The fact need not be emphasised that Eliot, the self-styled pupil of Pound, whom he called "il miglior fabbro", practiced the dramatic monologue form for nearly twenty years. "Prufrock", "Portrait of a Lady", "Gerontion", "Journey of the Magi", *The Waste Land* itself, are, if not in the precise manner of Browning, variations on the form he created. Browning's monologues are designed to proceed from one fragment of narrative or thought to another; the complete poem achieves a coalescence of these fragments into a consistent psychological whole displayed in a real action. Eliot, in his early monologues at least, substitutes for this narrative and ideological base the flow of fragmented images which by opposition, analogy, and repetition produce a vision of character in its moral *ambiance*. The arrangement of Eliot's images in the poem has been compared to the arrangement of musical sounds, and indeed it was his intention to assimilate the language of dramatic poetry to the language of music – "speech as song".

The Waste Land may be considered a cluster of dramatic monologues, some of them extremely fragmentary, but all of them meant (the poet tells us in his notes) to cohere in the vision of Tiresias, "the most important personage in the poem, uniting all the rest". "What Tiresias *sees*, in fact, is the substance of the poem." Eliot's handling of the conventional monologue may be compared to an abstract painter's rendering of an object in nature. The form is broken down and reassembled according to an expressive or analytic purpose. The locutor of Eliot's poem is Tiresias, who belongs to both past and present, contains multitudes, and speaks in many tongues. The attempt is to present an age and to reveal its nature through living speech; Eliot is a dramatic poet. However, the central figure of *The Waste Land* is not attached to a time or a place. Indeed, his appearance is so exiguous

[12] T. S. Eliot, "Donne in Our Time", *A Garland for John Donne 1631-1931*, ed. T. Spencer, Cambridge, Mass. (1931) p. 15.

that without the help of Eliot's notes his presence in the poem might not even be perceived.

It may be objected that once a poetic form has been so radically altered it has become another genre. But I think the structure of Eliot's poem cannot be fully understood without reference to the conventions of the dramatic monologue. It is worth our while to observe how distinctly Browning's example lurks beneath the intricate pattern of *The Waste Land*, and how vital the inspiration of that example has been in modern literature.

Eliot several times remarked that Browning had nothing to teach him about poetic diction. Perhaps one example will be sufficient to show that the younger poet has not been entirely deaf to the language of the "old mesmeriser". Here are some lines from Eliot's "Fragment of an Agon":

> When you're alone in the middle of the night
> and you wake in a sweat and a hell of a fright
> When you're alone in the middle of the bed and
> you wake like someone hit you on the head
> You've had a cream of a nightmare dream and
> you've got the hoo-ha's coming to you.[13]

This is slightly reminiscent of the verse of W. S. Gilbert, but I think it is more like this passage from Browning:

> If at night when doors are shut,
>   And the wood-worms picks,
>   And the death-watch ticks,
>   And the bar has a flag of smut,
>   And a cat's in the water-butt –
>
> And the socket floats and flares,
>   And the house-beams groan,
>   And a foot unknown
>   Is surmised on the garret-stairs,
>   And the locks slip unawares – [14]

The influences I have discussed so far have operated on the techniques of dramatic poetry, and to a lesser extent on the creation of poetic diction. It is in such matters that Browning's

[13] Eliot, *Collected Poems 1909-1932*, p. 132.
[14] "Mesmerism", 6-15.

inspiration has been most strongly felt. At first sight it would seem that very little common ground could be perceived between the poetic attitude and subject matter of Browning and those of the distinguished moderns. Modern poetry (and again the generalisation is reckless) has been marked by a tendency to pessimism, by the antirationalist bias of most modern thought, and by what can only be called a neo-classical approach to the nature of art. Now in spite of certain contradictory evidence (a few passages in *La Saisiaz* and elsewhere), it is difficult to prove that Browning's poetry displays a leaning toward pessimism. And in spite of the extraordinary discipline and devotion he brought to the practice of his art, he cannot be aligned with classic tradition. Browning's positions in both these respects have been rejected by most modern poets and by many readers. The "thought content" of his work, his "philosophy", is at a very low ebb of respectability. The picture of Browning as thinker does not appeal to the modern imagination, and the poems of his that are now most generally admired are those that contain the least philosophy.

And Browning was not, even as Victorian poets go, a very consistent thinker. In his crafty dissection of the truth he preferred leaps of logic, sudden pounces and illuminations, to consecutive reasoning. He explicitly suggested (primarily in *The Ring and the Book*) that the process of ratiocination could not carry one far toward perceiving the truth of a human situation. In this sense – and this connexion must be made very tentatively – he anticipated that distrust of abstract reason which is so marked a characteristic of the modern mind. What Browning substituted for a reasoning *about* man or history was a profound instinct for life, a magnificent sympathy for the rich energies, whether confused, disciplined, or misdirected, which inform the vital gestures of men and women. His subject was emotion, emotionally perceived. The object of his scrutiny was man in history, and he showed us not so much how men *thought* in certain epochs as how they *felt*, and how that feeling makes for the continuity of the human story.

No modern poet can equal Browning on this ground. Again, though, the course he marked out has been followed. Pound said the primary purpose of his "assaults on Provence" was to use the region as subject matter, "trying to do as R.B. had with Renaissance Italy".[15] In one of his essays on Pound, Eliot praises his treatment of the Middle Ages: "If one can really penetrate the life of another age, one is penetrating the life of one's own." Pound, he feels, sees his subjects as "contemporary with himself, that is to say, he has grasped certain things in Provence and Italy which are permanent in human nature." Eliot's comment applies to Browning as well as to Pound. It may be used to combat those supercilious critics who disparage Browning for having made all his historical figures contemporary to himself. The criticism is irrelevant. To the extent that Browning realised his conceptions he made his personages contemporary to us all, to the extent that he brought his characters to life he endowed them with his own emotional energy. Pound, as a practising poet, could recognise such a virtue where an *avant-garde* critic would fail to perceive it. Like Browning, Pound did not attempt an objectivity devoid of feeling. In answer to the question, "Do you agree that the great poet is never emotional?" Pound answered, in part, "The only kind of emotion worthy of a poet is the inspirational emotion which energizes and strengthens, and which is very remote from the everyday emotion of sloppiness and sentiment. . . ."[16] The comment is, once more, appropriate to Browning.

If, in examining the parallels between Browning's poetic practice and that of Pound and Eliot, we can discover debts so specific as conscious imitation and so tenuous as a common attitude toward emotion, we are clearly beginning a useful investigation. The inquiry could be extended almost indefinitely. To run through the list of artists who went to school to Browning would be to utter most of the great names of twentieth-century poetry. Hardy, whose work has been seminal to younger poets, expresses his obligation in most features of his practice. In Yeats's poetry Browning's influence is more difficult to trace; it is not central to his accomplishment, but I think there is a stronger parallel than has usually been suspected. The famous manifesto of the Imagists did not go much beyond Browning's innovations

---

[15] Letter of 8 Jul. 1922, to Felix E. Schelling. See *The Letters of Ezra Pound*, p. 179.

[16] T. S. Eliot, "Ezra Pound: His Metric and Poetry", *To Criticize the Critic*, New York (1965) p. 175.

in diction and dramatic concentration. E. A. Robinson and Robert Frost, masters of dramatic poetry, have built on Browning's discoveries. John Crowe Ransom has unexpectedly said, "It is a fact that Browning started me on my own, and no other poet did." And Robert Lowell has recently turned to an intensive study of Browning and to an exploration of the monologue form.

In discussing the effects that Browning's poetic principles have had on modern poets I have tried to avoid suggesting that tracing an influence is the same as finding a "source", or drawing a set, confining line which encloses and, somehow, reduces the object to which it leads. A great critic has remarked that it takes at least two to make an influence – the man who exerts it and the man who experiences it. By seeing how Browning's achievement has fertilised the imaginations of poets who followed him, Victorian poetry can be brought closer to us. If we know some of the roots of modern poetry we may examine the plant more curiously. The method of comparison is natural to criticism; it illuminates more than one age of literature, and more than any other method it increases one's sense of delight and wonder at the progress of poetry.

Geoffrey Tillotson

BROWNING[1]

In the *Fleshly School of Poetry* – Robert Buchanan's notorious pamphlet of 1872 that has so much to recommend it – a test was proposed for showing how far some of the vaunted poems of Rossetti and Swinburne fell short of what we expect of good, let alone great, poetry. Admirers of the poems were recommended to paraphrase them in prose. The worthlessness of the result, Buchanan claimed, would shock the paraphrasers into a sense of their infatuation. It may be that Buchanan's test is not a fair one, though we should all agree that good and great poetry would pass it. And it may be that more of Rossetti's poems than Buchanan predicted, and perhaps more of Swinburne's, would survive it – after all it was Rossetti who spoke of the "fundamental brain-work of poetry". What is certain is that a poet who would come out of the test very well would be Browning. Indeed he has already done so, for Mrs Orr's classic *Handbook* was to do to his poems what Buchanan proposed, and to show conclusively that the ideas in them were always interesting and sometimes brilliantly original as well.

Perhaps, however, Mrs Orr's versions flatter Browning – we may sometimes get more pleasure from reading her than from reading him. It is always a pleasure to read good prose, even when we are not warmly interested in its topic. Poetry when it is good gives us more pleasure still because, as Lascelles Abercrombie put it, poetry is language exerting the whole range of its powers. Browning is unusual in the use that he puts these powers

[1] Much of the present essay formed part of the Robert Spence Memorial Lecture 1965, which the author delivered to the Newcastle Literary and Philosophical Society.

198

to. He is interested in the power of language to be musical but seldom in its power to be musical in a mellifluous way. And few poets have been so intent on making the language of verse draw on its power to be conversational while remaining almost strictly metrical. For some reason or other, or perhaps for many reasons that operate together or singly and casually, he is sometimes, indeed often, defeated by language. Throughout his career Browning aroused complaints about his expression. It was always agreed that he had something to say. Whether or not he had always something to say that existed in his head firmly and clearly we may doubt, though it is quite possible that much of his imperfect expression may be due to the difficulties he made for himself by choosing to write in metres that would have made severe demands on metrists even more accomplished than he himself was. If only, one sighs, Browning could have attained as a matter of course the perfection of expression in a difficult metre that he attained in such a stanza as this from "Shop":

> I want to know a butcher paints,
>   A baker rhymes for his pursuit,
> Candlestick-maker much acquaints
>   His soul with song, or, haply mute,
>   Blows out his brains upon the flute![2]

That is even better in verse than it would be in prose because the adventurous rhymes fall so amusingly and neatly, and the word "candlestick-maker" is made to look delightfully self-conscious now that we say it slowly, and see its rhythm as falling rhythm; and, further, because words in their prose order delight when they coincide, as it were by chance, with metre. Of the tens of thousands of Browning's stanzas a great many pass muster. But a great many do not. And though, when he writes blank verse, the technical problems are not so teasing as those raised by complex stanza forms, they are still severe, and are not always solved.

That Browning's technique, greatly ambitious, was imperfect has something almost doctrinal about it. As a theologian he saw perfection as inevitably postponed for man. His concern with

[2] "Shop", 101-5.

heaven was almost a pre-occupation, and it was that just because everything on earth – including most of his poems – was imperfect:

On the earth the broken arcs; in the heaven, a perfect round.[3]

For him perfection was ruled out on principle. When he achieved it, it was almost by accident. His poems differ greatly from Tennyson's. They are never still. Any moment you feel they will explode. They do not sink into our hearts. They stir us up. They are too busy to be intense. Tennyson's poems are alive, but Browning's alive and kicking.

We have every sympathy with Browning in his acceptance of the principle of the inevitability of imperfection. But we also have every sympathy with those of his contemporaries who pleaded with him to come as near perfection as possible. When his grasp of his difficult ideas is slack, we cannot expect expression that is firm and sound. But when his grasp is quite firm he sometimes, and perhaps often, gives us imperfection that is far from inevitable. We are on slippery ground here because his imperfections in this kind lie so close to great virtues. In the first place, no poet has ever had so many splendid ideas for the shapes he wanted his poems to build up for themselves. For each poem, perhaps before he began to write it,[4] he hit on a quite novel and often a brilliant and interesting shape. G. K. Chesterton has praised Browning's architectural power.[5] But he has scarcely done him full justice because he failed to praise the construction, which meant much to writers, of some of the later poems. For instance in the long sensation-novel poem, *The Inn Album*, the MS book of the title keeps being referred to because the personages keep quoting its vapid entries to further the points they are making. In *Red Cotton Night-Cap Country* the story is introduced conversationally and recounted to a friend – it was Anne Thackeray, who had happened to nickname a sleepy bit of Normandy the White Cotton Night-Cap country – while she was walking with Browning about the place in which its events

[3] "Abt Vogler", 72.
[4] Cf. "A Grammarian's Funeral", 69: "Image the whole, then execute the parts. . . ."
[5] *Browning*, London (1903) pp. 136ff.

reached their climax. The "Parleying with Charles Avison"
begins with

> How strange! – but, first of all, the little fact
> Which led my fancy forth.[6]

We are then told that the poet that morning in March had
noticed a blackcap tugging at, and at last stealing,

> The cloth-shred, still a-flutter from its nail
> That fixed a spray once.[7]

The fact of March being the month started up an odd association:

> Yet – by the first pink blossom on the larch! –
> This was scarce stranger than that memory, –
> In want of what should cheer the stay-at-home,
> My soul, – must straight clap pinion, well nigh roam
> A century back, nor once close plume, descry
> The appropriate rag to plunder, till she pounced –
> Pray, on what relic of a brain long still?
> What old-world work proved forage for the bill
> Of memory the far-flyer? "March" announced,
> I verily believe, the dead and gone
> Name of a music-maker: one of such
> In England as did little or did much,
> But, doing, had their day once. Avison!
> Singly and solely for an air of thine,
> Bold-stepping "March", foot stept to ere my hand
> Could stretch an octave, I o'erlooked the band
> Of majesties familiar, to decline
> On thee – not too conspicuous on the list
> Of worthies who by help of pipe or wire
> Expressed in sound rough rage or soft desire –
> Thou, whilom of Newcastle organist![8]

And so we are launched on what is one of Browning's most en-
lightening explorations of a "dark passage" – music, which is
one thing in one age and a very different thing in another, and
what it expresses. (No other poet, not even Milton or Hopkins,

---

[6] "Parleying with Charles Avison", 1-2.
[7] *Op. cit.*, 18-19.   [8] *Op. cit.*, 37-57.

has lingered long in that passage, and most of our poets scarcely knew it existed).

The structure of Browning's poems is of great technical interest. It was when he came to fill out the grand structure with words that he often faltered. It was as if a great architect allowed shoddy workmanship from bricklayers. Here is an instance. A splendid poem of his, which must have been startlingly novel in 1855, is " 'De Gustibus – ' " (in the transcription of which I venture to add accents here and there to indicate where accents should not be missed in the reading):

I

Yóur ghóst will walk, you lover of trees,
  (If our loves remain)
  In an Énglish láne,
By a cornfield-side a-flutter with poppies.
Hark, those two in the hazel coppice –
A boy and a girl, if the good fates please,
  Making love, say, –
  The happier they!
Draw yourself up from the light of the moon,
And let them pass, as they will too soon,
  With the bean-flowers' boon,
  And the blackbird's tune,
And May, and June!

II

What Í love best in all the world
Is a castle, precipice-encurled,
In a gash of the wind-grieved Apennine.
Or look for me, old fellow of mine,
(If I get my head from out the mouth
O' the grave, and loose my spirit's bands,
And come again to the land of lands) –
In a sea-side house to the farther South,
Where the baked cicala dies of drouth,
And one sharp tree – 't is a cypress – stands,
By the many hundred years red-rusted,

Rough iron-spiked, ripe fruit-o'ercrusted,
My sentinel to guard the sands
To the water's edge. For, what expands
Before the house, but the great opaque
Blue breadth of sea without a break?
While, in the house, for ever crumbles
Some fragment of the frescoed walls,
From blisters where a scorpion sprawls.
A girl bare-footed brings, and tumbles
Down on the pavement, green-flesh melons,
And says there's news to-day – the king
Was shot at, touched in the liver-wing,
Goes with his Bourbon arm in a sling:
– She hopes they have not caught the felons.
Italy, my Italy!
Queen Mary's saying serves for me –
    (When fortune's malice
    Lost her – Calais) –
Open mý heart and you will see
Graved inside of it, "Ítaly."
Such lovers old are I and she:
So it always was, so shall ever be!

Now look at that couplet

> What I love best in all the world
> Is a castle, precipice-encurled.

We might almost say that one test of competence in a verse
technician is his power to get satisfactory rhymes for "world".
He has few choices. In "My Star" Browning had used "furled",
and when we really attend to the picture he is drawing the
rhyme does not offend us. Eminently satisfactory was the rhyme
to "world" that two great eighteenth-century technicians hit on:
the "character" of Man in the second Epistle of *The Essay on Man*
ends with:

> Sole judge of Truth, in endless Error hurl'd:
> The glory, jest, and riddle of the world!

and the equally splendid conclusion to Gray's "Descent of Odin":

> Never till substantial Night
> Has reassum'd her ancient right;
> Till wrap'd in flames, in ruin hurl'd,
> Sinks the fabric of the world.

Now in the poem we are discussing Browning badly wanted a rhyme to "world" because he could not bear to discard the excellent line –

> What I love best in all the world –

in which "I" is strongly accented. His rhyme, when it comes, is execrable. If it creates any picture at all it is a ludicrous one. How different from the fully-realised picture in the next line:

> In a gash of the wind-grieved Apennine.

But I said we were on slippery ground. Browning's failings are close to his virtues. The excellent line ending in "world" is an instance of what Browning can do so well as to have scarcely a rival. He can introduce actual speech – or speech we feel to be actual – into metre that remains metre. To measure his success here we might look at Wordsworth's failure, on one important occasion at least. "Resolution and Independence" is among Wordsworth's greatest poems, and in it he reproduces the speech he himself held with the leechgatherer. One line of it is as good as Browning would have made it:

> "This is a lonesome place for one like you."

But look at the others:

> "This morning gives us promise of a glorious day,"

and

> "What occupation do you there pursue?"

(which is a would-be improvement on the first version:

> "What kind of work is that which you pursue?"),

and

> "How is it that you live, and what is it you do?"

Wordsworth wanted faithful words here, and he got words that would be marked wrong in a foreigner's attempt to write down simple speech in an exercise book. A great deal of Browning's poetry is speech that strikes us as faithful to our ordinary habits of speaking but which miraculously coincides with metre. More than most poets, he demands to be read aloud. No doubt he wrote to be so read. And we find that if we read him aloud, after studying him, some of his apparently crabbed passages come out with forceful clarity. Recently the distinguished actor, Marius Goring, recited "Mr. Sludge, 'The Medium' " on the radio – he did it a portion at a time. The verse proved as speakable as that of a Hamlet soliloquy.

Keats saw that after Wordsworth English poetry would be different, because it would take up new matter. He saw that it would record the poet's exploration of what he called "dark passages" – a phrase I have already quoted – matter that was obscure, and which extended through time rather than existed momentarily:

> "We see not the ballance of good and evil, [and] are in a mist," [which] means that the life of a thinking man must be a search, and, perhaps, that poetry should take the path not of Shakespeare and Milton . . . but rather of Wordsworth, who "can make discoveries" in the "dark Passages."[9]

The poets were exploring the dark passages because those passages now confronted everybody who had a taste for thinking. We all know how knowledge had been widening throughout the seventeenth and eighteenth centuries, and how headlong was the process in the nineteenth century. It is enough to call as witnesses Lyell, who showed more fully than any of his predecessors that the world was billions of years old instead of the six thousand years that had been calculated on the evidence of the Bible; Renan, who greatly developed the idea that Jesus was man and no more; and Darwin, who put the seal of truth on the guesses of later eighteenth-century thinkers about the relation of man to the inferior animals. Nor should we forget that Locke's late seventeenth-century investigation of the human mind was proving more and more fruitful as time went on. Like everybody else – everybody who did any thinking – the poets, when they left the simplicities that they could readily master (things like sadness and joy), were wanderers in the dark passages.

[9] W. J. Bate, *John Keats*, Cambridge, Mass. (1963) p. 322.

I suggest we look at a few instances of Browning's many explorations of this sort, noticing the thoughts that came to him in the process.

At the point in his career when he had written the youthful *Pauline*, and *Paracelsus* and *Sordello* and the plays, and also some remarkable lyrics in the *Bells and Pomegranates* volumes – that is, when he had written some of his finest small things – the youthful Matthew Arnold represented him as

> a man with a moderate gift passionately desiring movement and fulness, and obtaining but a confused multitudinousness. . . .[10]

And Arnold went on to say that Browning and others

> will not be patient neither understand that they must begin with an Idea of the world in order not to be prevailed over by the world's multitudinousness: or if they cannot get that, at least with isolated ideas. . . .

Arnold's counsel was out of date by several centuries. He should have known that the people who were now coming to be called "thinkers" were remarkable because they let ideas start up and form while experience proceeded. Arnold himself was one of them! And by the time the remark was made Browning had already acquired for himself many ideas both of the "isolated" and further-spreading sort: for instance those of a bold passage in *Paracelsus*:

> Then all is still; earth is a wintry cold,
> But spring-wind, like a dancing psaltress, passes
> Over its breast to waken it – rare verdure
> Buds here & there upon rough banks, between
> The withered tree-roots & the cracks of frost,
> Like a smile striving with a wrinkled face;
> The grass grows bright, the boughs are swollen with
>   blooms
> Like chrysalids impatient for the air
> The shining dorrs are busy – beetles run

---

[10] *The Letters of Matthew Arnold to Arthur Hugh Clough*, ed. H. F. Lowry, London (1932) p. 97.

Along the furrows – ants make their ado –
Above, birds fly in merry flocks – the lark
Soars up & up, shivering for very joy;
Afar the ocean sleeps – white fishing gulls
Flit where the strand is purple with its tribe
Of nested limpets: savage creatures seek
Their loves in wood and plain – & God renews
His ancient rapture! Thus He dwells in all,
From Life's minute beginnings, up at last
To Man – the consummation of this Scheme
Of Being – the completion of this Sphere
Of Life: whose attributes had here & there
Been scattered o'er the visible world before,
Asking to be combined – dim fragments meant
To be united in some wondrous Whole, –
Imperfect qualities throughout Creation,
Suggesting some one Creature yet to make –
– (So would a Spirit deem, intent on watching
The purpose of the World from its faint rise
To its mature development) – some point
Whereto those wondering rays should all converge.[11]

That passage shows Browning's awareness of multitudinousness, but does not show him as confused or overwhelmed by it. It shows him helping to formulate an idea that was in the process of formulation in his day and generation, by himself (the printed versions of his poems show changes) and others, an idea that Arnold was not ready for, though Newman and Darwin were. And after the date of Arnold's remark came *Men and Women* and all the later poems with their abundance of ideas, isolated and further-spreading, ideas about human life and the universe so substantial and coordinated that whole books have been written

---

[11] v, *ad fin.* I transcribe from the MS in the hand of Browning's sister, preserved in the Dyce-Forster collection in the Victoria and Albert Museum. In transcribing I have regularised what in the original are dots as well as dashes. The first edition reads as does the MS, except for the interesting capitalisation and punctuation. Later revision, perhaps prompted by the wish to shorten syntax, cut out the lines containing the phrase "mature development", a nineteenth-century phrase which the compositor, finding it difficult, spelt "mature devolopment".

about them. Speaking for myself, I do not find these books readable, and I suggest that if life is too short to allow us to read both the books on Browning's philosophy and the poems that embody it, we should read the latter and not the former. It is one thing to read *about* Browning's ideas, and another to read them in their place in the poems. The ideas of a prose writer suffer less damage when abstracted from their context than the ideas of a poet. For there is so much more *to* a poem than ideas. Browning talks on one occasion of his "mere grey argument". That is to do his poems of thinking an injustice. His argument, even in "La Saisiaz", is never "mere" and never "grey". It is always vigorous and better still always breaking into pictures. These pictures can be very satisfying. Look at those in the arguments in the *Parleyings*, which are so many philosophical discourses. For instance this in the "Parleying With Bernard de Mandeville":

> Man speaks now: "What avails Sun's earth-felt thrill
> To me? Sun penetrates the ore, the plant –
> They feel and grow: perchance with subtler skill
> He interfuses fly, worm, brute, until
> Each favoured object pays life's ministrant
> By pressing, in obedience to his will,
> Up to completion of the task prescribed,
> So stands and stays a type. Myself imbibed
> Such influence also, stood and stand complete –
> The perfect Man, – head, body, hands and feet,
> True to the pattern: but does that suffice?
> How of my superadded mind which needs
> – Not to be, simply, but to do, and pleads
> For – more than knowledge that by some device
> Sun quickens matter: mind is nobly fain
> To realize the marvel, make – for sense
> As mind – the unseen visible, condense
> – Myself – Sun's all-pervading influence
> So as to serve the needs of mind, explain
> What now perplexes. Let the oak increase
> His corrugated strength on strength, the palm
> Lift joint by joint her fan-fruit, ball and balm, –
> Let the coiled serpent bask in bloated peace, –

The eagle, like some skyey derelict,
Drift in the blue, suspended, glorying, –
The lion lord it by the desert-spring, –
What know or care they of the power which pricked
Nothingness to perfection? I, instead,
When all-developed still am found a thing
All-incomplete: for what though flesh had force
Transcending theirs – hands able to unring
The tightened snake's coil, eyes that could outcourse
The eagle's soaring, voice whereat the king
Of carnage couched discrowned? Mind seeks to see,
Touch, understand, by mind inside of me,
The outside mind – whose quickening I attain
To recognize – I only.[12]

Or look at the pictures in "Bishop Blougram's Apology", which make it one of the most engaging of Browning's pieces of argument. I have space to remind you only of one of them: the bishop is talking about the difficulties, indeed the impossibility, of maintaining your faith in Christian doctrine fixed, and absolute, and conclusive. He likens a "faith diversified by doubt" to a track up a mountain:

> – That way
> Over the mountain, which who stands upon
> Is apt to doubt if it be meant for a road;
> While, if he views it from the waste itself,
> Up goes the line there, plain from base to brow,
> Not vague, mistakable! what's a break or two
> Seen from the unbroken desert either side?[13]

No one else has thought of writing about a mountain track in that way though we all know what he is speaking of, and have had experience of it – which in itself gives us pleasure, a pleasure that is increased because the picture exists to illuminate something which, whether we have any religious faith or not, is of universal interest – the belief in the supernatural, interrupted but maintained over the course of a lifetime. And look at "A Gram-

[12] "Parleying with Bernard de Mandeville", 235-71.
[13] "Bishop Blougram's Apology", 197-203.

marian's Funeral". There are many ideas in this poem, the main one being that life should not be taken aimlessly in instalments, but should have a single purpose grander than can be achieved here on earth. That idea is excellent even in prose. But in the poem its excellence is doubled by the sort of art that verse invites, provides occasion for. And not only by its metre and some of its brilliant rhymes, but also because it is so constructed that there are four distinct and simultaneous lines of progression active in the visualised topic and the scene: the men are marching up the mountain, carrying the coffin of the dead grammarian; they are marching while the dawn is in process of breaking; they are singing about a man who proceeded from handsome youth to decrepitude and *pari passu* advanced steadily in learning. The result of all this "business" is that we receive the ideas not as when I summarised one of them a moment ago, but as coming from men who are marching and singing lustily (Browning's metre is vigorous) – as coming from men we admire. We receive the ideas in a good humour, which takes us half way towards accepting them. And is not poetry very much like life in this – most of our ideas we get through living friends and living enemies, or from books by authors we like or dislike? The ideas are coloured by their sources in living human beings.

One of the poems in which Browning explores a very dark passage is his "Parleying With Charles Avison", the Newcastle musician and musicologist who lived in the first half of the eighteenth century. What is music, what does it do to us, why does it mean so much to us, and why does simple music delight in one age and more complicated in another – these are some of the themes explored in the poem. As a sample of the interest Browning finds in the topic take the fifth paragraph of the poem:

> And here's your music[14] all alive once more –
> As once it was alive, at least: just so
> The figured worthies of a waxwork-show
> Attest – such people, years and years ago,
> Looked thus when outside death had life below,
> – Could say "We are now," not "We were of yore,"

[14] The simple "March" in $\frac{3}{4}$ time by Avison, which Browning prints at the close of his poem.

– "Feel how our pulses leap!" and not "Explore –
Explain why quietude has settled o'er
Surface once all-awork!" Ay, such a "Suite"
Roused heart to rapture, such a "Fugue" would catch
Soul heavenwards up, when time was: why attach
Blame to exhausted faultlessness, no match
For fresh achievement? Feat once – ever feat!
How can completion grow still more complete?
Hear Avison! He tenders evidence
That music in his day as much absorbed
Heart and soul then as Wagner's music now.
Perfect from centre to circumference –
Orbed to the full can be but fully orbed:
And yet – and yet – whence comes it that "O Thou" –
Sighed by the soul at eve to Hesperus –
Will not again take wing and fly away
(Since fatal Wagner fixed it fast for us)
In some unmodulated minor? Nay,
Even by Handel's help![15]

And, to take an altogether different sort of instance, here are
more ideas in a passage which stands like a peak in nineteenth-
century literature: the aged Pope is concluding his speech in *The
Ring and the Book*:

For the main criminal I have no hope
Except in such a suddenness of fate.
I stood at Naples once, a night so dark
I could have scarce conjectured there was earth
Anywhere, sky or sea or world at all:
But the night's black was burst through by a blaze –
Thunder struck blow on blow, earth groaned and bore,
Through her whole length of mountain visible:
There lay the city thick and plain with spires,
And, like a ghost disshrouded, white the sea.
So may the truth be flashed out by one blow,
And Guido see, one instant, and be saved.
Else I avert my face, nor follow him
Into that sad obscure sequestered state

[15] "Parleying with Charles Avison", 113-37.

Where God unmakes but to remake the soul
He else made first in vain; which must not be.
Enough, for I may die this very night:
And how should I dare die, this man let live?

Carry this forthwith to the Governor![16]

Browning's ideas are rooted in human beings. For him the word human is paramount. A late poem is "Poetics":

"So say the foolish!" Say the foolish so, Love?
  "Flower she is, my rose" – or else "My very swan is she" –
Or perhaps "Yon maid-moon, blessing earth below, Love,
  That art thou!" – to them, belike: no such vain words from me.

"Hush, rose, blush! no balm like breath," I chide it:
  "Bend thy neck its best, swan, – hers the whiter curve!"
Be the moon the moon: my Love I place beside it:
  What is she? Her human self, – no lower word will serve.

It is the human that interests him – human beings and what happens to them, how they look and how and what they feel and fancy, and think, and how they act. And he is specially interested in men and women being and doing all these things when they are in love. Here is a sample of his ideas about love:

every lover knows
Love may use hate but – turn to hate, itself –
Turn even to indifference – no, indeed![17]

Or take one of his finest poems, "Any Wife to Any Husband", which becomes more interesting with every new reading. Or take this instance of lovers in action, "A Lovers' Quarrel", in which eight of the 22 stanzas show the lovers behaving with glorious ridiculousness: for instance:

Teach me to flirt a fan
As the Spanish ladies can,
  Or I tint your lip
  With a burnt stick's tip

[16] *The Ring and the Book*, x, 2117-35.
[17] *The Inn Album*, 1853-5.

> And you turn into such a man!
> Just the two spots that span
> Half the bill of the young male swan.[18]

What other poet has allowed lovers this degree of ridiculousness?
Shakespeare comes nearest, who makes Juliet imagine Romeo
cut out into little stars. How silly their antics, and how they play
with fire! In earlier writers such things had been laughed at
without sympathy. Browning honours them because he knows
what it is like to be in love, and is bold enough to say so.

One thing stands out – that a human being was for Browning
an indivisible whole. Nineteenth-century writers were becoming
more conscious of this indivisible unity, and Browning would
have been amused by the suggestion that his optimistic theology
was ascribable to his good digestion.[19] The suggestion merely
turns Browning on himself – for Bishop Blougram reminds
Gigadibs:

> . . . don't you know,
> I promised, if you'd watch a dinner out,
> We'd see truth dawn together? – truth that peeps
> Over the glasses' edge when dinner's done,
> And body gets its sop and holds its noise
> And leaves soul free a little?[20]

The idea of the indivisibility of body, mind, and soul had come
a good way even by the eighteenth century. It is strong in Swift
and Pope:

> Not always Actions shew the man: we find
> Who does a kindness, is not therefore kind;
> Perhaps Prosperity becalm'd his breast,
> Perhaps the Wind just shifted from the east.[21]

It has recently been shown how important the idea was for
Smollett, and how it affects the presentation of his personages.[22]
The importance ascribed to it by Smollett, who was a medical

[18] "A Lovers' Quarrel", 64-70.
[19] G. K. Chesterton, *Robert Browning*, London (1903) p. 180.
[20] "Bishop Blougram's Apology", 15-20.
[21] Pope, "Moral Essays", 1, 109 ff.
[22] Donald Bruce, *Radical Dr Smollett*, London (1964).

man, is expanded by novelists in the nineteenth century. Browning expands the idea to take in place as well as body. He sees people as sometimes affected on occasions of great importance – not simply when it is a matter merely of a kind act such as Pope had in mind – by what happens to be round and about them in the external world. It is not a case of

> How oft the sight of means to do ill deeds
> Makes ill deeds done! . . .

or of good deeds, for that matter. It is a case of the participation of what has no obvious relevance.[23] "By the Fire-side" is one of the greatest love poems in English, and the closely analysed process of falling in love is its unusual theme, the process by which love and marriage supervene on friendship. The process is the thing, and to get that the whole poem with its 53 stanzas calls to be read. The climax may, however, be represented by the following:

> We stoop and look in through the grate,
>   See the little porch and rustic door,
> Read duly the dead builder's date;
>   Then cross the bridge that we crossed before,
> Take the path again – but wait!
>
> Oh moment, one and infinite!
>   The water slips o'er stock and stone;
> The West is tender, hardly bright:
>   How grey at once is the evening grown –
> One star, its chrysolite!
>
> We two stood there with never a third,
>   But each by each, as each knew well:
> The sights we saw and the sounds we heard,
>   The lights and the shades made up a spell
> Till the trouble grew and stirred.

[23] Dickens suggests something like the same thing at the close of chapter xxxv of *Great Expectations*:
> Once more, the mists were rising as I walked away. If they disclosed to me, as I suspect they did, that I should *not* come back, and that Biddy was quite right, all I can say is – that they were quite right too.

Oh, the little more, and how much it is!
   And the little less, and what worlds away!
How a sound shall quicken content to bliss,
   Or a breath suspend the blood's best play,
And life be a proof of this!

Had she willed it, still had stood the screen
   So slight, so sure, 'twixt my love and her:
I could fix her face with a guard between,
   And find her soul as when friends confer,
Friends – lovers that might have been.

For my heart had a touch of the woodland-time,
   Wanting to sleep now over its best. . . .

You might have turned and tried a man,
   Set him a space to weary and wear,
And prove which suited more your plan,
   His best of hope or his worst despair,
Yet end as he began.

But you spared me this, like the heart you are,
   And filled my empty heart at a word.
If two lives join, there is oft a scar,
   They are one and one, with a shadowy third;
One near one is too far.

A moment after, and hands unseen
   Were hanging the night around us fast;
But we knew that a bar was broken between
   Life and life: we were mixed at last
In spite of the mortal screen.

The forests had done it; there they stood;
   We caught for a moment the powers at play:
They had mingled us so, for once and good,
   Their work was done – we might go or stay.
They relapsed to their ancient mood.[24]

The poem containing these stanzas is one of the nineteenth-
century poems that make us feel how far we have come not only

[24] "By the Fireside", 176-202, 221-40.

from the eighteenth century but from the poets of the early nineteenth century.

Browning uses the word "truth" more often than any other poet, and it is a different thing after he has thought about human life and the universe. He felt that truth existed for his special benefit in the first place, and he did his best to see as big a part of it as possible. Sometimes he saw things in it that not all of us agree to be there, but other discoveries of his are confirmed by our own experience as that experience has been enlightened for us by Browning or other discoverers. He discovered that forests "heaped and dim" can push friends beyond friendship. He discovered that social usage may not have the last word – a bold discovery in its time: for which see "Confessions" with its unrepentant ending:

> How sad and bad and mad it was –
> But then, how it was sweet!

He even discovered that his famous optimism might be a delusion – that it might indeed begin and end in the body, or, if the mind is not material, in that part and degree of it that cooperates with the body in love. The "Epilogue" to *Ferishtah's Fancies* is not one of his best poems, by any means. It is woolly. Mrs Sutherland Orr paraphrased it, however, into her excellently clear prose:

> The EPILOGUE is a vision of present and future, in which the woe and conflict of our mortal existence are absorbed in the widening glory of an eternal day. The vision comes to one cradled in the happiness of love; and he is startled from it by a presentiment that it has been an illusion created by his happiness.[25]

The last stanza at least is quite clear and straightforward:

> Only, at heart's utmost joy and triumph, terror
> Sudden turns the blood to ice: a chill wind disencharms
> All the late enchantment! What if all be error –
> If the halo irised round my head were, Love, thine arms?

Mrs Orr brushes the evidence of this "Epilogue" aside:

[25] *A Handbook to the Works of Robert Browning*, London (1890) p. 327.

But we know that from Mr Browning's point of view, Love, even in its illusions, may be accepted as a messenger of truth.

All we dare say is that from other poems of Browning we know that love is the messenger of the sort of truth that Mrs Orr has in mind, but that from this poem we know that it may not be a messenger of supernatural truth at all. If Browning is an optimist, it is on balance, and in Blougram's words there are "a thousand diamond weights between".

What is of interest in Browning's poetry is the experience it records and imagines, the way the bold and novel expression of it bobs in and out of shadow – shadow that is sometimes tiresome but which not infrequently disperses for the patient reader – and the indefatigable thinking that it prompts from him.

SELECT BIBLIOGRAPHY

Robert Browning: A Bibliography, 1830-50, ed. Leslie N. Broughton, Clark S. Northrup, and Robert Pearsall. Ithaca N.Y. (Cornell University Press) 1953.

[There is a selective listing of critical and biographical studies that appeared before 1955 in *The Cambridge Bibliography of English Literature*, Cambridge, 1940 and supplement 1957. For a list that is said to be complete of studies between 1950 and the end of May 1965 see Boyd Litzinger and K. L. Knickerbocker, *The Browning Critics*, University of Kentucky Press, 1965, pp. 391-417. For more recent studies the reader must consult the annual listings in *Victorian Studies*.]

I. Biographies and letters

Griffin, W. H., and H. C. Minchin. *Life of Robert Browning*. London (Methuen) 1910. Revised edition, 1938.

Letters of Robert Browning, ed. Thurman L. Hood. New Haven (Yale University Press) 1933.

Letters of Robert Browning and Elizabeth Barrett Barrett 1845-1846, ed. R. B B[rowning], 2 vols., London and New York (Harper) 1899.

Miller, Betty Bergson. *Robert Browning, A Portrait*. London (John Murray) 1952.

New Letters of Robert Browning, ed. W. C. DeVane and K. L. Knickerbocker. New Haven (Yale University Press) 1950.

II. Other Books

Chesterton, G. K. *Robert Browning*. London (Macmillan) 1903.

Cook, A. K. *A Commentary Upon Browning's* The Ring and the Book. London (Oxford University Press) 1920.

Cooke, G. W. *Guide-book to the Poetic and Dramatic Works of Robert Browning*. London, 1891. [A quarry of useful information but to be used with caution.]

DeVane, William Clyde. *A Browning Handbook*. New York (F. S. Crofts) 1935. New and enlarged edition 1955.

——— *Browning's Parleyings: The Autobiography of a Mind*. New Haven (Yale University Press) 1927.

SELECT BIBLIOGRAPHY   219

HATCHER, H. H. *The Versification of Robert Browning*. Columbus (Ohio State University Press) 1928.

HONAN, PARK. *Browning's Characters: A Study in Poetic Technique*. New Haven (Yale University Press) 1961.

JOHNSON, EDWARD DUDLEY HUME. *The Alien Vision of Victorian Poetry: Sources of the Poetic Imagination in Tennyson, Browning and Arnold*. Princeton (University Press) 1952.

JONES, HENRY. *Browning as a Philosophical and Religious Teacher*. Glasgow, 1892.

KING, ROMA A. *The Bow and the Lyre: The Art of Robert Browning*. Ann Arbor (University of Michigan Press) 1957.

LANGBAUM, ROBERT W. *The Poetry of Experience: The Dramatic Monologue in Modern Literary Tradition*. London (Chatto and Windus) 1957.

LITZINGER, BOYD. *Time's Revenges: Browning's Reputation as a Thinker, 1889-1962*. Knoxville (University of Tennessee Press) 1964.

MILLER, J. HILLIS. *The Disappearance of God: Five Nineteenth-Century Writers*. Cambridge (Harvard University Press). 1963. [On De-Quincey, Browning, Bronte, Arnold, and Hopkins]

ORR, MRS SUTHERLAND. *A Handbook to the Works of Robert Browning*. London 1885. Revised edition 1887.

RAYMOND, WILLIAM OBER. *The Infinite Moment and Other Essays in Robert Browning*. Toronto (University Press) 1950. Second edition with additional essays 1965.

SMITH, CHARLES WILLARD. *Browning's Star Imagery: The Study of a Detail in Poetic Design*. Princeton (University Press) 1941.

WHITLA, WILLIAM. *The Central Truth: The Incarnation in Browning's Poetry*. Toronto (University Press) 1963.

III. ARTICLES

ALTICK, RICHARD D. "Browning's 'Karshish' and St. Paul", in *Modern Language Notes*, LXXII (1957) pp. 494-6.

—— "Browning's 'Transcendentalism' ", in *Journal of English and Germanic Philology*, LVIII (1959) pp. 24-8.

—— " 'A Grammarian's Funeral': Browning's Praise of Folly?", in *Studies in English Literature, 1500-1900*, III (1963) pp. 449-60.

—— "The Private Life of Robert Browning", in *Yale Review*, XLI (1951) pp. 247-62.

—— "The Symbolism of Browning's 'Master Hugues of Saxe-Gotha' ", in *Victorian Poetry*, III (1965) pp. 1-7.

BADGER, KINGSBURY. " 'See the Christ Stand!': Browning's Religion", in *Boston University Studies in English*, I (1955) pp. 53-73.

BROWN, E. K. "The First Person in 'Caliban Upon Setebos' ", in *Modern Language Notes*, LXVI (1951) pp. 392-5.

CHARLTON, H. B. "Browning: The Poet's Aim", in *Bulletin of the John Rylands Library*, XXII (1938) pp. 98-121.

—— "Browning as Dramatist", *Ibid.*, XXIII (1939) pp. 33-67.

—— "Browning's Ethical Poetry", *Ibid.*, XXVII (1942) pp. 36-69.

—— "Browning as Poet of Religion", *Ibid.*, XXVII (1942) pp. 271-307.

—— "Poetry and Truth: An Aspect of Browning's *The Ring and the Book*", *Ibid.*, XXVIII (1944), pp. 43-57.

—— "Browning: The Making of the Dramatic Lyric", *Ibid.*, XXXV (1953) pp. 349-84.

CUNDIFF, PAUL A. "The Clarity of Browning's Ring Metaphor", in *PMLA*, LXIII (1948) pp. 1276-82.

DEVANE, WILLIAM CLYDE. "The Harlot and the Thoughtful Young Man: A Study of the Relation between Rossetti's 'Jenny' and Browning's 'Fifine at the Fair' ", in *Studies in Philology*, XXIX (1932) pp. 463-84.

—— "The Virgin and the Dragon", in *Yale Review*, XXXVII (1947) pp. 33-46.

DREW, PHILIP. "Henry Jones on Browning's Optimism", in *Victorian Poetry*, II (1964) pp. 29-41.

DUNCAN, JOSEPH E. "The Intellectual Kinship of John Donne and Robert Browning", in *Studies in Philology*, L (1953) pp. 81-100.

ERDMAN, D. V. "Browning's Industrial Nightmare", in *Philological Quarterly*, XXXVI (1957) pp. 417-35. [On "Childe Roland".]

GREENE, HERBERT E. "Browning's Knowledge of Music", in *PMLA*, LXII (1947) pp. 1095-9.

HOLMES, STEWART W. "Browning's *Sordello* and Jung", in *PMLA*, LVI (1941) pp. 758-96.

—— "Browning: Semantic Stutterer", in *PMLA*, LX (1945) pp. 231-55.

HONAN, PARK. "Belial upon Setebos", in *Tennessee Studies in Literature*, IX (1964) pp. 87-98.

—— "Browning's Poetic Laboratory: The Uses of *Sordello*", in *Modern Philology*, LVI (1959) pp. 162-6.

HOWARD, JOHN. "Caliban's Mind", *Victorian Poetry*, I (1963) pp. 249-57.

JOHNSON, E. D. H. "Robert Browning's Pluralistic Universe: A Reading of *The Ring and the Book*", *University of Toronto Quarterly*, XXXI (1961) pp. 20-41.

MCCORMICK, JAMES P. "Robert Browning and the Experimental Drama", *PMLA*, LXVIII (1953) pp. 982-91.

MCELDERRY, B. R. "The Narrative Structure of Browning's *The Ring and the Book*", in *Research Studies of the State College of Washington*, XI (1943) pp. 193-233.

MELCHIORI, BARBARA. "The Tapestry Horse: 'Childe Roland' and 'Metzengerstein' ", in *English Miscellany*, XIV (1963) pp. 185-93.

—— "Where the Bishop Ordered his Tomb", in *A Review of English Literature*, V (1964) pp. 7-26.

—— "Browning and the Bible: An Examination of 'Holy Cross Day' ", in *A Review of English Literature*, VII (1966) pp. 20-42.

—— "Browning's Don Juan", in *Studies in Criticism*, XVI (1966) pp. 416-40. [On "Fifine at the Fair".]

MONTEIRO, GEORGE. "A Proposal for Settling the Grammarian's Estate", in *Victorian Poetry*, III (1965) pp. 266-70.

PREYER, ROBERT. "Robert Browning: A Reading of the Early Narratives", in *ELH*, XXVI (1959) pp. 531-48.

—— "Two Styles in the Verse of Robert Browning", in *ELH*, XXXII (1965) pp. 62-84.

PRIESTLEY, F. E. L. "Blougram's Apologetics", in *University of Toronto Quarterly*, XV (1946) pp. 139-47.

—— "A Reading of *La Saisiaz*", in *University of Toronto Quarterly*, XXV (1955) pp. 47-59.

—— "The Ironic Pattern of Browning's *Paracelsus*", in *University of Toronto Quarterly*, XXXIV (1964) pp. 68-81.

SMALLEY, DONALD. Introduction to *Browning's Essay on Chatterton*. Cambridge (Harvard University Press), 1948. [Deals at length with *The Ring and the Book* and other works by Browning.]

SYPHER, WYLIE. Introduction to his edition of *The Ring and the Book*, New York (1961).

TILLOTSON, GEOFFREY. "A Word for Browning", in *Sewanee Review*, LXXII (1964) pp. 389-97.

TRACY, CLARENCE. "Browning's Heresies", in *Studies in Philology*, XXXIII (1936) pp. 610-25.

—— "Caliban Upon Setebos", in *Studies in Philology*, XXXV (1938) pp. 487-99.

INDEX